The Asia-Pacific in the Age of Transnational Mobility

Anthem Southeast Asian Studies

In tandem with its increasing strategic and market importance amidst the dramatic growth of the neighbouring economies of both China and India, Southeast Asia's own political, social and intellectual trajectories have challenged not only the expectations of policymakers and analysts alike, but also raised important new questions for academia. Not surprisingly, recent years have seen a dramatic growth in scholarship devoted to the region. The **Anthem Southeast Asian Studies** series is committed to offering a global audience the best of this new generation of original scholarship drawn from across the full range of academic disciplines in the humanities and social sciences. Uniformly subject to rigorous editorial and production standards, our books are directed to academic libraries as well as to researchers, university students and other sophisticated audiences.

Series Editor

Michael W. Charney – School of Oriental and African Studies, University of London, UK

Editorial Board

Barbara Andaya – University of Hawaii, USA
Anne Booth – School of Oriental and African Studies, University of London, UK
Elizabeth Collins – Ohio University, USA
Kate Crosby – King's College London, UK
Christopher Goscha – Université du Québec à Montréal, Canada
Eva-Lotta Hedman – London School of Economics and Political Science (LSE), UK
Hong Liu – Nanyang Technological University, Singapore
Akio Takahashi – Institute for Advanced Studies on Asia, University of Tokyo, Japan
Kerry Ward – Rice University, USA

The Asia-Pacific in the Age of Transnational Mobility

The Search for Community and Identity on and through Social Media

Edited by Catherine Gomes

ANTHEM PRESS

Anthem Press
An imprint of Wimbledon Publishing Company
www.anthempress.com

This edition first published in UK and USA 2020
by ANTHEM PRESS
75–76 Blackfriars Road, London SE1 8HA, UK
or PO Box 9779, London SW19 7ZG, UK
and
244 Madison Ave #116, New York, NY 10016, USA

First published in the UK and USA by Anthem Press 2016

© 2020 Catherine Gomes editorial matter and selection;
individual chapters © individual contributors

The moral right of the authors has been asserted.

All rights reserved. Without limiting the rights under copyright reserved above,
no part of this publication may be reproduced, stored or introduced into
a retrieval system, or transmitted, in any form or by any means
(electronic, mechanical, photocopying, recording or otherwise),
without the prior written permission of both the copyright
owner and the above publisher of this book.

British Library Cataloguing-in-Publication Data
A catalogue record for this book is available from the British Library.

Library of Congress Cataloging-in-Publication Data
Library of Congress Control Number: 2020930706

ISBN-13: 978-1-78527-249-3 (Pbk)
ISBN-10: 1-78527-249-7 (Pbk)

This title is also available as an e-book.

CONTENTS

List of Illustrations vii

Acknowledgements ix

        Introduction 1
        Catherine Gomes

Part 1.   **SOCIAL MEDIA, MOBILITY, TRANSIENCE AND TRANSNATIONAL RELATIONSHIPS**

Chapter 1.   Female Indonesian Migrant Domestic Workers in Hong Kong: A Case Study of Advocacy through Facebook and the Story of Erwiana Sulistyaningsih   19
Panizza Allmark and Irfan Wahyudi

Chapter 2.   Media and Mobilities in Australia: A Case Study of Southeast Asian International Students' Media Use for Well-Being   41
Joshua Wong and Larissa Hjorth

Chapter 3.   Connecting and Reconnecting with Vietnam: Migration, Vietnamese Overseas Communities and Social Media   63
Cate Gribble and Ly Thi Tran

Chapter 4.   Liking It, Not Loving It: International Students in Singapore and Their Navigation of Everyday Life in Transience   87
Catherine Gomes

Part 2.	**SOCIAL MEDIA AND EXISTING MULTICULTURAL RELATIONSHIPS IN A CONTROLLED COMMUNICATION ENVIRONMENT**	
Chapter 5.	Is 'Allah Just for Muslims'? Religion, Indigenization and Boundaries in Malaysia *Susan Leong*	119
Chapter 6.	Ethnic Minorities and Multi-ethnic Heritage in Melaka: Reconstructing Dutch Eurasian and Chitty Melaka Identities through Facebook *Loo Hong Chuang and Floris Müller*	143
Chapter 7.	Nostalgia and Memory: Remembering the Malayan Communist Revolution in the Online Age *Jason Sze Chieh Ng*	169
Chapter 8.	New and Traditional Media in Malaysia: Conflicting Choices for Seeking Useful and Trusted Information in Everyday Life *Sandra Hanchard*	197

Notes on Contributors 219

Index 223

ILLUSTRATIONS

FIGURES

2.1 Picture diary of Karen, female Malaysian undergraduate, showing websites and apps she uses — 58

5.1 Protester outside Malaysia's Federal Court — 120

8.1 Comparison between usefulness and trustworthiness of media sources — 205

TABLES

4.1 Demographics of participating international students studying in Singapore — 98

4.2 Social media use of participating international students studying in Singapore — 100

8.1 Percentage of users who identified media types as 'useful' sources of information — 207

8.2 Percentage of users who identified media types as 'trusted' sources of information — 210

ACKNOWLEDGEMENTS

I would like to thank the Australian Research Council for providing me with the time and space to work on this project while I was a Discovery Early Career Research Fellowship (DECRA) awardee in 2013–2016. This book is an outcome of the research I did during the fellowship. I am also appreciative of the support Tej P. S. Sood, Katy Miller, Brian Stone, Vincent Rajan and the production team from Anthem Press provided throughout the duration of this project. I am also grateful for the supportive comments and helpful feedback from the three anonymous reviewers of this collection. Their insights help lift this book to pioneering levels. Thanks also go out to Jonathan Tan, Cirila P. Limpangog and Katie Grichting who helped with advice on various chapters in this collection. I am incredibly indebted to Drew Roberts for the invaluable eagle-eyed editorial and proofreading work.

I would like to especially thank Panizza Allmark, Irfan Wahyudi, Larissa Hjorth, Joshua Wong, Cate Gribble, Ly Thi Tran, Susan Leong, Loo Hong-Chuang, Floris Müller, Jason Sze Chieh Ng and Sandra Harchard, who worked tirelessly to produce cutting-edge research for this collection.

No writing and editorial project would be accomplished without the patience of the closest of those around us. Thank you, Andrew Newlands, for putting up with my constant typing, and thank you, little Sally, for keeping me company whenever I was lost in a sea of words on my screen.

INTRODUCTION

Catherine Gomes

In his graphic memoir *The Kampong Boy* (1979), Mohammad Noor Khalid – otherwise better known as Lat, Malaysia's most popular cartoonist – features his experiences growing up in a Malay-Muslim *kampong* (village) in the rural state of Perak on the Peninsular Malaysia in the 1950s. Lat's memoir is a whimsical ride through the misadventures of a young Muslim boy as he gets into trouble at school, plays with friends in the forbidden tin mines near his *kampong*, and faces circumcision as part of his religious obligation. Besides being highly entertaining and humorous, Lat's memoir also provides us with a nostalgic account of the strong ties that exist within a *kampong* community, where people minded each other's business and provided communal support when needed. *The Kampong Boy* highlights the significance that community has in determining an individual's everyday life. The impact of the *kampong* communal identity on Lat the protagonist and Lat the author is also present in the sequels, *Town Boy* (1981) and *Kampong Boy: Yesterday and Today* (1993). Community, and identifying with community, are very much part of a person's life but there are limits to this, too, as Graham Day articulates in his book *Community and Everyday Life*:

> [Community] refers to those things which people have in common, which bind them together, and give them a sense of belonging with one another. […] But as soon as one tries to specify more firmly what these common bonds are, how they arise, and how they can be sustained, the problems begin. We would not be social beings if we did not feel some sense of identification and solidarity with others around us and share in their experiences and expectations; yet there are limits to how far we can empathize with every one of them, or feel obligated towards them, or look to them for succour and support. As humans, we are boundary-drawing animals, and we erect barriers between ourselves and others, quite as much as we identify with them. The idea of community captures

these elements of inclusion and exclusion, pointing towards those who belong together and those who are held apart. (Day 2006, 2–3)

Day's description of community involves being part of and identifying with that group while negotiating one's own differences within the group and its collective identity. Day's definition of community is useful to a point; however, it still assumes a community made up of static rather than dynamically mobile members. Lat's narratives reflect nostalgically on a relatively uncomplicated sense of community and identity within the context of *kampong* and its homogenous ethnic–cultural–religious makeup – and like Day they do not take into consideration the fluidity of membership and the creation of new communities. The microcosm of the Malaysian *kampong* in Lat's story in many ways reflects an Asia-Pacific that has not existed now for some time. Malaysia, like the rest of the Asia-Pacific, is increasingly seeing cultural diversity. The Asia-Pacific, like the rest of the world, is also becoming more globally connected while individuals are witnessing rapid social and cultural changes to their own and other communities because of the unstoppable spread of social media technologies.

The authors in this book address and discuss the challenges of community and identity in the evolving Asia-Pacific transnational migrant and ethnographic landscapes of the region in the era of social media. They cover countries such as Singapore and Hong Kong, which are open to a variety of new migrants; countries like Vietnam, which have the problem of attracting its diaspora back to contribute to development; and countries such as Malaysia, which has a historical heritage of multiple cultures coexisting with varying measures of strain and harmony. A distinctive characteristic of most of the Asian countries covered in this book, together with the countries of origin of the Asian subjects featured, is that their experience with social media has arguably been within a controlled communicative environment. The governments in most of these countries control the traditional media and seek to suppress comments and opinions that go against their dominant national narrative. While these governments may say they have a free Internet, people who express opinions are seen by the government as seditious and can still be targeted. People and opinions that are marginalized and do not challenge the dominance of the government may be allowed a voice, but the government retains the power to act against allegedly seditious opinions. Yet, the chapters in this book provide narratives on how people in such restricted communicative environments or who have experience of such environments, navigate through these constraints in order to find and express community and identity.

There are only a few case studies of the use of social media by distinctive groups in the Asia-Pacific. This book offers a detailed analysis of the impact of social media on the construction of identity and its interrelated engagement with community in very recent situations. Some of the case studies have recently been very controversial, such as migrants' rights in Hong Kong or the 'Allah issue' in Malaysia. As such, this book provides us with a tool to understand the role played by social media in current media discourses and social issues.

A Changing Asia-Pacific – Transnational Mobility and Multiculturalism

In his introduction to *The Emergence of Modern Southeast Asia,* Norman G. Owen (2005, 4) writes: 'Ideas, institutions, cultural priorities, and social values' in the region have evolved where '[i]ntimacy, familial obligation, piety, and cultural identity have been challenged by foreign values and modern ideas'. Owen's collection – which is required background reading for any undergraduate student of Southeast Asian studies – presents a narrative of postcolonial Southeast Asia, a region that has undergone tremendous change since the 1800s, and how ensuing political chaos, economic developments and new technologies have influenced movements of Southeast Asian people within the region and beyond. However, Owen also points out that Southeast Asian nations are distinct from each other, despite significant similarities such as religious affiliation (Malaysia and Indonesia as majority Muslim nations, while Burma and Thailand support a Buddhist majority) and common histories as former colonies of imperial Western powers – the Portuguese and Spanish in the sixteenth and seventeenth centuries, and the British, French, Dutch and Americans in the nineteenth and twentieth centuries – and the memories and scars of the Japanese invasions and occupations during World War II.

Owen suggests that the remarkable differences between the nations in Southeast Asia lie in the difficult and various directions each nation took in the decolonization processes, largely in the 1960s and 1970s, effects of which are still felt today in their respective political, economic, societal and cultural spheres. Here, Owen (2005) notes that nations such as Malaysia and Singapore are neither mono-ethnic nor monocultural, due to the interrelated factors of colonialism, war, migration and the economic growth of the eighteenth and nineteenth centuries. Both these nations support demographically strong ethnic Indian, Malay and Chinese communities as well as minority ethnic communities such as the Eurasians, Arabs and Armenians (Goh 2008).[1]

---

1 British colonists in the nineteenth and early-twentieth centuries recognized that the Malaysian peninsula was rich in tin deposits and had the potential to become a site for growing rubber. The British involved traders and indentured labourers from the region and elsewhere to work in the tin mines and rubber plantations in Malaysia and to develop Singapore into a global entrepôt that was highly cosmopolitan for its time. While in Malaysia labourers from China and India worked in the tin mines and on rubber plantations, respectively, traders from various regions of Asia and the Middle East

The authors in this book pick up where Owen and his colleagues left off and revisit the consequences of historical and contemporary migration – not only in Southeast Asia but in the wider Asia-Pacific region – taking place due to economic factors such as work and education.

Transnational mobility

The migration of people for work, study and lifestyle is a global phenomenon and part of everyday life in the Asia-Pacific. According to the United Nations Sustainable Development (2016) international migrants constitute 3.3 per cent of the world's population (244 million people). In the last 30 years in the Asia-Pacific, the high circulation of both skilled and unskilled labour and a growing number of international students from within and outside the region have become commonplace, particularly in the rapidly growing economies of China, India, Singapore, Malaysia, Hong Kong and Thailand. The presence of these migrants has been acknowledged to have favourable economic effects, such as contributing to the growth of host nation industries and remittances transferred to the home nation. At the same time this exchange contributes to a diversity of ethnicities and cultures never seen before. However, the increase of both permanent and temporary migrants has created a heightened sense of anxiety among some locals who perceive migrants to be competitors for employment and as direct threats to the social and cultural fabric of their nations.

To meet the high demand for unskilled labourers required to supply the modernity projects of countries such as Singapore, transient (male) workers from other Asian nations – such as Vietnam and Bangladesh – started entering these countries in order to work in industries such as construction. These modernity projects, which largely started around the 1980s, meant that there was a need for more women to enter the workforce in order to meet the skilled and low-skilled labour demands. The result was the employment of foreign domestic workers (FDWs) on a massive scale. The temporary female migrants come principally from other Southeast Asian countries: Indonesia, the Philippines, Myanmar and Thailand as well as Sri Lanka, India and Bangladesh.[2] Since the mid-1990s Singapore has also been actively hiring

---

visited Singapore and saw its potential for robust trade. These traders and labourers ended up settling in Malaysia and Singapore due to various push–pull factors such as fleeing armed conflict, poverty and natural disasters to a place offering an abundance of work and a safer environment for entrepreneurship. Chapter 7 deals with the history of colonial and postcolonial Malaysia in greater detail.

2 As of 2015, there were 671,600 unskilled workers and 204,400 FDWs working in Singapore, who make up 46% and 14% of the transient population, respectively

tertiary-educated professionals who take up local managerial positions (Yang 2014, 422). Coming predominantly from the Philippines and Mainland China, they are known locally as 'foreign talent'. Some white-collar workers have also previously been international students in Singapore and many current international students have the intention of taking up local employment, which causes much tension among the local Singaporean community.

There is also a huge movement of Asians going overseas for study. Students from former colonies of the British Commonwealth in Southeast Asia (Singapore, Malaysia, Burma) have had a presence in Australia, the United Kingdom and Canada since the commencement of the Colombo Plan in 1951. Sponsored students were trained in these English-speaking countries in skills that would assist in the economic, infrastructural and social (e.g., medical and dental) development of these nations. Today, education hubs such as Australia, New Zealand, the United Kingdom, Canada and the United States are host to large numbers of full-fee paying Southeast Asian students. These students are an economic gold mine, since they also support secondary industries such as building and construction, real estate, hospitality and tourism in the host nations. In 2014, in Australia alone, China had 152,898 international students, India 63,096, Vietnam 30,121, the Republic of Korea 28,016 and Thailand 25,642. These were the top five source countries for international students entering Australia (Australian Education International 2015).

Meanwhile, migrants from the Asia-Pacific working outside the region is commonplace. Countries such as the Philippines and Indonesia are well known exporters of domestic workers to the Middle East. Filipino citizens also circulate the globe as service-industry professionals with expertise in health (e.g., nurses and technicians) and hospitality. The increasing frequency of high-paying, fly-in and fly-out working environments associated with the mining, petroleum and gas industries means that skilled, semi-skilled and low-skilled workers are in demand. Australia's mining boom, for instance, has generated a significant number of jobs for Indonesians and Vietnamese who work in the mining and construction industries (Earl and Kerin 2012; Australian Embassy Vietnam 2013). These workers fill a void in industries that Australians are unable to fill because of the difficult transient lifestyle associated with the work, which takes a strain on personal health and well-being (Pickles 2015). Meanwhile skilled Australians and New Zealanders are often seen in professional and management positions in the financial hubs of Asia, while young

(National Population and Talent Division, Prime Minister's Office, Government of Singapore, n.d.).

people from these countries take gap years in their study and working lives in order to live as working holidaymakers throughout the Asia-Pacific.

The circulation of Asia-Pacific people within the region and beyond has also impacted on their home nations. Research on international students in Australia, for example, shows that these students do not necessarily go back to their home nations: many decide to stay in the host nation (Robertson 2013) or go elsewhere (Gomes 2015). International students and skilled workers in particular represent a growing middle class that has the advantage of applying for permanent residency in the countries where they work or study. This exodus of skilled workers poses a conundrum for the home nations. While countries in Southeast Asia benefit from the remittances generated by overseas workers, they are also seeing a brain drain of individuals with the potential to contribute to the economic, political, social and cultural aspects of their home nations. The ways in which governments respond to this phenomenon are explored in Chapter 3 by Cate Gribble and Ly Thi Tran.

Multicultures

Migration – both historical and contemporary – defines and continues to define the Asia-Pacific today. As stated earlier, countries such as Malaysia, Singapore and Australia support multicultural populations; however, the dominant ethnic group in each of these nations has political, cultural and economic control. In Malaysia for instance the Malays make up the ethnic majority, while in Singapore three quarters of Singapore-born citizens claim Chinese heritage. The political, cultural and economic dominance of the ethnic majorities in both these countries have caused ethnic tensions notable in recent social media discourse. Such tensions in Malaysia exist primarily because Malaysia is governed by the controversial *Bumiputera* (princes, or sons, of the soil) policy. This policy is an affirmative action strategy whereby ethnic Malays and (arguably) the indigenous people of Peninsular Malaysia (*orang asli*) and 'natives' of Sabah and Sarawak are privileged in the constitution of Malaysia in terms of employment and education. However, if a non-Malay converts to Islam, they will be accorded Bumiputera status. This is because in Malaysia Islam and 'being Malaysian' are inseparable as discussed in the chapter by Susan Leong.

Meanwhile in Singapore, the government purposefully chooses elements of Chinese cultural values as the template for a common Singaporean national identity (Gomes 2010, 299–301). The ruling People's Action Party (PAP) openly encourages and supports the strength of Confucian Chinese values as a model for Singapore and its people, since selected elements support an unquestioning obedience to government, hard work and self-sacrifice – and the non-ethnic Chinese have been told that Chinese Confucian culture is the template to follow if Singapore is to continue progressing as an economic powerhouse. The national template, at least on the surface, has the intended effect of maintaining a shared Singaporean identity amongst a population of people from different ethnic groups; however, this appears to work only because the Chinese dominate in terms of cultural influence. Only recently, however, has this Chinese privilege been publicly questioned by non-Chinese Singaporeans. In 2014 an independent scholar in Singapore, Sangeetha Thanapal, questioned online the privileged position of Chinese in Singapore, which led to her being 'trolled, threatened, attacked verbally' by (Chinese) Singaporeans (Hidayah 2015).

And while Singapore may be politically, socially and culturally dominated by an ethnic Chinese majority, many Singaporeans resent the presence of Mainland Chinese 'foreign talent' working in and eventually permanently migrating to Singapore. They express views both privately and publicly (in online blogs, through social media and in forums in online news dailies) to the effect that Mainlanders are incapable of assimilation and communicating in English, and that they are the cause of social and economic chaos in Singapore society. Ethnic and cultural similarities do not, in other words, make for easy integration or assimilation. Chinese Singaporeans and Mainland Chinese neither identify with each other nor feel a sense of belonging as a singular diasporic Chinese community.

The dominance of the ethnic Malays in multicultural Malaysia has also created simmering tensions between the various majority and minority ethnic groups. Non-Bumiputera Malaysians resent the lack of opportunities presented to them as well as the detrimental effects of an Islam-centric policy on both non-Bumiputeras and Bumiputeras. Even Former Malaysian prime minister Mahathir Mohamad has openly stated that he considers the Bumiputera policy one reason why ethnic Malays have not progressed within a globally competitive environment.

From 1901 to 1973 Australia was ruled by a racially based policy known as the White Australia policy, which governed migration into the country. Since this policy's abolition, Australia has made great strides in welcoming migrants from diverse ethnic communities. However, the effects of this policy can still be seen today in seething and violent tensions between Anglo- and non-Anglo-Australians and between Anglo-Australians and new migrants. In December 2005, for instance, violence erupted in Cronulla Beach in Sydney. Known as the Cronulla Riots, the area saw young Anglo-Australian and Lebanese-Australian men openly fight with each other.

The growing mobility of people circulating within the Asia-Pacific and beyond has created environments of increasing diversity as nations become host to both permanent and temporary multicultural societies. How do we, however, begin to unpack the impact of mobility and multiculturalism on Asia-Pacific individuals and groups today? This is where the authors in this volume turn to social media as a tool of inquiry in order to map the ways in which mobile subjects and minorities articulate their sense of community and identity. The authors see social media as a platform that allows users to document and express their individual and collective identities while providing a sense of belonging and agency. Primarily through content analysis, qualitative and quantitative surveys, visual ethnography, historiography and conceptual analysis, the authors present original empirical work that attempts to help us understand how mobile subjects create a sense of community for themselves and articulate their ethnic, ideological and national identities in the Asia-Pacific.

Social Media as an Ethnographic Tool of Inquiry

Social media is a significant part of contemporary everyday life. It enables users to create and share content or to participate in social networking, and platforms that include blogs, business networks, enterprise social networks, forums, microblogs, photo sharing, products and services reviews, social gaming, social networks, video sharing and virtual worlds (Aichner and Jacob 2015). At the time of writing Facebook is the most popular social networking site in the world, with about a sixth of the world's population registered as users (Ross 2014).

More than just presenting us with various ways of communicating with each other, social media has also expanded the social groups we communicate with. Never before have ordinary people been able to communicate with people on such a mass scale, and with people with whom they have no personal relationship. While social media is a platform of choice for everyday communication with family, friends and acquaintances, it also allows us to broadcast our thoughts, opinions, ideas and ideologies to a broad audience – across state and national lines. Sometimes these thoughts, opinions, ideas and ideologies can go viral, which in some cases has led to significant political, social and cultural change.

Politically, we have seen governments toppled (the Arab Spring in 2011), political and military figures shamed (Ugandan guerrilla leader Joseph Kony) and politicians elected into office (Barak Obama's successful 2008 US presidential campaign). We have seen global social and cultural change take place where fear is injected into the population (the Islamic State in Libya and Levant, or ISIL/Islamic State in Iraq and Syria or ISIS) showcasing violent acts such as beheadings); people galvanized into contributing to various causes (the

2014 'Ice Bucket Challenge' that raised awareness of motor neurone disease); industries forced to rethink traditional business models (news outlets' use of social media comments as primary resources); and the rise of ordinary people into figures of influence (videogame commentator PewDiePie with 38 million YouTube subscribers) (Jacobs 2014). The subversive power of social media has led to China banning Facebook, Twitter, Instagram, YouTube, Blogspot and Vimeo, while replacing these with Chinese-made platforms widely used by Chinese citizens both within China and overseas (Tencent QQ, WeChat and Sina Weibo are the Chinese equivalent of Facebook, Twitter and a hybridized version of Facebook and Twitter, respectively).

The impact of social media and its cross-disciplinary reach is recognized by academia in disciplines such as marketing, cultural studies and communication studies. It is also an area of study within emerging sub-disciplines within the humanities and social sciences, such as digital anthropology, digital humanities and digital ethnography with scholars such as danah boyd leading the field. Others, such as Litang Cui and Michael Prosser (2014), advocate analysing social media for better intercultural understanding – something the authors of this edited collection actively do. Recognizing the impact of social media within the context of society and culture, universities have been investing in research centres within these sub-disciplines, such as the Centre for Digital Anthropology at University College London, Digital Humanities at Stockton University, Digital Ethnography at Kansas State University, and the Digital Ethnography Research Centre (DERC) at my own RMIT University in Melbourne.

Social media and mobility

The significance of social media increases with global mobility. Work in the area of migration often points to new permanent and temporary migrants creating links to or participating in existing networks linking to their home countries and cultures through new advances in communication technology, such as social media and Skype, which allow them to keep in touch with family and friends in the home nation (Hjorth 2011; Wong 2014). In recent studies I conducted on transient migrants, including international students in Australia, I recognized the importance of social media as a form of connectedness between migrant and host nation (Gomes et al. 2014; Gomes 2015). In one study, my colleagues and I concluded:

> The use of social media to stay in contact with friends and family from the home nation may assist students with forming imaginary bonds with their homelands. Doing so provides international students with virtual home-based

support networks, which then allow them the opportunity to pursue and form local social networks with students other than those who come from their countries of birth. (Gomes et al. 2014, 13)

Social media and multicultural societies

Social media is a well-used platform for showcasing the effects and consequences of multicultural societies. Facebook is host to numerous groups dedicated to communicating their thoughts, ideas and opinions on multiculturalism within multi-ethnic, multilingual, multifaith and multicultural societies. Group pages may be positive (e.g., dedicated to ethnic and cultural diversity), negative (e.g., racist or xenophobic ideologies), empowering (e.g., highlighting minority groups and their issues) or incidental (e.g., about the products of multiculturalism, such as food and cultural hybridity). However, to date there has been very little in the way of research looking at the connections between social media and multicultural societies. This book addresses that gap by highlighting the ways in which multicultural societies express themselves and are responded to in social media.

Communities, identities and social media in the age of mobility and cultural diversity

In his work on the political impact of the Internet and social networking sites (SNS) in Southeast Asia, Jason Abbott argues that 'while there is no teleological determinism which necessitates that [social media] will bring about political transformations' (2015, 201) – a point I, too, acknowledge in my own chapter on international students in Singapore, where I suggest that social media use needs to be analysed in unison with other factors – he does recognise, instead, that 'we can expect significant variation in how [social media] impact[s] upon different states and societies' (2015, 217). Likewise, the authors in this collection generally consider social media to be a valuable tool that provides a voice and a networked community to individuals and groups as they navigate through an increasingly mobile, transnational and multicultural Asia-Pacific ethnographic landscape. Moreover, social media allows individuals and communities to map and to redefine their evolving communal and national identities, as well as to create a sense of belonging, agency and place in their respective homeland(s) in the Asia-Pacific as they connect to global networks.

Thematically, the chapters fall into two groups: social media, mobility, transience and transnational relationships are dominant in the first part of the book; the second part deals with social media and existing multicultural relationships in a controlled communication environment.

The first three chapters look specifically at mobility and the strategies mobile subjects use when dealing with the consequences of life overseas. Chapters here deal with social media in combination with issues such as advocacy, transnational relationships in a context of transience and mobility, and government's concern with migrant return. In Chapter 1, Panizza Allmark and Irfan Wahyudi consider the human rights abuses suffered by Indonesian migrant domestic workers in Hong Kong as well as how social media, particularly Facebook, plays a role in advocacy and the significance of grassroots activism in providing agency for migrant workers. In particular, they look at a case study of a 2014 incident in which 23-year-old Erwiana Sulistyaningsih, an Indonesian migrant worker in Hong Kong, was severely beaten by her employer and went on to become a symbol of the exploitation of female migrant workers. Within 24 hours, the photos of Erwiana's battered body posted on social media went viral and attracted worldwide attention to the plight of this young woman. Here, the authors look at the way social media enabled this story and the wider issues of the plight of migrant workers to be disseminated across national boundaries.

Investigating strategies for feeling a sense of belonging in transience, Larissa Hjorth and Joshua Wong (Chapter 2) ask how social media impacts on the ways in which international students from Southeast Asia conceptualize and experience their own well-being in a foreign land. They note that with the rapid rise of new media technologies accompanying the increased student mobility in the region, we are witnessing a multitude of ways in which international students are using social media to foster culturally specific notions of well-being. With this in mind, this chapter is an ethnographic study that explores some of the complexities of ethnicity and identity involved in the modern-day international student experience, as well as how social media has led to some very culturally specific dilemmas of connecting and interacting with people both back home and in other countries.

In Chapter 3, Cate Gribble and Ly Thi Tran take a different perspective to mobility when they look at the ways in which nations and their diaspora engage with each other. Using the Vietnamese skilled migrant diaspora as their case study, they discuss the various waves of skilled outmigration before considering how social media can be used to facilitate a constructive dialogue between Vietnam and its diaspora, while also examining potential barriers. A key focus of this chapter is the growing outflow of overseas students and how Vietnam can avoid brain drain from this potential loss of talent.

The second part of this book looks at social media situated within transnational relationships in a context of transience and mobility; boundaries of religious discussion on social media; the re-emergence of ethic identities of minority groups; remembering, and its place in terms of everyday usefulness and trust. Hence, situated between the themes of mobility and cultural diversity, in Chapter 4 I look at international students studying at Singaporean universities and their relationship with their host nation. While, on the one hand, Singapore is an attractive destination for international students because of scholarship opportunities, a high standard of living and job opportunities post-graduation, on the other hand, the city-state can be a challenging place to live, with many Singaporeans nursing deep anti-foreign sentiments as expressed online. Here, I point out that international students have a laissez-faire relationship with their host nation, expressing only a mild form of integration and demonstrating indifference to their host nation on social media and in their social relations. This emotional disconnect from Singapore takes place even though the Singapore government is uncompromisingly welcoming to international students, and despite the fact that most participants have studied in Singapore since their early teens and a majority intend to take up permanent residence.

By choosing to situate their discussions on multicultural, yet Malay-dominated, Malaysia, the authors of Chapters 5 to 8 examine the ways in which minority groups use social media to create a sense of community and identity. In Chapter 5 Susan Leong seeks to unpack the contemporary dispute in Malaysia over the use of the term 'Allah' to denote God in Malay-language Bibles. She points out that while the use of 'Allah' is a practice that goes back to the seventeenth century, and is a result of the intersecting cultures and socio-historical processes that form Malaysia's social imaginary, in recent years it has become a controversy that has drawn impassioned protests, dramatic seizures of Bibles, and has been fought over in the highest courts in the land. Using the concept of the social imaginary, Leong argues that 'Allah' is a signification borrowed and indigenized to Malaysia. The chapter illustrates this by examining social media as both tool and space whereby Facebook groups and online petitions representing opposing sides of the debate draw on current discourses of pan-Islamic consciousness and liberalism to strengthen their positions. Leong also contends that in a nation where Islam is the national religion and Malay the national language, the ideas and the words of Islam cannot fail to be part of the social imaginary. As such, granting the exclusive use of 'Allah' to followers of Islam is to tear apart the lived experience of being Malaysian.

By looking at the Malaysian government's mismanagement of UNESCO heritage site Melaka City, Andrew Hong and Floris Müller (Chapter 6) examine the online reactions of ethnic minorities: the Dutch Eurasians and the Chitty Melaka. The Malaysian government's assimilation of UNESCO's recognition of its ethnic diversity with its own multiculturalist ideology has resulted in a peculiarly artificial and 'Disneyfied' restyling of the city that blatantly disregards historical facts in favour of economic and political motives. This mismanagement of the UNESCO site has inadvertently summoned up significant grassroots activism. Using data gathered from their discussions on Facebook, Hong and Müller demonstrate how the Dutch Eurasians and the Chitty Melaka are beginning to recuperate their ethnic and cultural identities through their critical responses to the administration of Melaka City.

In his study of ideology, ethnicity and language, Jason Sze Chieh Ng (Chapter 7) investigates the renewed sense of community and identity of ageing members of the Malayan Communist Party (MCP) through their Chinese-language website-cum-blog known as the '21st Century Old Friends Association'. Party members use social media in order to 'correct' what they feel is a distorted version of history authored by the British colonial authorities and maintained by the Malaysian government. Moreover, the Communist Party retirees have taken advantage of the importance of social media by setting up a website to promote their activities for the new Internet-savvy generation of Malaysians.

Finally, in Chapter 8 Sandra Harchard considers social media to be a unifying force in a fractured Malaysian society. She argues that Malaysian users prefer different forms of media for trusted or useful information-seeking in everyday life, reflecting a complex and confusing media environment. Adopting a networked media framework, Harchard discusses how social media is distinct from other information and communication channels and how it affords the possibility for Malaysians to gain information and news that has not been censored by government authorities. The impact of social media here is seen as having significant implications for democratic participation in Malaysian society.

References

Abbot, Jason. 2015. '"Hype or Hubris?": The Political Impact of the Internet and Social Networking in Southeast Asia'. In *Routledge Handbook of Southeast Asian Democratization*, edited by William Case, 210–22. London and New York: Routledge.
Aichner, Thomas and Frank Jacob. 2015. 'Measuring the Degree of Corporate Social Media Use'. *International Journal of Market Research* 57, no. 2: 257–75.
Australian Education International. 2015. 'Research Snapshot: International Student Numbers 2014'. Online: https://internationaleducation.gov.au/research/Research-Snapshots/Documents/International%20Student%20Numbers%202014.pdf (accessed 3 February 2016).
Australian Embassy Vietnam. 2013. 'Ozmine Vietnam 2013 Mining Mission Australia and Vietnam Partnering in Energy Development'. Online: http://vietnam.embassy.gov.au/hnoi/MR130411OZmine.html (accessed 7 June 2015).

Cui, Litang, and Michael Prosser (eds). 2014. *Social Media in Asia*. Lake Oswego, OR: Dignity Press.
Day, Graham. 2006. *Community and Everyday Life*. Oxford and New York: Routledge.
Earl, Greg, and John Kerin. 2012. 'Plan Calls for Indonesian Guest Workers'. *Australian Financial Review*, 20 November. Online: http://www.afr.com/news/policy/industrial-relations/plan-calls-for-indonesian-guest-workers-20121119-j1g3r (accessed 7 June 2015).
Goh, Daniel P. S. 2008. 'From Colonial Pluralism to Postcolonial Multiculturalism: Race, State Formation and the Question of Cultural Diversity in Malaysia and Singapore', *Sociology Compass* 2, no. 1: 232–52.
Gomes, Catherine. 2010. 'Active Remembering in Utopia'. In *Narratives of Community: Museums and Ethnicity*, edited by Olivia Guntarik, 290–397. Edinburgh: Museums Etc.
———. 2015. 'Footloose Transients: International Students in Australia and Their Aspirations for Transnational Mobility after Graduation'. *Crossings: Journal of Migration & Culture* 6, no. 1: 41–57.
Gomes, Catherine, Marsha Berry, Basil Alzougool and Shanton Chang. 2014. 'Home Away from Home: International Students and Their Identity-Based Social Networks in Australia'. *Journal of International Students* 4, no. 1: 2–15.
Hjorth, Larissa. 2011. 'Still Mobile: Cross-generational SNS Usage in Shanghai'. In *Mobile Technologies and Place*, edited by R. Wilken and G. Goggin, 140–56. London & New York: Routledge.
Hidayah, Salamat. 2014. 'Local Woman Breaks Silence on "Chinese Privilege"'. *Coconuts Singapore*, 2 September. Online: http://singapore.coconuts.co/2014/09/02/local-women-break-silence-chinese-privilege (accessed 9 June 2015).
Jacobs, Harrison. 2014. 'The 20 Most Popular YouTubers in the World'. *Business Insider Australia*, 11 November. Online: http://www.businessinsider.com.au/top-20-most-popular-youtube-stars-2014-11?op=1#1-pewdiepie-20 (accessed 9 June 2015).
Mohammad, Noor Khalid. 1975. *The Kampung Boy*. Kuala Lumpur: Berita Publishing.
———. 1981. *Town Boy*. Kuala Lumpur: Berita Publishing.
———. 1993. *Kampung Boy: Yesterday and Today*. Kuala Lumpur: Berita Publishing.
National Population and Talent Division, Prime Minister's Office, Government of Singapore. n.d. 'Composition of Singapore's Total Population'. Online: http://population.sg/resources/population-composition/ (accessed 5 June 2015).
Owen, Norman. 2005. 'Introduction: Places and Peoples'. *The Emergence of Modern Southeast Asia*, 26–41. Honolulu: University of Hawai'i Press.
Pickles, Saskia. 2015. 'Some FIFO Workers Pay High Price for Riches'. *Sydney Morning Herald*, 11 January. Online: http://www.smh.com.au/national/some-fifo-workers-pay-high-price-for-riches-20150110-12ioki.html (accessed 10 June 2015).
Robertson, Shanthi. 2013. *Transnational Student Migrants and the State: The Education-Migration Nexus Transnational Student-Migrants and the State*. Basingstoke: Palgrave-Macmillan.
Ross, Monique. 2014. 'Facebook Turns 10: The World's Largest Social Network in Numbers'. ABC News, 4 February. Online: http://www.abc.net.au/news/2014-02-04/facebook-turns-10-the-social-network-in-numbers/5237128 (accessed 4 July 2014).
United Nations Sustainable Development Platform, 2016. '244 international migrants living abroad worldwide, new UN statistics reveal', UN Sustainable Development Platform Homepage. Online: http://www.un.org/sustainabledevelopment/blog/2016/01/244-million-international-migrants-living-abroad-worldwide-new-un-statistics-reveal/ (accessed 15 September 2016).

Wong, Joshua. 2014. 'Media, Mobility and International Student Well-being'. In *Conference Proceedings of the 25th ISANA International Education Conference*, 2–5 December: 1–15. Online: http://proceedings.com.au/isana/docs/2014/Wong_Joshua_PAPER.pdf (accessed 10 June 2015).

Yang, Peidong, 2014. '"Authenticity" and "Foreign Talent" in Singapore: The Relative and Negative Logic of National Identity'. *Sojourn: Journal of Social Issues in Southeast Asia* 29, no. 2: 408–37.

Part 1

SOCIAL MEDIA, MOBILITY, TRANSIENCE AND TRANSNATIONAL RELATIONSHIPS

Chapter 1

FEMALE INDONESIAN MIGRANT DOMESTIC WORKERS IN HONG KONG: A CASE STUDY OF ADVOCACY THROUGH FACEBOOK AND THE STORY OF ERWIANA SULISTYANINGSIH

Panizza Allmark and Irfan Wahyudi

Hong Kong is a major receiving country for migrant workers, particularly women from Southeast Asia who work as domestic assistants or caregivers. One in five Hong Kong households employs migrant domestic workers (Sim 2003, 479) and there are over three hundred thousand migrant domestic workers in the country, with just about half of them from Indonesia (Amnesty International 2013). The Asian Migrant Centre (2007, 6) claims that Hong Kong is the premium destination for Indonesian migrant workers because of its moderately higher salaries, the perception of superior laws and regulations and an ambience of independence. Previous research on Indonesian migrant workers' lives in Hong Kong has mostly focused on the relationship between migrant workers and law, human rights and inequality, gender issues, political action and civil rights (Lai 2007; Ignacio and Mejia 2009; Liu 2010). However, there has been very little significant research relating Indonesian female domestic workers' activities to social media activism.

In Indonesia and Hong Kong the governments do not play an active role in controlling social media. Hence, both regions share similarities of easily accessible social media. In Indonesia, in particular, new media has impacted on political processes (Nugroho and Syarief 2013). Similarly, in Hong Kong, social media played a pivotal role in publicizing the Umbrella Revolution – the youth-led protest movement of 2014. 'The activists treated social media and new media as their basic information source' (Lee and Ting 2015, 382). Social media provides opportunities as a source for knowledge and for building community. Furthermore, the reach of social media provides a wider potential for impact and transnational connections.

Indonesian migrant domestic workers (IMDWs) in Hong Kong are heavy social media users. Most use Facebook as their communication channel with fellow migrants from Indonesia. They are live-in maids and generally work in households for more than twelve hours per day. Most cannot go outside without the permission of their employers. Female migrant domestic workers are routinely secluded in the employers' households, and this can constitute a challenge for them in negotiating their collective diasporic identity. Facebook, accessed via mobile phones, provides the opportunity for these women to create status updates and wait for responses from fellow migrant workers. This activity helps them cope with the isolation and loneliness of their daily lives. Engagement with fellow IMDWs via Facebook is not only a network of friendship, but also a way to communicate and share similar concerns and interests. Between 2013 and 2014, as a part of his PhD research on IMDWs in Hong Kong, Irfan Wahyudi conducted in-depth interviews with IMDW group representatives and nongovernmental organizations and held four focus group discussions with around twenty female IMDWs aged between 20 and 40. His research also provided some insight into the Facebook practices of IMDWs.

The following comments describe some of the restrictions encountered by one IMDW and their behaviours to circumvent them.

> I access Facebook frequently, from my cell phone even while I am working. To camouflage the mobile phone, I put it under my apron, or secretly go to the toilet and access Facebook and reply to messages. After five or seven minutes, I flush the toilet as if I were really using it. This has become a common secret. Actually, it is not our fault, since they [employers] want us to be available 24 hours. (Interview with Irfan Wahyudi, 6 June 2013)

Access to mobile phones with Internet capability, and access to social media sites such as Facebook, provide not only an opportunity for social connection but also for social activism (Lim 2013; Abbott 2013; Weiss 2013). For example, participants in Wahyudi's research asserted that Facebook was used for forwarding relevant news (from online news portals) about migrant workers and human rights abuses.

This chapter considers human rights abuses of IMDWs in Hong Kong and how social media, particularly Facebook, plays a role in advocacy. In particular, we look at a case study of a January 2014 event in which 23-year-old Erwiana Sulistyaningsih, an IMDW in Hong Kong, was severely beaten by her employer and became a symbol of the exploitation of female migrant workers. When photographs of Erwiana's bruised and battered body were uploaded to Facebook, they evoked widespread outrage. Within 24 hours, the photos went viral and attracted worldwide attention to the plight of this young woman. As Carol Chan asserts, migrant activists managed to provoke enough public uproar that led to unprecedented attention being given to the case by state actors in Hong Kong and Indonesia (2014, 6964).

In this chapter, we investigate, through a qualitative case study, the way social media enabled this story and the wider issue of migrant workers' plights to be disseminated across national boundaries. It highlights how social media 'operates as an interdependent grassroots community of individuals, organisations, and sites whose relevance and authority are established through interaction and participation' (Andreas 2007, 2). These groups might even be considered a 'counterpublic'. Hjorth and Arnold (2013, 11) assert that through social media, multiple publics are formed, which allows for affinity and political action.

A useful framework for the analysis of social media and activism is Nancy Fraser's (1997) term the *subaltern counterpublic*. She draws attention to the fact that

> in stratified societies, subaltern counterpublics have a dual character. On the one hand, they function as spaces of withdrawal and regroupment; on the other hand, they also function as bases and training grounds for agitational activities directed toward wider publics. It is precisely in the dialectic between these two functions that their emancipatory potential resides. (Fraser 1997, 82)

In the case of Erwiana the activist groups may be considered a counterpublic that is concerned with issues of human rights, of conveying solidarity and seeking justice for domestic migrant workers.

Issues Indonesian Migrant Domestic Workers Encounter in Hong Kong

A discussion of migrant labour and the activities of migrants in the host country cannot be separated from issues of diaspora. Rogers Brubaker asserts that the most common definition of diaspora refers to part of a population that 'lives as a minority outside its ethnonational "homeland"' (2005, 5). Keiko Yamanaka and Nicole Piper (2005), in their report for the United Nations, tell us that currently there are over two million migrant women workers in the Southeast and East Asia. In Hong Kong over 80 per cent of migrant workers are women (Amnesty International 2013). Female IMDWs in Hong Kong need to work hard in the host country without legal assurance of their citizenship and with the added pressure of maintaining connections and responsibilities to their families in their homeland.

Significantly, female domestic workers' contracts often last for no more than two years and exclude them from legal settlement in Hong Kong; however, they are able to continually renew their contracts. This situation has produced high numbers of migrant domestic workers who have lived in Hong Kong for more than ten years, and who have spent their working lives as provisional workers with few rights. Aihwa Ong's notion of Hong Kong as a space of neoliberal exception, which refers to how 'neoliberalism interacts with regimes of ruling and regimes of citizenship practices' reflect practices such as this, where the migrant domestic workers do not gain the benefit of citizenship but are rather subject to the disturbing cultural logic of transnationality (2006, 6).

At the same time, we also need to recognize that the use of domestic workers has existed for centuries in Chinese cultures, where there is a long tradition of servitude. Hsieh Bao Hua (2014), in her study of China from the sixteenth to the nineteenth centuries, suggests that in Imperial China those in servitude were part of the vast social stratum, and its practice was widespread in urban areas, in 'which most servile labourers migrated from agricultural villages' (xxii). The tradition of middle-class and affluent households employing house servants was prevalent in the late twentieth century and still prevails in the early twenty-first century. Domestic labourers now migrate from agricultural villages in nearby foreign countries such as Indonesia.

The practice of acquiring domestic labourers is necessitated by Hong Kong's modernity, which has led to a rise in local Hong Kong women entering the workforce, thus creating a demand for domestic labour that cannot be met by the local population. Hence, there is a need for foreign workers to take on the domestic duties. The labour of the domestic migrants 'privileges the upper and middle classes of Hong Kong', where migrant women might be considered the prey of 'neoliberal global capitalist forces' (Constable 2009, 155). Thus, worldwide rapid economic growth, which is evident from the United Arab Emirates to Hong Kong and other economically thriving areas, has brought increased income due to developments in manufacturing and services, an increase in the number of graduates from the tertiary sector, and an increase in local women entering the workforce. As a result of higher disposable incomes and two-income families, locals (and expatriates) who do not have the time or are reluctant to engage in domestic work have also created a demand for female migrant labour.

In her report for Human Rights Watch, Nisha Varia explains that 'countries with a highly-educated, highly-skilled workforce often have difficulty finding local workers for low-paying jobs and have created special immigration schemes for domestic workers' (2007, 5, 9). Furthermore, the sanctioning of foreign domestic workers was a way of increasing the labour supply by encouraging more women from rural areas to enter the urban workforce (Athukorala and Manning 1999, 141). There has been previous research concerning migrant domestic workers in the Asian region (Ford and Piper 2007; Yeoh 2007; Rahman et al. 2005). This work builds on the idea that in economic globalization, trade and capital are linked to the global movements of people. Much like Singapore, Hong Kong's modernization and the corresponding increase in women in the workforce have created a subordinate group of transnational migrants who are subject to social and cultural upheaval and exploitation.

Stereotypes of the Domestic Migrant Worker in Hong Kong

In Indonesia the IMDWs have been popularly known as 'the foreign-exchange heroes' as they attract billions of dollars of income for their country (Chan 2014; Nurchyati 2010). The financial remittances from transnational labour migration to Indonesia have been extremely beneficial for the nation. For example, in 2013 Indonesia received US$7.4 billion worth of remittances from about six million migrant workers abroad (Chan 2014, 6954). In major airports in Indonesia, the officials greet arriving Indonesian migrant workers with large signs displaying 'Welcome Foreign Exchange Heroes'. Nurchayati (2010) describes the government's policy to send migrant workers abroad as a significant part of their solution to solve economic challenges. She states, 'Since the end of the oil boom era in the early 1980s, migrant workers have become one of Indonesia's major contributors of foreign exchange' (2010, 13). Chan highlights that 'the Indonesian state is one among many neoliberalizing states that actively promote labor migration as a temporary solution to national unemployment and poverty' (2014, 6951). Chan further asserts that the 'Indonesian state and recruitment agents promote migration not only in its economic promises and advantages, but also in terms of gendered, moral, and religious or spiritual development – such as representing migration in terms of carrying out a patriotic or (feminine) familial duty' (2014, 6956). As such, Indonesia has promoted transnational female labour migration as positively contributing to the nation. Furthermore, there is direct targeting of women with little education, and from rural areas, to engage in labour migration and become the 'heroes' of Indonesia.

Hong Kong has been identified as one of the most popular countries for female IMDWs who work in domestic service as maids or caregivers. (Lai 2011; Hsia 2009). According to Susan Blackburn (2004), the prospect of work overseas has attracted many Indonesian women because of opportunities to earn a higher income than they receive back home. The Asian Migrant

Centre notes that IMDWs started to arrive in Hong Kong in 1985 (2007, 6). In the 1990s, the Indonesian government collaborated with the Hong Kong government on developing labour policies for IMDWs to work in Hong Kong. This resulted in a boom of Indonesian migration to Hong Kong (2007, 6). In 2013, more than one hundred and sixty thousand IMDWs lived in Hong Kong (Amnesty International, 2013).

Hong Kong's flourishing economy has resulted in a high demand for foreign maids (Ignacio and Mejia 2009, 12). Hsia (2009, 128) notes that to 'ensure that local workers would not complain when the migrant domestic workers began to arrive, the Hong Kong government made the hiring appear to be a "privilege"', suggesting that employers had to be wealthy enough to provide full accommodation and board for the migrant worker. At first, the maids were imported from neighbouring countries, such as the Philippines and Thailand. Between 2002 and 2007 there was a huge increase in the number of maids, with a very high demand for maids from the Philippines (Ignacio and Mejia 2009, 12). In general, Filipina maids are more proficient in English, older, better educated, and better informed of their legal rights than Indonesians (12); however, there is a growing preference for Indonesian maids by employers, possibly because Indonesian maids tend to be young, poorly educated, and lacking in knowledge of their legal rights (11). For many, it is only when they arrive in Hong Kong that they first learn of the strict constraints to their mobility while employed as domestic workers. Most Indonesians who arrive as migrant workers have low levels of education and many have not completed high school. Workers are from rural areas and regions where there is long-term poverty. The differences in educational level and status between Filipinas and Indonesians have also resulted in damaging stereotypes that circulate not only among employers but also between the two migrant groups.

Hsiao-Chuan Hsia explains that migrant domestic workers in Hong Kong are distinguished by the construction of 'stereotypes and prejudices against other nationalities' and asserts that

> negative impressions of migrants of other nationalities are constructed in the context of capitalist globalization where developing countries compete with one another to expand labor export markets. To become more competitive in the global labor markets, labor-sending states often need to demonstrate their comparative advantages, that is, how workers from their countries are 'better' than others. (2009, 118–19)

Hsia further adds: 'For governments that are latecomers in formalizing labor export policies, their marketing niche is workers who are cheaper and more docile' (119). The Indonesian female migrant workers cater to this niche as they are poorly educated and regarded by Hong Kong employers as more culturally subservient than Filipina workers. Nicole Constable aptly states that female IMDWs are viewed as 'less savvy, more passive, and appropriately submissive' (2009, 149). In addition, recruiting agencies in Indonesia play a crucial role in 'actively engaging in creating conditions that could be seen as detrimental to its emigrants' (Hsia, 119). Paul (2011) claims that placement agencies gain an economic benefit in higher profit margins from certain racial groups. The agencies 'perpetuate a hierarchy through their construction and propagation of racialized stereotypes about migrant domestic workers' who, in turn, may become exploited (2011, 1073).

Hsia asserts that 'recruiting agencies not only encourage Indonesian migrants to be 'docile' but also themselves perpetuate 'negative images of migrants to other nationalities' (2009, 119). He cites the chairperson of the Association of Indonesian Migrant Workers in Hong Kong (AKTI) who commented:

> All Indonesians are told many times by agency: don't befriend Filipinos. Ordinary Indonesian migrants feel that it's OK to have lower wages because Filipinos speak English, they know how to fight, so only they deserve higher wages. (Hsia 2009, 119)

The notion of Indonesians being told not to befriend Filipinos (or Filipinas) relates to the perceived danger that Filipina workers will encourage activism and political agency. This is because migrant domestic workers from the Philippines have a longer history of migrant worker presence and of activism in Hong Kong. They have a legacy of organizing protests, support groups and networks for migrant domestic workers. As Constable suggests, 'Filipino domestic workers are widely considered to be shrewd and politically savvy activists whose "negative" influence is rubbing off on formerly less assertive Indonesian workers' (2009, 161–62).

Female Indonesian migrant workers are preferred by the majority Chinese population in Hong Kong because they have been trained to speak Cantonese by recruitment agencies, are considered submissive and are willing to work overtime (Annggraeni 2006). The working conditions, such as the long arduous hours inside the employer's home, create social isolation for many IMDWs. The use of technology such as the Internet and mobile phones constitutes an opportunity for outside engagement and for the women to move away from the submissive Indonesian stereotype.

The Use of Social Media and Activism by Indonesian Migrant Workers

For IMDWs who have lived for many years away from their homelands and families, the Internet and social media provide a forum for community, advice and support. For women who have mobile phones with Internet capabilities, social media provides accessibility in a simple, empowering manner, allowing them to develop a voice, create their own space, participate in culture, and share information. Because of the restricted free time outside the workplace/home, IMDW use the Internet and social media to seek contact and advocacy. Anik Setyo, former chairperson of the Indonesian Migrant Workers Union (IMWU), confirms that Facebook is not only used to disseminate information but also to coordinate with members via Facebook messenger. Anik also states 'Facebook is used as a tool to interact socially, and at certain times, Facebook is a very useful tool in member coordination for collective action. WhatsApp is used as a discussion forum while Facebook is used for campaigns and socializing' (Interview with Wahyudi, 9 June 2013).

Social media also provides migrant domestic workers with a means of maintaining contact with their families. Female migrant domestic workers spend a high proportion of their adult life in Hong Kong striving to meet the financial and other needs of their families back home. This transnational connection is enacted in their position as caring mothers and obedient wives who often sacrifice themselves for the sake of the family (Yeoh and Huang 2000, 418–22). In his work on transnationalism, Lee Komito (2011, 1084,) suggests that social media helps 'maintain a sense of continuity with each other [...] regardless of where the members' of the community live. One female migrant worker interviewed by Wahyudi stated:

> I've been active using Facebook almost all the time, except when I am asleep. I access Facebook also during my work time, especially during the break time. I use social media to get various information from my friends. I also use Facebook to keep contact with family. I use Tango and Line to communicate virtually. (Interview with Irfan Wahyudi, 9 June 2013)

Facebook usage may be considered a type of emancipatory activity. In addition, social media provides a channel for information and social connection with other women for support. Social media could be seen as virtual counterpublic to the mainstream public sphere, in which participants can connect and group together (Uldam and Vestergaard 2015). It is a space for civic engagement. As research by Human Rights Watch (2013) suggests, the working conditions of female migrant workers make them vulnerable to abuse and exploitation. Advocacy and support groups play a vital role, via social media, in providing assistance to these workers.

Labour Organizations in Hong Kong

Notably, in Hong Kong 'the administrative and legal system inherited from the British colonial period established labour laws that were inclusive of migrant workers and provided institutional channels for redressing their rights' (Yamanaka and Piper 2005, 40). However, as pointed out by the Human Rights Watch,

> in countries where domestic workers are included under labour laws, enforcement is the greatest challenge. Labour officials and police may not be trained to identify or handle complaints from domestic workers competently and may treat them dismissively. (2013, 13)

There has been a long tradition of collective action to address the inequities and human rights violations in Hong Kong. Since the 1980s it 'has been a site of vibrant and well-organized migrant worker activism, particularly by Filipino women, staging very visible demonstrations on a regular basis' (Yamanaka and Piper 2005, 40). As discussed earlier, IMDWs in Hong Kong have been discouraged to associate with Filipinas due to the fear that the Indonesians will become more active in asserting their rights. However, by the early 2000s IMDWs in Hong Kong have 'succeeded in organising themselves' and have been successful in staging protest rallies 'against the exploitation by employers, recruitment agencies, and the Indonesian government', as well as uniting with the Filipina migrant domestic workers in protest movements (Blackburn 2004, 191). As Constable (2009, 149) reports, 'Indonesians have become emboldened in the more democratic post-Suharto period; they are aware of workers' rights and of the legality of labor organizing in Hong Kong'. The Hong Kong government has allowed trade unions – for example The Coalition of Indonesian Migrant Workers' Organisations (KOTKIHO) and the Indonesian Migrant Workers Union (IMWU) – to organize and demonstrate for migrant rights, such as a fair wages and working conditions. Nevertheless, the Asian Migrant Centre (2007) study, 'Underpayment: Systematic Extortion of Indonesian Migrant Workers in Hong Kong', highlighted the multiple vulnerabilities of the IMDWs, especially those who work in the domestic sphere. The report stated that '42 per cent of Indonesian migrant domestic workers in Hong Kong were underpaid' (2007, 7). The income of migrant domestic workers has become a central issue in migrant workers' activism in Hong

Kong. Hong Kong grassroots activist groups, such as the Asian Migrant's Coordinating Body (AMCB), represents a united coalition to address these issues. Such groups have helped forge relations across migrant groups from different nationalities and with local trade unions, as well as women's and community-based organizations (Hsia 2009, 123). Intensive communication and interaction are important elements in forming the sense of community and participatory action.

Solidarity through Facebook

According to Constable (2009, 143) it is unusual for migrant workers to take part in a public protest in the countries where they work. Constable points out 'public protests are virtually unheard of among migrant domestic workers in Singapore, Taiwan, and Malaysia, and especially in the Middle East and the Gulf states' (143). However, she emphasizes that in the past 15 years migrant workers in Hong Kong have become highly active in organizing and participating in political protests (14). Freedom of speech and the freedom to protest are supported by the government of Hong Kong. These advantages are used by migrant workers' organizations to raise the subject of migrant rights activism. KOTKIHO, whose mission is to serve as a unifier of Indonesian migrant worker associations, lists seven active affiliate organizations. These organizations work together mainly to manage advocacy and public campaigns on migrant workers' rights, and many have an Internet and/or social media presence. KOTKIHO's web page provides details of what they offer Indonesian migrant workers, such as shelter, training, advocacy, counselling and cultural activities. Lisa Law (2003), in her research on the electronic telecommunication networks of the Migrant Forum in Asia (MFA) and its advocacy for migrant workers, argues that this form of communication shapes political action and encourages new voices and perspectives.

Significantly, Law (2002, 219) also contends that in the diasporic public sphere 'new forms of politics and new kinds of political spaces are opening in response to transnational populations' and this may be evidenced in the use of social media. There is also a flow of communication that creates an intimacy of perspectives, as well as an openness of ideas. For example, in their consideration of the politics of social media in everyday life in the Asia-Pacific region, Larissa Hjorth and Michael Arnold's (2013, 6–7) focus on migrant workers and diaspora and on the creation of a 'mobile intimacy' that they suggest engenders non-geographic mobility and mobile phone practices that follow the trope of fluidity. They contend that 'fluids have moving surfaces (inner and outer), moving boundaries (private and public), often caused by moving currents (flows of communication)' (2013, 7). The intimacy created in this fluid movement is a way of understanding the significance of social media for migrant workers and transnationalism.

Facebook, through its participatory structure, invokes notions of community – although, we might add, it is ephemeral and based on contingent forms of solidarity. Social media offers a platform to engage in activism and to widen civic participation as well as mobilizing support. Experienced as a counter-public, social media provides a separate discursive space in which there are opportunities for community building. The notions of the community are twofold: one in terms of individuals coming together for a cause or shared interests, the other more formal notions of community building deployed by non-governmental organizations (NGOs).

Anis Hidayah, coordinator of Migrant Care, an Indonesian NGO concentrating on migrant workers' advocacy, shares the notion of Facebook as community: 'Migrant workers send news and information through Facebook since they can access it from cellular phones and perform this during their working activities. It is a flexible instrument to bridge their communication limitations and keep them engaged with the community' (interview with Wahyudi, 7 May 2013). Social media enhances the notion of community in its emphasis on social relations and provides a space for 'participatory culture' which involves, as Henry Jenkins et al. (2009) assert, not only affiliation and distribution but expression, collaboration and circulation. Sites such as Facebook provide a space for social participation and affiliation, as well as for commentating. On these sites 'participants believe their contributions matter' (Jenkins 2006, xi). The sites create a mobile intimacy that is concerned with the everyday lives and advocacy of its participants, and this is evident in the Facebook campaigns that document the human rights issues of migrant workers. The sites allow a social participation and presence that lets otherwise unheard voices to be heard

Merlyna Lim's (2013) research into social media activism in Indonesia provides some insights into the kind of social media events that gain popular attention. Lim also emphasizes the importance of 'framing the moment' of an issue. She asserts:

> Not every issue is widely diffused. In the social media environment, networks are vast, the content is over-abundant, attention spans short and conversations are parsed into short incomplete sentences instead of complete paragraphs. This circumstance is evident in Indonesia, where a majority of social media users access the networking platform from mobile phones. In such an environment, those that go 'viral' are of a light package, they tap into headline appetites and they embrace a trailer vision. In other words, only simple or simplified narratives can usually go viral. (2013, 644)

The use of captions that are pithy and seek to capture the readers' interests were used in 2014 and 2015 on the story of the abuse a Hong Kong Indonesian domestic migrant worker, Erwiana Sulistyaningsih. It sought to pique readers' interests and emotions by utilizing the terms such as 'young maid', 'torture' and 'prisoner'. Chan asserts that Erwiana's case was able to garner outrage, public support and media coverage because she 'fits representations of the extreme moral victim, as a very young, fresh-faced woman whose experiences in Hong Kong reduced her to an undernourished, barely walking, heavily bruised body' (2014, 6964).

The tragic story of domestic migrant worker Erwiana Sulistyaningsih is one recent example where social media activism and civic engagement were utilized to highlight migrant worker abuse. It was also an event that was able to 'frame the moment' by presenting an account of a victim's suffering accompanied by horrific photographs of the abuse, and thus go viral and become symbolic of the mistreatment that some female migrant domestic workers endure.

Prior to this, reports of abuse and exploitation of migrant workers in Hong Kong and elsewhere had circulated for several years in print and online media, but they had failed to gain national or international news prominence. Following the impact of the social media recording of Erwiana's abuse, her ordeal rapidly gained international media attention.

Unlike many other migrant domestic workers disempowered through mistreatment, Erwiana was able, with the public support of the Facebook campaigns about her story and the subsequent call for protest action, to report the abuse and testify against her abusive employer. Her employer was sentenced to six years in prison. Erwiana is now a spokesperson and advocate for justice for migrant domestic workers.

Facebook advocacy and the case of Erwiana Sulistyaningsih

Erwiana was tormented and abused by her Hong Kong employer for eight months. She received no days off during this time and was confined to her employer's apartment. Her treatment has been described as slavery by Amnesty International (2014). The abuse was so severe that her physical wounds never fully healed. Beatings and death threats finally ceased when her employer left Erwiana at Hong Kong airport with less than US$10 as remuneration and a ticket to return to Indonesia. She was told never to speak out about her mistreatment. Erwiana claims that her employer said that 'she knew a lot of people in Indonesia and if I said anything she would have my parents killed' (Hewson 2014). Riyanti, a fellow Indonesia domestic worker en route to Indonesia, saw that Erwiana could barely walk and offered her assistance. He encouraged her to go to the Hong Kong police, but Erwiana was scared that her employer would cancel her ticket home. On arriving in Indonesia, Riyanti escorted her to a hospital for medical assistance.

Law (2011, 248) has argued that 'viewing photos might form a situated practice of cross-cultural communication' that fosters an imagined sense of community and evokes action. The first photo portraying Erwiana's bruised and battered body at Hong Kong airport was uploaded to the Facebook account of a fellow migrant domestic worker, named Bunga, on 11 January 2014. This initial image and the subsequent photographs were important in garnering support for Erwiana's plight. The photographs of Erwiana were quickly shared by Yuni Sze, an Indonesian journalist living in Hong Kong. On 14 January 2014, just three days later, the Facebook page, 'Justice for Erwiana and all Migrant Domestic Workers Committee', appeared and received widespread attention. The creators of this page are still unknown, but is most likely affiliated with the Indonesian Migrant Domestic Workers Union in Hong Kong, as it was the leaders of this union who documented her case and supported Erwiana during her hospitalization.

The Facebook page collected around 9,000 'likes'. Of course, the number of likes may be the result of click activism or Morosov's (2011) notion of *slacktivism*, in reference to the ease of liking and joining online communities. By liking the page participants 'feel' like activists, but the 'like' may not have any real-world impact. Nevertheless, the support for the page could be seen as a discursive performance of political affinity just for Erwiana. As Jose Marcichal has argued: 'identifying with a public cause helps in presenting a self that can be affirmed or legitimated for one's public choices. As such, performing a political identity is an important public statement of affiliation with and/or opposition to a set of categories. This identification can be thought of as a small-scale form of activism' (2013).

In the case of Erwiana, the Facebook group soon rallied for action. Within a few days they posted a press release further describing Erwiana's ordeal and the need for the Hong Kong government to take more responsibility for the cases of mistreatment of migrant domestic workers. The Facebook group recorded the protests and calls for actions through updates and posting further photographs and information about Erwiana and other migrant workers' issues. On 16 January 2014 the group organized picketing, in conjunction with the AMCB, in front of the recruitment agency that hired Erwiana. In just one month news of her case had spread rapidly and widely via social media. It serves as a strong example of grassroots action drawing attention to the abuse of migrant workers.

The story of Erwiana's plight provoked further calls for action. The Facebook group supporting her case organized protests outside Hong Kong government offices and the Indonesian consulate in Hong Kong, as well as vigils and multiple submissions to the Hong Kong government. This is evidence of the power of the Indonesian migrant associations using social media to mobilize action, with a rally and protest occurring only days after the revelation of the abuse. It is important to consider that in Hong Kong there is a tension for domestic migrant workers who are allowed some form of civil rights, such as the right to protest, yet are not given the benefits of citizenship. Constable drawing upon the work of Aihwa Ong notes 'these flexible noncitizens, who are transnational in the sense of both transforming and transcending the borders of nation-states, work in a space of exception that simultaneously permits their protests (within limits) and denies them the rights of citizens and citizenship' (2009, 155).

During the campaign, the organizers of the Facebook page 'Justice for Erwiana and All Migrant Domestic Workers' provided information about a street stand where they invited passers-by to take photos expressing support for Erwiana and to distribute flyers appealing to the public to contact the Hong Kong Confederation of Trade Unions (HKCTU) if they suspected the mistreatment of domestic workers. Furthermore, on 19 January 2014, about a week after Erwiana's story went viral, the Facebook page organizers promoted a march entitled 'Justice for Erwiana! No to Modern Slavery! End Social Exclusion of Migrant Workers in Hong Kong!' Details about the march were given in Indonesian, English and Cantonese. The rally attracted around five thousand protesters, a clear example of participatory and advocacy culture in social media. The rally received worldwide attention and was featured in various of media outlets such as the *South China Morning Post*, *NewsForAfrica*, the *Daily Mail*, the *New York Times* and *ABC* news (Australia). Mainstream media also played a significant role in drawing attention to Erwiana and the working conditions of migrant domestic workers; however, the involvement of the mainstream media only came about due to the prominence of the story in social media, the success of which relies on its participatory nature. Lim (2013, 643) aptly points out that 'with Facebook, the act of writing-creating and reading-watching-listening is changed to joining and sharing' and this is particularly well evidenced in social media support for Erwiana.

Erwiana's story of abuse resonated strongly with migrant workers in Hong Kong as well as with the broader 'imagined community' of transnational migrant domestic workers. In April 2015, a Google search for 'Erwiana Sulistyaningsih' came up with around 103,000 results. Erwiana was in *Time* magazine's 2014 list of the '100 most influential people in the world' (Mam 2014). Her plight and the protest actions by migrant domestic workers have been documented in various global news sources such as *The Guardian*, *News.com*, *CNN* and *Al Jazeera*. Young, bruised and helpless, Erwiana became the poster girl for many transnational domestic worker migrants who had also been victims of abuse, while her image and her story of survival resonated with human rights advocates. The protest movement in Hong Kong calling for improvements to the working conditions of migrant workers, and the global media attention that followed, all began with social-media advocacy, and social media continued to play a role for this cause.

International support for Erwiana

An example of the transnational reach of Erwiana's cause, facilitated by the Facebook page, 'Justice for Erwiana and All Migrant domestic workers Committee', was the posting of information and a photograph from Filipino migrant au pairs and domestic workers living in Amsterdam. While Hong Kong employment agencies perpetuated stereotypes of migrant groups to disempower and discourage unity, the Facebook post suggests contrary supportive behaviour. As such, there seems to be a sense of solidarity conveyed in the labour diaspora, a community based on labour practices and understandings that transcend the migrant domestic workers' local country of employment. The global alliance of overseas Filipinos, Migrante International, had covered the story of Erwiana and conveyed their expressions of support for her, such as solidarity in protest actions. Migrante International stated:

> Erwiana's case as the latest most gruesome case depicting the suffering and plight of domestic workers, especially women domestic workers, is testament to how forced migration and labor export have become the worst cause and manifestation of all forms of abuse, oppression and exploitation of women all over the world. (Admin 2014)

The Filipino Parish, Migrante-Netherlands, Migrante Europe/IMA-Europe held a prayer service for Erwiana and all domestic workers who had been victims of abuse. In the photograph on this page, protesters posed together and held placards with calls for justice and solidarity with Erwiana. This grassroots expression is an example of a transnational solidarity that could only be achieved and broadcast through social media.

Social media activism is also prevalent in migrant workers' home in Indonesia. Globally, Indonesia has the third-largest number of Facebook users and around 90 per cent of all online activities in Indonesia relate to social media usage (Lim 2013, 639). As Lim states, 'In the political history of Indonesia, the Internet has acted as a "cyber-civic space" in which individuals and groups generate collective activism online and translate it into real-world movements' (2013, 639). Lim also asserts that social media involves 'greater collaboration and social interactivity' than does an offline setting (638). To take this point further, 'social media such as Facebook have acquired an increasingly important role in shaping Hong Kong people's political attitudes and behaviours' (Leung and Lee 2014, 345). As a result of social media's politicizing drive there is an increase in civic engagement, and this can be understood in the context of participatory politics. In the case of Erwiana, details of protests, vigils and links to petitions were broadcast on social media. An international online petition urging an end to the exploitation of migrant domestic workers was organized by Amnesty International, Hong Kong Confederation of Trade Unions, International Domestic Workers Federation and Walk Free: it gathered over a hundred thousand signatures from 160 countries and was delivered to the Government of Hong Kong in April 2014. According to Amnesty International (2014) 'the unprecedented international response to the petition demonstrates huge public concern on this issue'.

The global online organization, One Billion Rising for Justice (OBR), also rallied support for 'Erwiana and the rise for justice for all migrant workers' (One Billion Rising, 2014). The OBR takes its name from the United Nations figure that one billion women, or one in three globally, will be raped or beaten in their lifetimes. About a month after Erwiana's story went viral, OBR organized an event in Victoria Park, Hong Kong, in line with their annual worldwide dance event in which people from 207 countries had participated in 2013. Significantly, dance is seen by OBR as an act of defiance and a means of connection with others. The dance event in February 2014 in Hong Kong was organized primarily on Facebook and aimed to bring together people united in their outrage about Erwiana's abuse by her employer. It brought together Hong Kong locals and migrants, as well as fellow Filipina migrant domestic workers, in what may be described as a flash mob event of around a thousand participants – dressed in purple and joined in synchronized dance, along with speeches and chants (*China Worker* 2014). The event was streamed live and was a joint initiative with a wide range of activist groups in Hong Kong. The Hong Kong organizer, Rama Kulkarni, commented that while Erwiana had experienced violence as a migrant worker, violence against women in general was much broader issue and there was still much to be done to raise awareness of it: 'Erwiana's case did raise the profile of what we are fighting for' (Ngo 2015).

Information about and updates on Erwiana's case have also been made available on a number of websites, such as walkfree.org and the hkhelperscampaign.com (HK Helpers Campaign: A Campaign for Hong Kong Domestic Workers), which also have active Facebook pages with information about Erwiana and other migrant domestic worker news. The original Facebook page, 'Justice for Erwiana and All Migrant Domestic Workers Committee', has had the most activity, providing regular updates about

Erwiana's case, political lobbying, and a forum to share similar personal and public statements of abuse from other migrant domestic workers. Erwiana's case has drawn attention to further stories of abuse of migrant workers and has increased the number of victims coming forward with their stories via Facebook. For example, Filipina domestic migrant worker Rowena Uychiat's personal account of abuse by her Hong Kong employer has had over a thousand shares and has garnered hundreds of comments of support. Similarly, a press release about Indonesian migrant domestic worker Anis Adriana, who had her finger chopped off by her Hong Kong employer, received over 2,000 shares, hundreds of supportive comments and advice from fellow migrant domestic workers on how to take action and escape from her abusive situation.

The success of the Facebook campaign for Erwiana and migrant domestic workers may be measured through online participation and the strength of the transnational community that it has created. Furthermore, stronger forms of advocacy for human rights issues have been instituted because of the activity in social media, such as migrant workers' groups collaborating to raise awareness of the issues of migrant domestic workers. The social media campaign to raise awareness of Erwiana's story and the conditions of migrant domestic workers is an example of the rise and power of an alternative media in Hong Kong, where there is an increasing public distrust in the mainstream media because of increasing political control (Leung and Lee 2014, 344). Importantly, the alternative media may have an influence on the broader public sentiment through Facebook's extended networks through which information is shared with 'friends'. In the case of the Facebook pages for Erwiana, their overwhelming public support suggest that Facebook users, 'though constituting a minority in the society, may nonetheless exert a disproportionately large influence on public opinion' and mainstream media (Leung and Lee 2014, 355). As such, social media has played a pivotal role in gaining wider public awareness of the circumstances of female migrant domestic workers. The Facebook campaign generated visibility for the story of the abuse of Erwiana, at the same time thrusting the plight of migrant domestic workers from many regions, such as Europe, Asia and the Middle East into the global spotlight. It consolidated many activist groups to call for justice. The program coordinator for the Asia Pacific Mission for Migrants, Aaron Ceradoy, stated: 'It would be good if the migrant community can use this case to strengthen their position on their demands for changes in policies' (ABC News 2015). It is unclear how much the campaign and international outrage has effected the high-profile legal case and sentencing of the former employer of Erwiana. Nevertheless, The Mission for

Migrant Workers, the authorized representative of Erwiana in her civil case, asserts:

> This historic decision ushers in a pool of opportunities for the Hong Kong government to reform its policies for the protection of the rights and welfare of foreign domestic workers (FDWs). (Mission for Migrant Workers 2015)

Furthermore, Erwiana's story has precipitated a great deal of online awareness and generated pressure groups whose existence could have only come to be because of the presence of social media.

Conclusion

In Hong Kong, female migrant domestic workers bond through the shared social experiences as a poorly paid, marginalized and exploited group. But this bond does not reflect any passivity. Migrant domestic workers engage in counter-hegemonic practices by engaging in collective action through the use of alternative media, such as Facebook. Catherine Squires (2002, 460) notes that counter-publics 'test the reactions of wider publics by stating previously hidden opinions, launching persuasive campaigns to change the minds of dominant publics, or seeking solidarity with other marginal groups'. The campaign for Erwiana is just one example in which solidarity between marginal groups was achieved and campaigns were launched to raise awareness about human rights injustice.

Erwiana's case highlights the significance of grassroots activism in providing agency for migrant workers and social media sites providing a forum for civic engagement. In the examples provided in this chapter, collective action on Facebook by migrant domestic workers in Hong Kong has created transnational allegiances between migrant workers in other nations: a new diasporic consciousness. This solidarity was evident in the sharing of Erwiana's horrific tale of maltreatment that powerfully symbolized the abuse experienced by migrant domestic workers around the world.

References

Abbott, J. 2013. 'Introduction: Assessing the Social and Political Impact of the Internet and New Social Media in Asia'. *Journal of Contemporary Asia* 43, no. 4: 579–90.

ABC News. 2015. 'Hong Kong Court Finds Indonesian Maid Erwiana Sulistyaningsih "Tortured" by Former Employee'. ABC News, 10 February. Online: http://www.abc.net.au/news/2015-02-10/hong-kong-woman-found-guilty-of-torturing-indonesian-maid/6083474 (accessed 20 March 2015).

Admin. 2014. 'In Solidarity with Tortured Indonesian Domestic worker Erwiana Justice for all Abused Domestic Workers, End Forced Migration, Junk Labor Export! – Migrante'.

Migrante International, 6 February. Online: http://migranteinternational.org/2014/02/06/in-solidarity-with-tortured-indonesian-domestic-worker-erwiana-justice-for-all-abused-domestic-workers-end-forced-migration-junk-labor-export-migrante/ (accessed 27 February 2016).

Amnesty International. 2013. 'Exploited for Profit, Failed by Governments: Indonesian Migrant Domestic Workers Trafficked to Hong Kong'. Online: https://www.amnesty.org/download/Documents/.../asa170292013en.pdf (accessed 10 August 2014).

Amnesty International. 2014. 'Hong Kong Must End Exploitation of Migrant Domestic Workers'. *Amnesty International News*, 28 April. Online: http://www.amnesty.org.au/news/comments/34418/ (accessed 30 July 2014).

Anderson, B. 1983. *Imagined Communities: Reflections on the Origin and Spread of Nationalism*. London: Verso.

Andreas, C. S. 2007. 'Web 2.0 and the Culture-Producing Public'. Online: http://www.scribd.com/doc/40127/Web-20-and-the-CultureProducing-Public (accessed 30 July 2004).

Anggraeni, D. 2006. *Dreamseekers: Indonesian Women as Domestic Workers in Asia*. Jakarta: Equinox.

Asian Migrant Centre. 2007. 'Underpayment 2: The Continuing Systematic Extortion of Indonesian Migrant Workers in Hong Kong: An In-Depth Study'. Online: http://www.ilo.org/wcmsp5/groups/public/---asia/---ro-bangkok/---ilo-jakarta/documents/publication/wcms_116888.pdf (accessed 10 August 2014).

Athukorala, P., and C. Manning. 1999. *Structural Change and International Migration in East Asia: Adjusting to Labour Scarcity*. Melbourne: Oxford University Press.

Blackburn, S. 2004. *Women and the State in Modern Indonesia*. Cambridge: Cambridge University Press.

Brubaker, R. 2005. 'The "Diaspora" Diaspora'. *Ethnic and Racial Studies* 28, no. 1: 1–19.

Bryceson, D., and U. Vuorela (eds). 2002. *The Transnational Family: New European Frontiers and Global Networks*. Oxford: Berg.

Chan, C. 2014. 'Gendered Morality and Development Narratives: The Case of Female Labor Migration from Indonesia'. *Sustainability*. Online: www.mdpi.com/2071-1050/6/10/6949/pdf (accessed 27 February 2016).

China Worker. 2014. 'Hong Kong: "One Billion Rising" Protest for Migrant Rights'. China Worker, 10 February. Online: http://chinaworker.info/en/2014/02/10/5795/ (accessed 31 July 2014).

Constable, N. 2009. 'Migrant Workers and the Many States of Protest in Hong Kong'. *Critical Asian Studies* 41, no. 1: 143–64.

Ford, M., and N. Piper. 2007. 'Southern Sites of Female Agency: Informal Regimes and Female Migrant Labour Resistance in East and Southeast Asia'. In *Everyday Politics of the World Economy*, edited by J. M. Hobson, 63–80. Cambridge: Cambridge University Press.

Fouron, G., and N. Glick Schiller. 2001. 'All in the Family: Gender, Transnational Migration, and the Nation State'. *Identities* 7, no. 4: 539–82.

Hewson, J. 2014. 'Hong Kong's Domestic Worker Abuse'. Al Jazeera, 19 January. Online: http://www.aljazeera.com/indepth/features/2014/01/hong-kong-domestic-worker-abuse-20141199347455882.html (accessed 10 August 2014).

Hjorth, L., and M. Arnold. 2013. *Online@AsiaPacific: Mobile, Social and Locative Media in the Asia-Pacific*. New York: Routledge.

Hsia, H. 2009. 'The Making of a Transnational Grassroots Migrant Movement'. *Critical Asian Studies* 41, no. 1: 113–41.

Hua, H. 2014. *Concubinage and Servitude in Late Imperial China*. Lanham, MD: Lexington Books.

Human Rights Watch. 2013. *Claiming Rights: Domestic Workers' Movements and Global Advances for Labor Reform*. Online: http://www.hrw.org/sites/default/files/related_material/2013_Global_DomesticWorkers.pdf (accessed 15 August 2014).

Ignacio, E., and Y. Mejia. 2009. 'Managing Labour Migration: The Case of Filipino and Indonesian Domestic Helper Market in Hong Kong'. ILO Asian Regional Programme on Governance of Labour Migration, working paper no. 23. Online: http://www.ilo.org/wcmsp5/groups/public/–asia/–ro-bangkok/documents/publication/wcms_101824.pdf (accessed 10 August 2014).

Jenkins, H. 2006. 'Confronting the Challenges of Participatory Culture: Media Education for the 21st Century'. *Confessions of an Aca-Fan* (blog). Online: http://henryjenkins.org/2006/10/confronting_the_challenges_of.html (accessed 10 August 2014).

Jenkins, H., R. Purushotma, M. Weigel, K. Clinton and A. Robinson. 2009. *Confronting the Challenges of Participatory Culture: Media Education for the 21st Century*. Cambridge: The MIT Press.

Jones, Q. 1997. 'Virtual Communities, Virtual Settlements and Cyber-archaeology'. *Journal of Computer Mediated Communications* 2, no. 3. doi: 10.1111/j.1083–6101.1997.tb00075.x.

Komito, L. 2011. 'Social Media and Migration: Virtual Community 2.0'. *Journal of the American Society of Information Science and Technology* 62, no. 6: 1075–86.

Lai, M. 2007. 'Field Note: In Your Face: Indonesian Domestic Workers' Activism at the World Trade Organization Ministerial in Hong Kong'. *Women's Studies Quarterly* 35, no. 3: 123–27.

———. 2011. 'The Present of Forgetting: Diaspora Identity and Migrant Domestic Workers in Hong Kong'. *Social Identities: Journal for the Study of Race, Nation and Culture* 17, no. 4: 565–85.

Law, L. 2002. 'Sites of Transnational Activism: Filipino Non-governmental Organisations in Hong Kong'. In *Gender Politics in the Asia-Pacific Region*, edited by B. S. A. Yeoh, P. Teo and S. Huang, 205–22. London and New York: Routledge.

———. 2003. 'Transnational Cyberpublics: New Political Spaces for Labour Migrants in Asia'. *Ethnic and Racial Studies* 26, no. 2: 234–52.

Lee, A. Y. L and Ting K. W. 2015. 'Media and Information Praxis of Young Activists in the Umbrella Movement'. *Chinese Journal of Communication* 8, no. 4: 376–92.

Leung, K. K., and L. F. Lee. 2014. 'Cultivating an Active Online Counterpublic: Examining Usage and Political Impact of Internet Alternative Media'. *The International Journal of Press/Politics* 19, no. 3: 340–59.

Lim, M. 2013. 'Many Clicks but Little Sticks: Social Media Activism in Indonesia'. *Journal of Contemporary Asia* 43, no. 4: 636–57.

Liu, D. 2010. 'Ethnic Community Media and Social Change: A Case Study in the United States'. In *Understanding Community Media*, edited by K. Howley, 250–59. Thousand Oaks, CA: SAGE.

Liu, J. 2014. 'Are Indonesian Maids Safe in Hong Kong?'. BBC News, 28 April. Online: http://www.bbc.com/news/world-asia-china-27184521 (accessed 5 August 2014).

Mam, S. 2014. 'The 100 Most Influential People: Erwiana Sulistyaningsih'. *Time*, 23 April. Online: http://time.com/70820/erwiana-sulistyaningsih-2014-time-100/ (accessed 15 August 2014).

Marichal, J. 2013. 'Political Facebook Groups: Micro-activism and the Digital Front Stage'. *First Monday* 18, no. 12. Online: http://firstmonday.org/article/view/4653/3800 (accessed 27 February 2016).

Morozov, E. 2011. *The Net Delusion – The Dark Side of Internet Freedom*. New York: Public Affairs.
Mission for Migrant Workers. 2015. 'Erwiana's Victory Calls for Immediate Policy Reforms for FDWs in HK'. Mission for Migrant Workers. Online: http://www.migrants.net/erwianas-victory-calls-for-immediate-policy-reforms-for-fdws-in-hk/ (accessed 5 April 2015).
Nugroho, Y. and Syarief S. S. 2012. *Beyond Click-Activism? New and Political Processes in Contemporary Indonesia*. Berlin: Friedrich-Ebert-Stiftung.
Nurchayati, N. 2010. 'Foreign Exchange Heroes or Family Builders? The Life Histories of Three Indonesian Migrant Workers'. Master of Arts. Center for International Studies of Ohio University. Online: https://etd.ohiolink.edu/rws_etd/document/get/ohiou1289411593/inline (accessed 28 February 2016).
Ngo, J. 2015. 'Erwiana in One Billion Rising Dance Campaign to End Violence against Women'. *South China Morning Post*. Online: http://www.scmp.com/news/hong-kong/article/1713560/erwiana-one-billion-rising-dance-campaign-end-violence-against-women (accessed 10 March 2015).
Ong, A. 2006. *Neoliberalism as Exception: Mutations in Citizenship and Sovereignty*. Durham, NC: Duke University Press.
Paul, A. M. 2011. 'The "Other" Looks Back: Racial Distancing and Racial Alignment in Migrant Domestic Workers' Stereotypes about White and Chinese Employers'. *Ethnic and Racial Studies* 34, no. 6: 1068–87.
Rahman, A. N., B. S. A. Yeoh and S. Huang. 2005. 'Dignity Overdue: Transnational Domestic Workers in Singapore'. In *Asian Women as Transnational Domestic Workers*, edited by S. Huang, B.S.A. Yeoh and N. Abdul Rahman. Singapore: Marshall Cavendish Academic.
Sim, A. 2003. 'Organising Discontent: NGOs for Southeast Asian Migrant Workers in Hong Kong'. *Asian Journal of Social Sciences* 31, no. 3: 478–510.
Squires, C. R. 2002. 'Rethinking the Black Public Sphere: An Alternative Vocabulary for Multiple Public Spheres'. *Communication Theory* 12, no. 4: 446–68.
Uldam, J. and Vestergaard, A. (eds). 2015. *Civic Engagement and Social Media: Political Participation beyond Protest*. Basingstoke: *Palgrave-Macmillan*.
Varia, N. 2007. 'Globalization Comes Home: Protecting Migrant Domestic Workers' Rights'. Human Rights Watch. Online: http://www.hrw.org/legacy/wr2k7/essays/globalization/globalizationcomeshome.pdf (accessed 20 August 2014).
Walkfree. 2014. 'Help End Modern Slavery in Hong Kong'. Walkfree. Online: http://www.walkfree.org/hong-kong-domestic-workers/ (accessed 20 August 2014).
Weiss, M. 2013. 'Parsing the Power of "New Media" in Malaysia'. *Journal of Contemporary Asia* 43, no. 4: 591–612.
Yamanaka, K., and N. Piper. 2005. 'Feminized Migration in East and Southeast Asia: Policies, Actions and Empowerment'. (December) Occasional paper, United Nations Research Institute for Social Development. Online: http://www.unrisd.org/80256B3C005BCCF9/%28httpPublications%29/06C975DEC6217D4EC12571390029829A?OpenDocument (accessed 20 August 2014).
Yeoh, B., and S. Huang. 2000. '"Home" and "Away": Foreign Domestic Workers and Negotiations of Diasporic Identity in Singapore'. *Women's Studies International Forum* 23, no. 4: 413–29.
Yeoh, B. S. A, 2007. 'Singapore: Hungry for Foreign Workers at All Skill Levels'. Migration Information Source. Online: http://www.migrationinformation.org/Profiles/display.cfm?ID=570 (accessed 20 August 2014).

Chapter 2

MEDIA AND MOBILITIES IN AUSTRALIA: A CASE STUDY OF SOUTHEAST ASIAN INTERNATIONAL STUDENTS' MEDIA USE FOR WELL-BEING

Joshua Wong and Larissa Hjorth

Introduction

In recent years, social media has become an integral part of everyday life in Asia. In India, one can find the world's third-largest number of Facebook users, with over 57 million users. Dubbed 'Twitter Nation', Indonesia is home to nearly 43 million Twitter users (Nugroho 2012). In China, where Facebook is banned, a healthy diet of QQ, Weibo and WeChat dominate, highlighting the significance of media-rich mobile media. With a strong *shanzhai* (pirate or copy) phone culture that keeps smartphone prices down through the creation of imitation phones, we see over 420 million of China's total 564 million online users accessing the Internet from their mobiles. It was estimated that Internet users in Asia stood at more than 1 billion in mid-June 2012, 44.8 per cent of the world's Internet users and representing an 841 per cent growth over 2000. In Southeast Asia, the survey showed locations like Indonesia, Vietnam and Thailand as boasting the highest penetration rates of social media use.

This accelerated growth in social media – predominantly through the mobile phone – highlights the changing mobilities, cultural and ethnic entanglements playing out in the region's media practices. This is no more apparent than with the highly visible mobility of Asian students within the region. This leads us to ask: How are media practices – often deployed to negotiate being simultaneously home and abroad (Hjorth 2007) – used to pursue culturally specific notions of well-being while also engaging with global mobility? This chapter explores the intersection between culturally specific notions of well-being by Asian international students as they negotiate media usage while studying in Australia.

By exploring some detailed case studies, this chapter highlights the complex and often conflicting ways in which mobility and well-being intersect, overlay and entangle. The fieldwork was conducted by Joshua Wong as part of his PhD with the Young and Well CRC. As an international student from Southeast Asia, Wong was interested in how experiences of mobility were shaped by cultural contexts. To explore this idea, Wong interviewed approximately 40 students from various locations and asked them to compile pictorial diaries of media use in their daily lives in 2013–2015 in Melbourne. The students were recruited through international student groups and online advertisements. Through the fieldwork it became apparent that more research into culturally specific notions of well-being was required. This chapter seeks to consolidate the work done on student mobility and media usage with more nuanced notions of well-being.

International Students

Mobility has become one of the key features of the twenty-first century, aided by the rise of globalization and technologies that facilitate the movement of people, resources and ideas across different national, cultural and socioeconomic boundaries (Urry 2012). International students are one example of mobile migrant populations that are experiencing radical changes in life and aspirations because of the rise of mobile technologies and global media such as the smartphone and Internet services. This is particularly the case in some parts of Asia, such as China, whereby generation Y (*ba ling hou*) is undergoing a type of socio-economic mobility that informs geographic and cultural capital mobility unimagined by their parents (Hjorth and Arnold 2013). In this mobility, media technologies feature both symbolically and literally. The rise of these media technologies has created a very different socio-cultural and technological environment, one that separates the international students of today from the international students of the previous two decades.

Firstly, the rise of global media results in a breed of international students who are exposed to a much wider range of cultural flows and ideas than ever before. For example, cultural studies scholar Fran Martin has been exploring how female students from China undertake higher education in Australia and how this reshapes notions of selfhood and cultural identity (Martin 2014). Even though students may originate from one country, they are not bound by the media of that country, and instead can consume media from many other cultures via the Internet. With the rise of online access through mobile phone ubiquity in the Southeast Asia region, the imagining of communities and how this relates to place is changing. Far from a Benedict Anderson 'imagined community' whereby the rise of the printing press and then broadcast media sees the demise of the local through the online, the vernacular is actually given new currency and importance.

This phenomenon is especially true of students from Southeast Asia, who consume media as diverse as Indian movies, Hong Kong dramas, Korean pop music, Japanese animation and television shows from the United States, the United Kingdom and Australia in addition to their local or regional media. As cultural studies scholars such as Chua Beng Huat and Koichi Iwabuchi have highlighted, media entanglements flow through and across local and regional boundaries. For Chen (2010), nuanced and regional cultural studies approaches provide ways in which to recalibrate East Asian history. Expanding upon the work of Giovanni Arrighi, who argued for acknowledgement of internal imperialism within the region, Chen argues that Cold War concepts after World War II stalled de-imperialization efforts. Through his revised notion of 'Asia as a method', Chen calls upon 'Asian studies in Asia' (2010). While a highly significant approach, such a concept does not fully engage with the multiple forces of mobility (chosen and thrust upon) constituting the region. As Bryan Turner has noted, the rise of mobility in the region has been augmented by the growth of enclaves (2007). As Turner argues, mobility has been accommodated by immobility: with the birth of 'mobility studies' by the likes of Urry and Sheller we have also witnessed what Turner calls 'the sociology of immobility', whereby societies become enclaves rather than increasingly open.

These debates about mobility are amplified by international students whereby movements across geographies, socio-economic and socio-cultural enclaves are perpetually traversed. As the region has unevenly grown socio-economically (growth rendered into ideological power), it has been international students who are both demonstrative and instrumental in this growth. Instead of viewing culture as a monolithic environment and international students as moving from one static culture to another, the modern experience of international students is of a much more fluid amalgam of different cultural flows that continue to be present in their lives even after they physically travel to a different location – as long as they have access to the Internet. In a sense, then, many international students are *already* transcultural – even before they leave their home country – due to the ubiquity of global media flows.

Secondly, being exposed to different cultural flows means that students have the possibility to challenge traditional and culturally specific notions of 'a good life'. While the influence of their familial environment and home culture probably would play the biggest part in the determination of what goals to aim for in order to better their lives, the access to information and different cultural worldviews through media technologies may also play a role in their definitions of well-being. A greater awareness of what people in other countries consider important for success in life – or what things to value, or how to deal with problems – will lead to a reconsideration of their own aspirations and resources for well-being. The increase in global student mobility also comes into play here, as students are no longer limited to their own countries, but can start thinking about and aspiring to a better life in another country, or using the resources gained through travel to improve their future situation at home. Thus, as a result of the flow across the world of ideas and people, international students are starting to plan for and construct factors in their lives that will improve their well-being both in the present and in the future, and in ways that may be very different from the approaches supported by official well-being organizations.

While there have been many studies of international student well-being, most have approached it from the perspective of addressing systematic problems through the efforts of university administrations and well-being organizations (Burns 1991; Iwamoto 2010; Kell and Vogl 2012; Khawaja 2008; Menzies 2014; Mori 2000; Quintrell 1994; Ramburuth 2001). In this literature, not much has yet been done on how international students themselves are *active agents* pursuing their own well-being. At the same time, there is growing academic interest in studying international student mobility – not just as economic flows of labour or capital (e.g., 'brain drain') – but also as a sociocultural process in which social or cultural factors play a role in influencing student mobility (King 2003). Mobility then can be linked to the socio-cultural processes that surround student aspirations for 'a better life', and their current or future well-being.

Well-Being

The substantial amount of literature on well-being indicates that it is a complex and controversial concept – one that has been defined and measured variously in different fields. Although the bulk of the literature has come from psychologists, there have also been inputs from sociologists, medical professionals, economists and cross-cultural researchers in the debate about how to define and measure well-being. At the turn of the century, research into psychological well-being had roughly fallen into one of two schools of thought: *hedonic* and *eudaimonic* approaches. (Ryan and Deci 2001). Hedonic approaches are those studies that focus on well-being as happiness or pleasure. Eudaimonic approaches focus on well-being as 'flourishing' – the realization of human potential and living a full and self-actualized life.

Within the hedonic paradigm of well-being, happiness is usually measured through 'subjective well-being', which consists of people's subjective reports of their well-being. Subjective well-being can be said to consist of two factors: a cognitive appraisal of life satisfaction, and affect balance (the balance of positive and negative emotions felt by the person). (Argyle 2001) The contrast to subjective well-being is 'objective well-being', which is measured through indicators such as income levels and socio-economic status, physical health indicators, and other material properties that are independent of subjective reports. The greater proportion of literature in the field of psychological well-being research, however, has focused on using subjective well-being, and this is also the approach used by the majority of studies done on the well-being of international students.

Cultural approaches to subjective well-being suggest that there are cultural factors that do not just co-vary with well-being, but these factors actually have a causal or determining influence on well-being (Diener and Lucas 2000). Some researchers have also pointed out that the very way well-being is *defined* (and not just measured) is culturally influenced. Montgomery (2013) showed in an ethnographic study of Central Asian cultures how notions of well-being can emerge from culture and can be conceived of not as 'happiness', but as 'contentedness'. This flies against the positive psychological emphasis on happiness maximization, but makes perfect sense for people living under difficult conditions in Central Asia. Other researchers are starting to explore how different cultures understand what 'happiness' (Pflug 2009) and 'goodness' (Smith 2007) mean, according to the peoples of that country.

However, there are also alternative approaches to well-being that arise from health studies and economics, such as the resilience and capability approaches. Studies of resilience focus on thinking about an individual's well-being as his ability to weather difficult times and achieve positive outcomes in negative circumstances (Gilligan 1999; Waaktaar et al. 2004). Amartya's Sen's capability approach (Sen 1985, 1993), however, considers quality of life or well-being as something individually determined, based on the individual's capacity to choose from a range of options on ways of being and of doing things. These various things that an individual chooses to be or do in the course of leading a life, Sen terms as 'functionings', examples of which include 'being well-nourished' or 'maintaining good relationships with family'. The capability of a person is total range of functionings that she or he can achieve or be, from which individuals choose one particular combination of functionings to be active in their lives. As such, Sen's approach to well-being is one in which individuals determine which functionings are important to their concept of 'well-being' and then choose or work towards gaining the capability to have those functionings active in their lives.

Sen's approach is particularly useful in the examination of the conjunction between media and well-being. Media technologies massively expand the set of capabilities that a person could have. For example, consider the capability of 'communicating with family members in a different country'. Media technologies not only expand the range of choices to fulfil that particular functioning – expanding phone calls and snail-mail letters to mobile text messages, social-media updates, video chat, e-mails, and many more – but they also spread knowledge of such choices through information. Thus, both the information and communication afforded by new media technologies serve to expand the capability of international students to communicate with family members overseas. However, it must be said that these are just capabilities – *potential* functionings, if you will – and the specific form of communicating with family members in a different country still needs to be determined by the student. The next section provides an overview of some of the ways in which migrant and mobile populations have used media technologies to pursue functionings they consider important to their well-being.

Mobility, Migration and Media

The study of transnational migrants (which includes international students) often falls under the new mobilities paradigm – studies that focus on the movements of people, ideas and resources and the wider social impacts of such movements. (Urry 2007) From migrant workers in China (Qiu 2014; Wallis 2011) to Filipino care workers across the world (Madianou 2011), mobility – and particularly the role of mobile technologies – has impacted well-being in various ways. For many transnational communities – which includes students – media technologies help to maintain intimate relationships with home as well as negotiating being simultaneously 'home and away' (Hjorth 2007). In the case of Filipino care workers in Hong Kong, mobile technologies facilitate both a sense of independence and a constant co-presence with family, ranging from raising children at a distance to establishing and extending networks of community support (McKay 2006; 2007). For others, such as rural-to-urban migrant workers in China, these technologies provide not only connection with their hometowns, but also ways to connect with their fellow migrant worker communities, and even to develop romantic attachments (Wallis 2011). While some theorists, such as Sherry Turkle (2012), argue that these technologies merely mediate 'real' intimacy, others point out that ideas about face-to-face being 'unmediated' are also problematic, especially when language, accents, gestures and memories serve to further mediate the experience of intimacy (Jamieson 1998).

Mobile and new media technologies have not only been a source of connection and intimacy, but also a platform that allows the disenfranchised to challenge existing hegemonies of power (Qiu 2014; Qiu 2010; Schwittay

2011). Voices that have been traditionally silenced now have a say in their local communities, ranging from lower-class migrant workers protesting exploitation (Qiu 2014) to youth in Korea and China organizing protests around political and social issues (Qiu 2010) to Indian women expressing their thoughts about the gender divide (Schwittay 2011). In other cases, media technologies have allowed new structures of power in terms of media access to emerge. For the aforementioned Chinese generation Y (*ba ling hou*), growing up in a media-rich environment allows them to teach their elders – parents and grandparents – new media literacy skills in order pursue co-presence with them (Hjorth 2012).

Contradictions and paradoxes are apparent. On one hand, there have been growing concerns about addiction to numerous forms of new media, concerns that have culminated in various governmental initiatives to curb the problem (Ok 2011; Wallis 2011). On the other hand, young people have argued that participation in games and new media have a wide range of positive effects, ranging from learning economic and trading skills in MMORPGs (Wallis 2011) to fostering useful social connections and promoting socialization (Schwittay 2011).

With regard to international student mobility and how it relates to well-being in particular, a growing number of studies focus on the social and cultural motivations for acquiring an international education. These include accumulation of cultural capital in the form of degrees from 'Western' universities in Asian societies (Waters 2006), acquisition of new languages and exposure to different cultures and mobility aspirations for future international careers (Findlay 2012), and the development of a multicultural or cosmopolitan identity (Gu 2009; King 2003). At the same time, there are also problematic assumptions about international student mobility being a great equalizer regarding socio-economic class distinctions. However, as Findlay et al. (2012) show, more often than not class distinctions are extended and reproduced through the globalization of higher education, with students from well-to-do families having more opportunities and aspirations to seek an international education and thus maintaining established class differences. In the next section we discuss fieldwork conducted into understanding the entanglement between divergent understandings of well-being, mobility and media practice through a case study in Melbourne, Australia.

Methodology: A Case Study of Home and Away

To explore a more nuanced understanding of international student well-being and media usage, a pilot study following an ethnographic approach was conducted from September to December 2013 in Melbourne. The ethnographic methods included interviewing, participant observation, scenarios of media use and 'a day in your life' re-enactments. These methods sought to provide nuanced understandings of well-being in, and through, practice. The pilot study was an exploratory one, seeking to examine the problems they faced as international students, their thoughts about well-being and connections to sources of well-being, as well as how their usage of media technologies for playful or leisure purposes impacted their well-being. A total of 19 international undergraduate and postgraduate students took part in this study. Students came from a variety of countries, including Colombia, Fiji, France, Indonesia, Malaysia, Mauritius, Russia, Singapore, Sri Lanka and Vietnam. They were interviewed individually or in groups of two to three people.

While discussing the problems they faced as international students, a number of them revealed some interesting themes that are relevant to the discussion about migrant identities, well-being and the usage of social media. From these themes we identified some key rubrics informing mobility, well-being and media. Below are three examples of topic areas in which the confluence of mobility and media interact with international students' identity and well-being: Maintaining Home Connections; Sharing Life Narratives and Vicarious Hanging Out; and 'Inauthentic' Connections and Online Communities of Diaspora. (Note that in all cases of quotes from participants in this chapter, pseudonyms have been used to protect the privacy of the participants.) These sample topics illustrate how mobility, well-being and media are informed, both by global and yet culturally specific local notions. Now we will discuss five rubrics for understanding the overlay between media, mobility and well-being.

Maintaining home connections

Social media has often been seen as a channel through which migrants can maintain connections with their home communities and families while away in another country. While this is still true to some extent, the role of online media becomes more complex as one probes deeper. For many international students, the co-presence (electronic proximity) afforded by Skype teleconferencing has allowed them to alleviate their sense of homesickness during their early days in Australia. Two girls, Carol[1] from Malaysia and Samantha from Singapore, describe the Skyping experience in informing maintaining intimacy with home and family:

---

1   All names of participants used are pseudonyms.

Excerpt 1 – Carol, female Malaysian-Chinese undergrad.

CAROL: Yeah, usually I would Skype my family – you know, like just leave it on the whole day while I do my work and they do their thing. Just like you know, the sound of home and the noises and their voices, and things like that.

INTERVIEWER: And who was on the other side of the Skype connection that you turned on?

CAROL: Anyone. Like my sister, my father, my mom[, …] sometimes they're just busy – no one's actually sitting in front of the computer, they're just moving around, things like that, but I just leave it on.

INTERVIEWER: Okay. What made you decide to use that way of doing things rather than just talking face-to-face on Skype?

CAROL: Well we talked, but after a while obviously everyone's going to get on with their own things, so we just left it on. And like if anyone has anything to say to me, just come over and talk to me, things like that.

INTERVIEWER: Right. How did you feel then, using that way of –?

CAROL: It was a bit comforting. It was like […] my sister was initially supposed to stay with me, but she missed her enrolment so she had to go back to Malaysia and do another semester there. So, like, we rented a place that was fairly big, for the two of us. So the house was just very, very quiet, for just one person. So like, the noise back at home, seeing home and stuff, was just very comforting.

INTERVIEWER: Okay. What were some of the noises that were comforting for you?

CAROL: My dog. I could hear him. The computer I usually Skype them faces the dining table, so they eat and things like that. They sometimes talk to me while eating, and things like that.

Excerpt 2 – Samantha, female Singaporean-Chinese undergrad.

Because everyone was back home, sometime my parents would like just be[, …] they just switch on the Skype and I just switch on my Skype and then, whether is it we're talking or not, it's just switched on. I know that they worry, 'cos I'm alone in the room, with four walls and all, they just – I think they just worry I'll just [go] crazy out in the quietness, and you know, want to go out, 'cos not familiar too much and usually after school it's quite late already. Five-thirty, six, yeah.

The contrast between these two female students' experiences of how Skype connects them to home is interesting in their perceptions of space. In Carol's case, Skype was used primarily to bring the immediacy of the home *environment* into her life to stave off loneliness – particularly the sounds of home, such as her dog's barking. What was comforting to her was the everyday noises and routines of home. In Samantha's case, however, Skype helped her connect to the freedom and safety of home in a very spatial way. Her mention of going 'crazy out in the quietness' and 'want[ing] to go out' implies that she felt hemmed in, yet was uncertain about the safety of wandering around after dark. By connecting with Skype to the family home, it somehow expands her spatial horizons virtually, alleviating any claustrophobic reactions or boredom, while still keeping her safe in her own room. This may also be linked to Samantha's cultural background as a student from Singapore, which would influence her expectations of city nightlife.

Singapore is a city where most shops, neighbourhood cafes and urban amenities stay open much later than Melbourne (usually until 9 or 10 p.m.), and thus the overall level of activity of city residents at night is much higher. Added to the fact that Singapore is a relatively more densely crowded city than Melbourne, the noise and bustle of the city at night is significantly higher, even in the suburbs. Therefore, when Samantha arrived in Melbourne, the relative 'quietness' of the city was unfamiliar and disturbing to her.

In addition to this, Singapore has very high standards for night-time safety, and it is generally safe for women to walk around alone at night – it was recently ranked as the top city in the world with regard to personal safety, while Melbourne was ranked eighth (*The Economist* Intelligence Unit, 2015). Furthermore, it is fairly common for university students living alone in Singapore to eat out for dinner or supper rather than cooking at home (due to the relatively cheap and prevalent hawker food). As such, it was probably unusual for Samantha to return to her room so early in the evening (6 p.m.), but concerns for her safety in a new environment forced this upon her. Many Singaporean families are aware that their country's high levels of safety are not found elsewhere, and thus Singaporeans who go overseas are often cautioned to be wary of their surroundings when living in other countries. Samantha had to remain in her room to alleviate parental worries about safety in Melbourne, but at the same time she felt a dissonance with the lifestyle expected of a university student in Singapore. This physical confinement to her room felt unnatural to her, and thus Skype afforded a way of expanding her perception of spatial freedom in a way that does not compromise her safety in Australia, while at the same time bringing some of the pervasive closeness of her family into her room, so that she would not feel alone.

Sharing life narratives and vicarious hanging out

In Ito et al.'s study of new media, the authors noted the important literacy of new media for 'hanging out' and 'messing around' (2009). Being ambiently there or always on are key features of contemporary new media – characteristics that bring both positive and negative affordances. In Samantha's case, above, Skype also served as a way for her parents to monitor her activities and well-being – thus providing a layer of security in alleviating parental worries. While familial monitoring in many Asian families is apparent, with social media apps we are witnessing new ways in which families can keep a friendly eye on children, especially as they travel (Sengupta 2012). Social media such as Skype provides a type of ambient hanging out that allows more and different types of co-presence than previously afforded. As Hjorth and Arnold (2013) noted in their study of parents of university students studying away from home, media such as online games afforded a type of ambient co-presence that served to ease feelings of loneliness and sadness.

As Daniel Miller and Jolynna Sinanan note in *Webcam* (2013), the 'always-on' nature of the webcam exemplifies a theory of attainment that views media technologies as an integral part of being human. In these technologies, uneven power relations are amplified, with those seeking to watch (such as parents) becoming more apparent. For many young people, negotiating their parents watching, and also using social media to construct notions of self beyond the parental eye, is a balancing act (Clark 2013). Social media services are not merely a communications technology to bring the familiar presence of home to the user – they are also sites that allow international students to construct narratives about their lives in Australia for their families to vicariously and ambivalently be co-present.

Excerpt 3 – Carol, female Malaysian-Chinese undergrad.

INTERVIEWER: Okay. Did you use Facebook for posting your own photos, or –?
CAROL: I did. Because my Mum uses Facebook as well – she would always ask me to upload photos so she could see […] and things if I, you know, go out with friends or things like that, then I would post it up for her to see.
INTERVIEWER: I see. So it was primarily a way to update your mother […] what the things you were doing?
CAROL: Yeah.

Excerpt 4 – Samantha, female Singaporean-Chinese undergrad.

A lot of my friends in Singapore, they do ask, 'What's going on in your life, you know? What do you see that, you know, you find interesting about Melbourne that we don't see?' and stuff. Yeah. So, after they requested, [I] started to put some more photos up so that they get to know what's going on and what's there here that we don't see in Singapore. Yeah.

The passages above show how Facebook and Skype are being used as tools for identifying, documenting and sharing the student's life to family and friends back home. For Carol, it was a way to let her mother see what is happening in her life. For others, such as Samantha, it was a way to demonstrate what is interesting and different about her new country to friends back home who would otherwise not have a chance to see these things. This activity of selectively showing photos that contrast the two countries may also play a role in Samantha's understanding of her national identity. What becomes apparent in these quotes, however, is that it is the people who are back home who request the students to construct these narratives for them. In Carol's case, her mother requested it, and in Samantha's case, it was her friends.

In some ways, this practice of requesting narratives about lives in a different country parallels the travel storytelling that existed prior to social media, when travellers would return from their voyages and then tell their stories to the eager listeners at home. In discussions about social media and intimacy we see how the new media remediates – that is, revisits and amplifies existing and older practices (Bolter and Grusin 1999). Technologically, Facebook photos have merely replaced the slideshow photo reel. However, the key difference is that the slideshow reel was a fixed narrative based on events that have happened in the past, which travellers would only show at the end of their travels, whereas the Facebook photo album or Skype video feed can be shared across temporal and geographic distances to multiple and instantaneously intimate publics. This means that the time gap between the activities of the narrator and the feedback of the audience is much smaller.

For parents who might be worried that their child may be going astray or encounter troubles, this almost instantaneous feed allows them to be actively involved in giving advice, monitoring for trouble and generally fulfil their parental roles while they are still in a position to influence the future events in the child's travel story. So the narratives that students construct, on the one hand, enable people from home to vicariously experience their lives in a different country. On the other hand, they also serve as a tool for parental monitoring because of the relative immediacy of the feedback loop. Of course, the parental monitoring function only applies in cases in which the student has been truthful about the events that they disclose in the narratives they construct for their family and friends. Which leads us to our next topic.

'Inauthentic' connections

Definitions of being 'true' or 'real' on social media differ across generational and cultural divides. These definitions are often tacit and shape what activities and practices are deemed fine for sharing and which ones should not be disclosed. While social media seems to promote over-sharing of personal information, often there are culturally specific nuances as to what is respectable to over-share. In those uneven expectations, perceptions about being true or fake ensue. Even though social media can be, and often is, used by international students as a tool for identity formation and sharing, other students raise doubts about the validity and authenticity of narratives constructed via social media:

Excerpt 5 – Eric, male Singaporean-Chinese postgrad.

Since Facebook came out, for me I'm quite imaginative about it. I feel that it puts on a false appearance or a false outlook on a person. It diminishes what the true person is. He portrays how he wants to look like through what he likes on Facebook, what he doesn't like.

For Eric, the problem with Facebook was that people crafted an image of their best self and left out the bad parts. This was problematic because it provided an incomplete picture. A second problem students mention is the insincerity of expressions of friendship often posted on Facebook:

Excerpt 6 – Camille, female Malaysian-Chinese undergrad. Rebecca, female Singaporean-Chinese undergrad.

CAMILLE: I used to play Facebook a lot more, but then like […] I actually deactivated for a while, and then I think I deactivated it for like almost a year, and then after that I just didn't really feel the need to play anymore. I just – like, I have it there, but I just don't touch it.
INTERVIEWER: Okay. How come? What made you want to deactivate it?
CAMILLE: Mmm […] I was annoyed at it. <laugh> 'Cos there were some people that only […] they just write things on Facebook and interact with you on Facebook, but then like in real life, in the 'now' time, they don't actually interact with you. So I got really annoyed with some people, 'cos they just say stuff like, 'Oh, we miss you', and I'm like, 'You guys don't even *look* for me', and I just got annoyed and I was like, 'Okay, I don't want […] I don't want to do this', and I just shut it away. And then I just go, like, if they want to contact me, contact me on the phone.
INTERVIEWER: Okay. So I see a lot of nodding in you guys <looking at others>. Do you also have similar experiences?
REBECCA: Yeah. But just never deactivate. I think for international students, I find that […] people, especially at the start, 'Oh, yeah, we miss you, we miss you',

but then most of the time, I feel that I'm the one making the effort to keep in contact with them. And then they'll be like, 'Yeah, yeah, we always think of you, and we miss you', and stuff[. ...] I'm like – 'Okay, true, but why is it I'm always the only one initiating contact?' – so [...] yeah, Facebook [...] a bit wrong.

Excerpt 7 – Nicholas, male Singaporean-Chinese undergrad.

Some people, they like to post on each other's walls and whatever, having conversations where everyone can see – yeah, I don't like that kind of stuff. It's too public. As in [...] it feels very artificial, it feels like you're posting on each other's walls not to talk to the person, but to tell everyone 'Hey, I'm talking to my friend here, have a look, I'm so close to this person'. Or 'I am whatever, whatever, I'm doing this'. It's sort of an advertisement to the world. You're not really talking to that friend. I prefer to have a private chat where you message the friend or you talk to the friend individually rather than you broadcast to the entire world. Some people like that, as in, whatever – if they like that it's cool, that's their choice – but I tend not to like that. I tend to like conversations where you don't tell everyone 'Oh I'm talking to this person'. It just feels very fake and very artificial to me. So I think just mainly messaging apps – Whatsapp, Lime, Viber, Callin – that sort of stuff. Not public social media but private social media.

Both these excerpts talk about the insincerity of people posting on Facebook. In these excerpts we see the often-tacit expectations around what is perceived as 'real' or inauthentic playing out. In this perception, differing notions of public/private and real/fake come to the foreground. The young women point out that there is a dichotomy sometimes between expressions of friendship and interest on Facebook versus real life. Nicholas suggests that the motives of people posting on Facebook are more about showing off the relationship than actually connecting with the person. Thus, what appeals most to him as an international student is 'private social media', in which small, intimate messaging is perceived as being more authentic than conversations on the public walls of Facebook.

Rebecca also points out that it is usually the international students who have to make more effort in reconnecting to their home communities and friends. The question of effort and who has to make the effort to maintain the relationship is an important part of the uneven expectations informing media usage. For international students, they initially are cut off from much of their social support structures upon moving to a different country. Therefore, the relationships with friends and family back home comprise a greater proportion of the social support they need, compared to their friends back home. In a paper that examines how usage of mobile phones for maintaining friendships influences friendship satisfaction, Hall and Baym (2012) discuss the dialectic between dependence and autonomy in close friendships that mobile communications impacts in an ironic way. They note that mobile phone use for relationship maintenance among close friends contributes to both mutual dependence (which increases friendship satisfaction), but also over-dependence and lack of autonomy, which decreases satisfaction and can lead to entrapment (feelings of guilt and pressure). For international students, moving to a new country means that their autonomy sharply rises in *all* of their relationships, leading to them feeling the need for increased dependence in their close relationships in order to bring the dependence–autonomy relational dialectic in their lives back into balance. This leads them to pursue greater interaction and inclusion into the everyday lives of their family and friends overseas, through communications media. On the other hand, for the friends back home, the overall balance between dependence and autonomy among their close relationships has only been changed to a minor extent by the loss of one friend overseas. However, when that overseas friend starts demanding greater inclusion and interaction in order to fulfil her need for mutual dependence in her friendships, this may instead feel like an impingement on the home friend's autonomy, leading to dissatisfaction in the friendship. Furthermore, attempts by the home friend to preserve autonomy are viewed negatively by the international student as denial of support or rejection of efforts to maintain the friendship, thus also leading to dissatisfaction on the international student's side of things. This problem is further exacerbated by the dispersal of many 'home communities', as seen in the next section.

Online communities of diaspora

Finally, we come to the problem of what it means to connect to a 'home community'. David Morley has written extensively about the tensions around notions of 'home' in the age of mobile technologies. Mobile technologies both tether us to notions of home at the same time as setting us free (Morley 2000). With online media entangling in offline everyday practices, notions of community and public are as much defined by the online as the offline (Hjorth and Arnold 2013). Participatory media like Twitter and Facebook mean that Western binaries between online and offline, public and private/intimate, home and away are eschewed. Multiple communities take the form of intimate publics that play out, and through, online and offline co-presence.

With the rise in global mobility, students are increasingly seeking tertiary education overseas. For many of our participants an overseas education is seen as a ticket to moving out of their country and finding a permanent residence in their new country. Thus, old certainties about international students going away from home for a short while to study and then returning are starting to fade away. Joseph, an undergraduate from Malaysia, shares how he has difficulties reconnecting with school friends:

> Excerpt 8 – Joseph, male Malaysian-Chinese undergrad.
>
> JOSEPH: I was from a high school where sixty students in my class, one-quarter went to UK, another quarter went to US, another quarter went to Hong Kong and Taiwan, another quarter went to Singapore. So when you go back to Malaysia, you have no community to go back to. And then suddenly you realise – hmm, the only people you can ever talk with or ask out, or even just eat a meal with, is your relatives or your parents or whatnot. Where are all my friends? Huh. They're all overseas somewhere.
>
> INTERVIEWER: Okay, alright. So, it was a lack of community back home that was a big factor as well?
>
> JOSEPH: Yeah. And I think it occurs for particularly Malaysian communities where everyone really tries to go overseas. Like Australians, I think, if they study – one of the Australians tried to go, like say UCL [University College London] or something, when they come back their community is still back home, like everybody's still here. Very few [Australian students] go overseas. Malaysia, every single person will go overseas. So I had to build a new community here. And that was a very challenging thing.

Joseph highlights a unique aspect of the Malaysian higher education system, which features a host of partnerships with foreign universities, resulting in many students who can afford it travelling overseas for their further education. Not only does affordability increase, but Joseph also mentions that everyone 'really tries to go overseas'. In Malaysia, there are a number of push factors that drive students overseas in hopes of perhaps securing a permanent residency in another country – the first step of which is gaining a university degree from that country. These push factors include racial and religious discrimination, perceptions of high levels of governmental corruption and incompetence, perceived low educational standards of local institutions and rising costs of living in comparison to starting pay. Many students, especially from middle-class families, see moving to another country as the best option.

As a consequence, the sense of community among Malaysian international students returning home becomes fragmented. Their usual patterns of friendship activities – face-to-face chats and eating out together (Gomes 2014) – become disrupted due to the increased global mobility of their high school friends. Their 'home community' is no longer a group of friends bounded by a physical locality, but rather a diaspora of fellow travellers scattered across various countries, united only by past memories of shared experiences together. While this diasporic community can provide some elements of support to international students living alone in another country, Joseph is also aware of the problems of relying on such an online community:

Excerpt 9 – Joseph, male Malaysian-Chinese undergrad.

INTERVIEWER: How connected do you feel to sources of social support? That means people you go to for encouragement, for advice, when times are difficult. In your early days at Melbourne.

JOSEPH: Social support? Unfortunately, regrettably as well, um, turned back to my gaming communities. So basically, friends who have separated, but went to UK or Singapore while I was in Australia. True, there are some delays, because [I]nternet connection and the distance [...] when we played games together it's like, we're back in high school again. So those were the initial support. But I've since discovered that such things cannot be permanent. So, it must be stopped. I encouraged friends to stop also. [...] That was the initial support. Beneficial up to a certain extent. But if you rely on it solely to be your social support, then destructive.

INTERVIEWER: Why do you say that it can be destructive if it's your only source of social support?

JOSEPH: Then, you won't learn at all. Because [...] I think, uh, social life has a lot of learning involved. And, if you've already learnt a way to interact, which is through gaming, then that's it. Like the next time you go into the gaming community you know how to interact again. And you never learn, uh, outside world, how they interact. Professionals interact differently, Master's students interact differently, undergraduate students interact differently, high school students in Australia also interact differently. But when you're part of different social circles, with different personalities grouped together, then there's a whole new learning process involved. So that's what I meant by if you rely on it too much, it'll be destructive because you don't build up your social skills.

For Joseph, even though he initially relied on existing communities online that were formed in his home country for social support, he eventually broke it off. This was not because there was anything particularly unsatisfying with his online friends, but because he was aware that he needed to learn how to interact with other groups of people rather than relying on his online gaming community comfort zone. This also relates to his conscious shaping of his self-identity – he is aware of multiple roles in society that he may one day play as a working professional or a Master's student – and he wants to learn the social skills required to interact with these groups of people. Thus, in order to step into his future identity, he slowly detached himself from his online 'home' community.

At the other end of the spectrum, several students are using social media and online technologies to help them build local communities in Melbourne. Karen, another female undergraduate from Malaysia, shares pictures of how online social media helps her connect to other international students, as well as keep up with news from her home country.

For Karen, social media has greatly helped her to develop and maintain friendships with both the local community here as well as her home country. She seamlessly navigates between all of these apps to maintain a network of friends that constitutes a new home environment for herself and that combines offline and online elements that feed off each other in a virtuous cycle: the online networking site informs her of offline events where she meets people with whom she then maintains contact through social media apps on

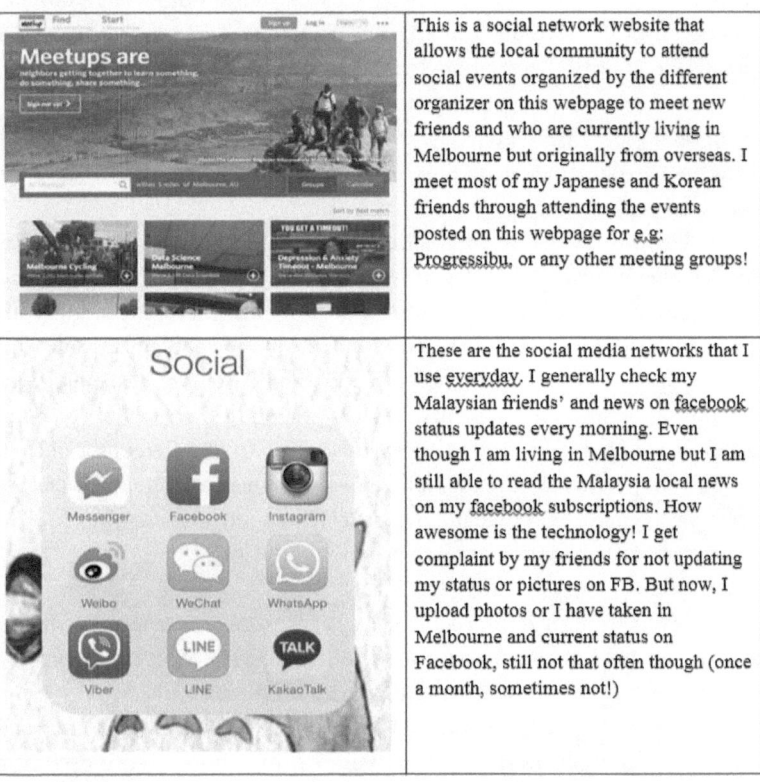

Figure 2.1 Picture diary of Karen, female Malaysian undergraduate, showing websites and apps she uses.

her phone. The apps on her phone also reflect the diversity of the people she forms a community with – LINE and KakaoTalk are both preferred social media applications used by students from Japan and Korea; WeChat and Weibo are used by Chinese-speaking Malaysian youth; while the rest are for English speakers. The offline activities she does with her friends in Melbourne also form the basis of her sharing of her life narrative with people in Malaysia.

Besides keeping in touch with her friends from Malaysia through Facebook, Karen also subscribes to newsfeeds from Malaysian news outlets. As Tapsell (2013) explains, news in Malaysia is often problematic, due to strong governmental controls over traditional print/broadcast news media and crackdowns on independent journalism. The Internet and social media has allowed for greater media liberalization and the organization of activist campaigns in the short term – particularly during the Malaysian general elections in 2013. However, very few of the students interviewed reported much interest in politics or following political news in their home countries. Having grown up in a country where media freedom has not been valued, nor critical analysis of the government encouraged, most of these students express political apathy in their usage and consumption of news media from home, and self-censorship when posting political content online. In fact, a few have suggested that their reason for going overseas to study was because the political situation in their home country was deemed impossible to change, and thus they would rather escape to start a new life in Australia than care about changing their home country. While news media helped them stay in touch with their origin countries, the road to their future well-being lay outside their home countries – in the diasporic community linked together by social media and online communications technologies. Their true homes are now found ambivalently through the multiple digital screens that negotiate an entanglement between various forms of co-presence that navigate an electronic proximity when face-to-face is not a reality.

Conclusion

In this chapter we have explored the entanglement between mobility, media and well-being through a case study of Southeast Asian international students in Melbourne. Drawing on fieldwork with 40 participants, we have studied some of the key notions involving the relationship between mobility, media and well-being – Encountering the Cross-Cultural; Maintaining Home Connections; Sharing Life Narratives and Vicarious Hanging Out; 'Inauthentic' Connections; and Online Communities of Diaspora. These rubrics are by no means definitive or exhaustive, rather they provide ways in which to understand the complex overlay between media, mobility and well-being. Through these rubrics we have sought to tease out some of the ways uneven transnational narratives play out through individual practices. For some students, home attitudes towards ethnicity and race are replicated and reinforced through social media connections. For others, the connections facilitated by social media help to alleviate loneliness, but at the same time increase the cultural patterns of constant monitoring of their lives by friends and family. And for still others, the problem lies in whether social media really helps or hinders relationship-building with family or friends back home – and whether or not that sort of home community really exists anymore, outside of the Internet.

The case study examples are but a few ways in which media and mobility are changing the way international students live and think well-being. There are plenty of new challenges and much more to be done in exploring and mapping out how international students and other migrants cope with the new conditions under which they will live in the twenty-first century.

References

Argyle, M. 2001. *The Psychology of Happiness*. New York: Routledge.
Bolter, D. and R. Grusin. 1999. *Remediation*. Cambridge, MA: MIT Press.
Burns, R. B. 1991. 'Study and Stress among First Year Overseas Students in an Australian University'. *Higher Education Research & Development* 10, no. 1: 61–77.
Chen, K. H. 2010. *Asia as Method: Toward Deimperialization*. Cambridge and London: Duke University Press.
Clark, L. S. 2013. *The Parent App: Understanding Families in the Digital Age*. New York: Oxford University Press.
Diener, E. and R. Lucas. 2000. 'Explaining Differences in Societal Levels of Happiness: Relative Standards, Need Fulfillment, Culture, and Evaluation Theory'. *Journal of Happiness Studies* 1 no. 1: 41–78.
Findlay, A. M., R. King, F. M. Smith, A. Geddes and R. Skeldon. 2012. 'World class? An Investigation of Globalisation, Difference and International Student Mobility'. *Transactions of the Institute of British Geographers* 37, no. 1: 118–31.
Gilligan, R. 1999. 'Enhancing the resilience of children and young people in public care by mentoring their talents and interests'. *Child & Family Social Work* 4, no. 3: 187–96.
Gomes, C., M. Berry, B. Alzougool and S. Chang. 2014. 'Home Away from Home: International Students and Their Identity-Based Social Networks in Australia'. *Journal of International Students* 4, no. 1: 2–15.
Gu, Q., M. Schweisfurth and C. Day. 2009. 'Learning and Growing in a "Foreign" Context: Intercultural Experiences of International Students'. *Compare: A Journal of Comparative and International Education* 40, no. 1: 7–23.
Hall, J. A., N. Baym. 2012. 'Calling and Texting (Too Much): Mobile Maintenance Expectations, (Over) Dependence, Entrapment, and Friendship Satisfaction'. *New Media and Society* 14, no. 2: 316–31.
Hjorth, L. 2007. 'Home and Away: A Case Study of the Use of Cyworld Mini-hompy by Korean Students Studying in Australia'. *Asian Studies Review* 31, no. 4: 397–407.
Hjorth, L. and M. Arnold. 2012. 'Home and Away: A Case Study of Students and Social Media in Shanghai'. In *New Connectivities in China: Virtual, Actual and Local Interactions*, edited

by Pui-lam Law, 171–82. Dordrecht, Heidelberg, London and New York: Springer Netherlands.
Hjorth, L. and M. Arnold. 2013. *Online@AsiaPacific*. New York: Routledge.
Ito, M. et al. 2009. *Hanging Out, Messing Around, and Geeking Out*. Cambridge, MA: MIT Press.
Iwamoto, D. K. and W. M. Liu. 2010. 'The Impact of Racial Identity, Ethnic Identity, Asian Values, and Race-related Stress on Asian Americans and Asian International College Students' Psychological Well-being'. *Journal of Counseling Psychology* 57, no. 1: 79–91.
Jamieson, L. 1998. *Intimacy*. Cambridge: Polity Press.
Kell, P. and G. Vogl. 2012. *International Students in the Asia-Pacific – Mobility, Risks and Global Optimism*. Heidelberg: Springer.
Khawaja, N. G. and J. Dempsey. 2008. 'A Comparison of International and Domestic Tertiary Students in Australia'. *Australian Journal of Guidance and Counselling* 18, no. 1: 30–46.
King, R. and E. Ruiz-Gelices. 2003. 'International Student Migration and the European 'Year Abroad': Effects on European Identity and Subsequent Migration Behaviour'. *International Journal of Population Geography* 9, no. 3: 229–52.
Kobayashi, E., H. R. Kerbo and S. F. Sharp. 2010. 'Differences in Individualistic and Collectivistic Tendencies among College Students in Japan and the United States'. *International Journal of Comparative Sociology* 51, no. 1–2: 59–84.
Miller, D. and J. Sinanan. 2013. *Webcam*. London: Polity Press.
Madianou, M. and D. Miller. 2011. *Migration and New Media: Transnational Families and Polymedia*. Abingdon and New York: Routledge.
Martin, F. 2014. 'The Gender of Mobility: Chinese Women Students' Self-Making through Transnational Education'. *Intersections: Gender and Sexuality in Asia and the Pacific* no. 35. http://intersections.anu.edu.au/issue35/martin.htm (accessed 28 February 2016).
McKay, D. 2006. 'Translocal Circulation: Place and Subjectivity in an Extended Filipino Community'. *The Asia Pacific Journal of Anthropology* 7, no. 3: 265–78.
———. 2007. "Sending Dollars Shows Feeling' – Emotions and Economies in Filipino Migration'. *Mobilities* 2, no. 2: 175–94.
Menzies, J. L. and R. Baron. 2014. 'International Postgraduate Student Transition Experiences: The Importance of Student Societies and Friends'. *Innovations in Education and Teaching International* 51, no. 1: 84–94.
Montgomery, D. W. 2013. 'Negotiating Well-being in Central Asia'. *Central Asian Survey* 32, vol. 4: 423–31.
Mori, S. C. 2000. 'Addressing the Mental Health Concerns of International Students'. *Journal of Counseling & Development* 78, 2: 137–44.
Morley, D. 2000. *Home Territories – Media, Mobility and Identity*. London: Routledge.
Nugroho, Y. and S. S. Syarief. 2012. 'Beyond Click-Activism? New Media and Political Processes in Contemporary Indonesia'. *FES Media Asia Series*. Jakarta: Friedrich-Ebert Stiftung.
Ok, H. 2011. 'New Media Practices in Korea'. *International Journal of Communication* vol. 5: 320–48. http://ijoc.org/index.php/ijoc/article/view/701 (accessed 12 November 2013).
Pflug, J. 2009. 'Folk Theories of Happiness: A Cross-cultural Comparison of Conceptions of Happiness in Germany and South Africa'. *Social Indicators Research* 92, no. 3: 551–63.
Qiu, J. L. 2014. "Power to the People!": Mobiles, Migrants, and Social Movements in Asia'. *International Journal of Communication* vol. 8: 376–91 http://ijoc.org/index.php/ijoc/article/view/2076 (accessed 9 February 2016).

Qiu, J. L. and K. Yeran. 2010. 'Recession and Progression? Notes on Media, Labor, and Youth from East Asia'. *International Journal of Communication* vol. 4: 630–49.

Quintrell, N. and M. Westwood. 1994. 'The Influence of a Peer–Pairing Program on International Students' First Year Experience and Use of Student Services'. *Higher Education Research & Development* 13, no. 1: 49–58.

Ramburuth, P. and J. McCormick. 2001. 'Learning Diversity in Higher Education: A Comparative Study of Asian International and Australian Students'. *Higher Education* 42, no. 3: 333–50.

Ryan, R. M., and E. L. Deci. 2001. 'On Happiness and Human Potentials: A Review of Research on Hedonic and Eudaimonic Well-being'. *Annual Review of Psychology* 52, no. 1: 141–66.

Schwittay, A. 2011. 'New Media Practices in India: Bridging Past and Future, Markets and Development'. *International Journal of Communication* vol. 5: 349–79. http://ijoc.org/index.php/ijoc/article/view/702 (accessed 12 November 2013).

Sen, A. 1985. 'Well-being, Agency and Freedom: The Dewey Lectures 1984' *The Journal of Philosophy*, 82, no. 4: 169–221.

Sen, A. 1993. 'Capability and Well-being'. In *The Quality of Life*, edited by M. Nussbaum and A. Sen. London: Oxford University Press.

Sengupta, S. 2012. "Big Brother'? No, It's Parents'. *New York Times*, 25 June. http://tinyurl.com/aysm5ud (accessed 12 November 2013).

Sheller, M. and J. Urry. 2006. 'The New Mobilities Paradigm'. *Environment and Planning A* 38, no. 2: 207–26.

Smith, K. D., S. T. Smith and J. C. Christopher. 2007. 'What Defines the Good Person? Cross-Cultural Comparisons of Experts' Models with Lay Prototypes'. *Journal of Cross-Cultural Psychology* 38, no. 3: 333–60.

Suh, E., E. Diener, S. Oishi and H. C. Triandis. 1998. 'The Shifting Basis of Life Satisfaction Judgments across Cultures: Emotions Versus Norms'. *Journal of Personality and Social Psychology* 74, no. 2: 482–93.

Tapsell, Ross. 2013. 'The Media Freedom Movement in Malaysia and the Electoral Authoritarian Regime'. *Journal of Contemporary Asia* 43, no. 4: 613–35.

The Economist Intelligence Unit. 2015. 'Safe Cities Index 2015 White Paper'. *The Economist*. http://safecities.economist.com/whitepapers/safe-cities-index-white-paper/. (accessed 28 February 2016).

Turkle, S. 2012. *Alone Together: Why We Expect More from Technology and Less from Each Other*. New York: Basic Books.

Turner, B. S. 2007. 'The Enclave Society: Towards a Sociology of Immobility'. *European Journal of Social Theory* 10, no. 2: 287–304.

Urry, J. 2007. *Mobilities*. Cambridge: Polity Press.

———. 2012. *Sociology beyond Societies: Mobilities for the Twenty-first Century*. London and New York: Routledge.

Waaktaar, T., H. J. Christie, A. Borge, and S. Torgersen. 2004. 'How Can Young People's Resilience Be Enhanced? Experiences from a Clinical Intervention Project'. *Clinical Child Psychology and Psychiatry* vol. 9: 167–83.

Wallis, C. 2011. 'New Media Practices in China: Youth Patterns, Processes, and Politics'. *International Journal of Communication* vol. 5: 406–36. http://ijoc.org/index.php/ijoc/article/view/698 (accessed 12 November 2013).

Waters, J. L. 2006. 'Geographies of Cultural Capital: Education, International Migration and Family Strategies between Hong Kong and Canada'. *Transactions of the Institute of British Geographers* 31, no. 2: 179–92.

Chapter 3

CONNECTING AND RECONNECTING WITH VIETNAM: MIGRATION, VIETNAMESE OVERSEAS COMMUNITIES AND SOCIAL MEDIA

Cate Gribble and Ly Thi Tran

Over the last fifty years, Vietnam has experienced significant outmigration closely linked with the nation's social, political and economic fortunes. Many of those who left in the various waves of migration have been highly skilled, including the most recent flows of Vietnamese overseas students. Losing highly skilled human capital has been a major concern for a nation like Vietnam, which has been transitioning from a centrally planned socialist economy to a market economy, and has the ambition to become a modern, industrialized economy by 2020 (World Bank 2012). However, in recent years, there has been less concern surrounding a 'brain drain'. This has arisen from the belief that there are in fact many advantages associated with being a 'sending country', including the financial benefits of remittances, the cultural engagement with diaspora communities, and the benefits of return migration (Gribble 2008). The rapid development and widespread availability of information communication technologies (ICTs) has facilitated the formation, growth and maintenance of diaspora communities' transnational social networks. In addition, both traditional and social media provide opportunities for nations such as Vietnam to harness their diaspora's skills, knowledge, finances and networks in order to boost local social and economic development.

This chapter examines the complex relationship that Vietnam has with Vietnamese overseas communities. It starts with a review of existing literature on Vietnam's major migration trends and groups since the reunification of the country, including war-related *Việt Kiều*, overseas Vietnamese students and temporary migrant workers. It then discusses the current practices and approaches to harnessing the diaspora. A review of how some other Asian nations with large diaspora populations have engaged with their diaspora via social media is included as it provides some useful implications for Vietnam to develop stronger and more sustained connections with its diaspora. The chapter concludes by considering the role of social media and the recent developments in facilitating constructive dialogues between Vietnam and its diaspora via social media.

There have been three main phases of outmigration in Vietnam. The first phase was the outflow of Vietnamese refugees, including *thuyền nhân* (boat people), during the Vietnam war and the post-reunification period. The second wave of outmigration has been the movement of skilled students and workers to developed countries over the past two decades, and this includes the phenomenon of international education. The third emerging trend in contemporary Vietnam is the temporary migration of unskilled and semi-skilled to skilled workers under the Vietnamese government's labour dispatch program. This chapter is mainly concerned with these three distinctive groups and will not address the relatively small trend of migration under the marriage and family union programs.

A key focus of this chapter is the growing outflow of Vietnamese overseas students and how Vietnam can avoid a brain drain from this potential loss of skills and talent. For countries experiencing an outflow of skilled labour, there are three main policy options available. Governments can attempt to retain students at the tertiary level by ensuring that they complete the greater part of their tertiary studies in their home country, therefore reducing the likelihood of student emigration – although not necessarily the skilled migration flow. The second option is to allow or even encourage students to pursue their tertiary studies abroad and then promote their return home. This approach requires the adoption of polices that aim to facilitate student repatriation. The third option is to accept that many students may not return upon graduation and employ policies that will enable the student graduate diaspora to contribute to their home country's development from afar (Gribble 2008). While there is evidence of Vietnamese policy initiatives designed to facilitate the return of overseas talent, we suggest that more effort needs to be invested in engaging with those Vietnamese students who choose to remain overseas, especially via social media. While establishing and fostering lines of communication is critical to Vietnam benefitting from its diaspora, without real progress on some of the diaspora's key concerns – such as employment opportunities and local bureaucracy and corruption – many overseas Vietnamese will continue to seek opportunities elsewhere.

Post-1975 Migration

The first major wave of Vietnamese outmigration occurred at the end of the Vietnam War in 1975, when an estimated 210,000 Vietnamese were resettled, primarily in four countries: the United States, France, Canada and Australia (A. T. Pham 2011). Following the fall of the South Vietnamese regime and the reunification of the country in 1975, there was a further outflow of refugees known as *thuyền nhân* (boat people). The period of economic reform aiming to shift from a centrally planned socialist economy to a socialist-oriented market economy and to promote international integration, known as *Đổi Mới*, began in 1986 and led to a further outflow of Vietnamese, as closer economic ties with other nations in the region expanded opportunities for Vietnamese to work abroad (Dang et al. 2003). It is estimated that between 1975 and 1995 a total of 1.3 million Vietnamese resettled in Western countries, including those leaving to pursue opportunities abroad following the economic, political and social transformations associated with Đổi Mới (A. T. Pham 2011).

In more recent years, self-financed and scholarship-funded overseas Vietnamese tertiary students have represented a large and expanding source of skilled migrants. While the trend for self-financed overseas study began in the 1990s, the numbers have risen dramatically over the last decade. According to UNESCO, the number of Vietnamese students studying abroad has grown from 23,334 in 2006 to 53,802 in 2012 (Schulmann 2014). In addition, an emerging group of temporary migrants of around 500,000 Vietnamese workers was resettled in 40 countries under the government's labour export program (V. H. Pham 2012). Together these distinct groups of temporary and permanent migrants have contributed to a large and growing diaspora. The following section examines the contribution of the diaspora to Vietnam's economic and social development, providing insights into how shifts in government policy and attitude have influenced diaspora engagement.

War-Related Việt Kiều: Shifts in Attitudes and Increasing Involvement in the Homeland

Two distinctive groups who are commonly referred to as Việt kiều are war-related migrants and skilled or work migrants. Their attitudes towards the Vietnamese government as well as their forms and manner of engaging with the homeland might differ due to their distinct political and social backgrounds and their different reasons for leaving Vietnam. There are significant populations of Việt Kiều in the United States, Australia, Canada and France. As many Việt Kiều left Vietnam when the communists seized power following the Vietnam War, relations between the Vietnamese government and this group of Việt Kiều have been, at least historically, strained. Initially, those who left Vietnam were considered traitors to the communist regime and were spurned by the government. However, in the period following Đổi Mới, relationships with the West were viewed more favourably, resulting in the

Vietnamese government actively courting overseas Vietnamese. Official policy and attitudes towards Việt Kiều have changed dramatically in recent years with the government now recognizing the enormous political, economic and social potential associated with Việt Kiều communities.

In recent years the Vietnamese government has repeatedly sent out positive messages to overseas migrants, encouraging them to return to contribute to their motherland's development, announcing a policy to appeal to Việt Kiều, calling for the construction of 'great solidarity' in the Vietnamese nation both inside and outside Vietnam. This was followed in 2004 by 'Resolution 36' validating a new political stand for welcoming and incorporating overseas Vietnamese back to the motherland (Chan and Tran 2011). Importantly, in Vietnam public perception of overseas Vietnamese also appears to be more favourable, which may in part be attributed to the government's positive promotion of the Việt Kiều as 'brilliant young professionals' (Chan and Tran 2011). Reciprocally, the attitudes of many (especially second- or third-generation) Việt Kiều towards the homeland have also changed as they have more possibilities of visiting their cultural homeland and have witnessed the country's reform and integration into the global economy. Both traditional and social media also play an important role in providing a more updated picture of contemporary Vietnam for Việt Kiều – a significantly different image of the Vietnam they or their family left behind.

Local shifts in attitudes and changes in policy have undoubtedly enhanced the economic contribution of Việt Kiều. By the late 1990s, the Vietnamese government's official attitude towards the Việt Kiều had shifted, and the contribution of overseas Vietnamese was actively encouraged. By 2000 the Vietnamese government was even more aware of the key economic opportunities, and it implemented a series of policies designed to expand and strengthen the contribution of the Việt Kiều to the nation's economic and social development. Key government policies designed to encourage Việt Kiều economic investment began with the 1988 Foreign Investment Law, which was amended in 1993 to include incentives for Việt Kiều investment (A. T. Pham 2011). More recently there have been a number of key policies aimed at strengthening relations and facilitating involvement of Việt Kiều in Vietnam's development, including Resolution 36 which both recognizes the Việt Kiều community and their economic potential and acknowledges the disconnect between the government and the Việt Kiều community. The overall aim of Resolution 36 is to make policies more transparent and offer more support to Việt Kiều (A. T. Pham 2011). In 2004, the Vietnamese government began a series of legal changes to give Việt Kiều rights to reclaim their Vietnamese citizenship and own property in Vietnam. In 2008 the government introduced visa exemptions for overseas Việt Kiều and, in 2010, a presidential decree relaxed the eligibility for home purchase and provided more transparent procedures (A. T. Pham 2011).

In addition, the government has actively promoted the positive contribution of Việt Kiều and advocated for their inclusion in the nation. Via newspaper articles and the government's official magazine, *Homeland*, Việt Kiều are portrayed as talented professionals who are an important asset to the entire Vietnamese community. In recent years the Vietnamese media has been awash with articles highlighting the Việt Kiều's role in the nation's development, including charity work, business investment, education and research, remittances and the acceleration of Vietnam's international integration. Return visits have also increased dramatically. At the beginning of Đổi Mới, only 8,000 Việt Kiều returned annually to Vietnam, but by 2004 around 500,000 Việt Kiều returned to Vietnam, injecting substantial amounts into the local economy. In recent years Việt Kiều have invested an estimated US$5.7 billion into over 3,200 projects, mainly in the manufacturing, tourism and service sectors (Ministry of Foreign Affairs 2012).

While government policy, community attitudes and economic incentives have clearly led to a shift in relations between the Vietnamese government and the Việt Kiều, resulting in significant economic benefits, for many overseas Vietnamese it is not sufficient for them to consider re-establishing relations with their homeland. An examination of the literature suggests that while the government has been generally successful in shifting both policy and attitudes towards Việt Kiều, there is further scope to develop closer relations between Vietnam and the diaspora. In recent times, the government has introduced a number of initiatives designed to attract talented Vietnamese to work in high-tech industrial parks or take up academic positions in Vietnam's university sector. The Ministry of Foreign Affairs has implemented a project designed to create a database of Vietnamese nationals living abroad in order to better understand population flows (Ministry of Foreign Affairs 2012). While these initiatives are laudable, many Việt Kiều believe that without addressing issues around government corruption and excessive bureaucracy, certain sections of the overseas Vietnamese diaspora will remain suspicious of the government's motives and remain reluctant to reconnect with Vietnam.

Overseas Vietnamese Students

Those Vietnamese leaving now are likely to have different attitudes to previous generations of Việt Kiều because of their different social and political circumstances, as well as their experiences of contemporary Vietnam. Vietnam is experiencing an outmigration of Vietnamese students seeking educational opportunities in English-speaking countries, Europe and some neighbouring countries in the Asia Pacific region such as Singapore, Japan, South Korea and China. Since Đổi Mới and the resulting expansion of the middle-class and increased opportunities to live and work overseas, these students have come to represent a new wave of migration and a high risk of a future brain drain.

The outbound mobility of staff and students is a key element of the Vietnamese government's Strategy for Education Development (2011–2020). Funding has been allocated to increase the number of teaching staff and students trained overseas while the government encourages self-funded overseas study (Tran et al. 2014). Approximately 90 per cent of Vietnamese international students are self-funded (Clark 2013). The government views the rapid increase in Vietnamese students studying abroad as a positive development. International education augments the supply of qualified human capital for the nation as it allows young Vietnamese students to receive high-quality education in countries such as the United States, United Kingdom and Australia at no expense to the state. The trend for Vietnamese students to study abroad also relieves pressure on the strained domestic tertiary sector. While the government has nominated improving domestic higher education provision as a key priority, the sector is struggling to keep up with demand, as a large youth population and a rapid increase in participation rates at the secondary school level have led to growing demand for higher education. In 2012, 1.8 million students registered for the national higher education entrance exam; however, the admission quota was only 560,000. Concerns over quality and overcrowded classes in a country that places a high value on education has led to a growing numbers of middle-class families sending their children abroad (Tran et al. 2014; Tran 2015; Truong and Tran 2014).

Vietnam's Ministry for Education and Training estimates that in 2011 there were over a hundred thousand Vietnamese students studying abroad in 49 countries (Dantri International 2012). Australia is the most popular destination, followed by the United States and then China. While there is evidence to suggest that the Vietnamese government, at both the national and local level, recognizes the importance of tapping into the Vietnamese diaspora, the focus appears to be largely on senior or well-established Việt Kiều who have particular expertise or interests in the fields of science and technology, business and finance (BBC News 2009; Pham 2011). Little mention is made of Vietnamese students who have gone abroad to study and failed to return. While in the short term it makes sense to focus on attracting those overseas Vietnamese who are experienced in their field and are well placed financially and professionally, efforts should also be made to establish and maintain links with current overseas students. Overseas students represent an important pool of expertise, and any policy that fails to recognize the importance of maintaining links with these students is potentially flawed.

Members of Vietnam's educational diaspora contribute their skills and knowledge to many other countries, especially in the English-speaking world and Western Europe, while their contribution to Vietnam is minimal. Highlighting the diaspora as a broad and deep resource for Vietnam, Tran et al. (2014) argue that 'the national interest lies in facilitating the flow of people and being open to new knowledge, while at the same time attracting mobile talent into the country and "Vietnamizing" the wisdom that people acquire abroad' (233). The migration rate of Vietnamese overseas graduates is 27 per cent (Docquier and Rapoport 2012) and many others living abroad seek the opportunity to work or pursue further study in other countries rather than return. Despite their close links with the homeland and their desire to contribute to future national development, overseas students have a low return rate that is largely due to the variety of challenges Vietnamese returnees often encounter. These range from dealing with bureaucracy, housing and working culture, to being allocated an unsuitable job that fails to allow them to contribute at their full potential (Tran et al. 2014). Returnees and overseas investors complain of excessively long waiting periods for investment applications and a lack of guidelines surrounding the implementation of government incentives for overseas investors (Tuoi Tre News 2015). In the university sector, the Vietnamese government has implemented a number of programs designed to encourage the return of overseas Vietnamese academics, but barriers to return persist. These include low salaries, lack of academic freedom and a culture of 'seniorism' that hinders the career progression of young scholars (H. Pham 2011).

In an effort to minimize brain drain and encourage Vietnamese overseas students and diaspora to return, the government has recently offered several incentives in terms of visa conditions, legal status and citizenship in order to mitigate the current situation and attract the return of expatriates. Notably, Vietnam issued a decree which allows Vietnamese expatriates to have dual citizenship and retain their Vietnamese citizenship (Nguyen 2013). Through the decree, the government also offers visa exemption for Việt Kiều who can stay up to 90 days in Vietnam (Nguyen 2013). Furthermore, in December 2012 the government released a draft regulation that highlighted specific initiatives designed to attract qualified Vietnamese academics who were living overseas to come and teach and conduct research at Vietnamese universities (H. Pham 2013). These strategies address returnee concerns such as bureaucracy and red tape, housing, finance and adaptation to the working environment and the community (Tran et al. 2014). It is a 'coordinated policy that involves a wide range of organizations, including higher education institutions and the ministries of education and training, finance, foreign affairs, public securities, and science and technology' (H. Pham 2013, 2). These steps show the government's effort in lowering barriers and providing opportunities to encourage the country's talented human capital to return and contribute to national development. But whether these cross-sectoral coordinated policies achieve results is yet to be seen.

Temporary Migrant Workers

A growing migration trend in recent years has been the export of labour from Vietnam to foreign countries under the government's labour dispatch program. In 2012 the Vietnamese Department of Overseas Labour estimates that around 500,000 Vietnamese temporary migrant workers were working in 40 countries and territories (V. H. Pham 2012). This dispatch workforce includes unskilled, semi-skilled and skilled workers and technicians, and around 251,000 of these are female workers (Vietnam Steel Corporation 2014). Fifty-three per cent of the labour dispatch workforce work is in the services sector and 42 per cent in industries, agriculture and aquaculture (*Viet Nam News* 2011). Steel, mechanic, electrical, construction and textile and garment industries are the main sectors involved (Vietnam Steel Corporation 2014) and the main labour markets for Vietnam are Taiwan, South Korea, Malaysia and Laos. Taiwan is the biggest market for Vietnamese female workers (61% of the total), followed by Malaysia (20.9%) and the Republic of Korea (4.4%). The dispatch labour force send home an average of $US1.7 billion every year (*Viet Nam News* 2011).

According to Nguyen (2014), the Vietnamese labour dispatch trend has been shaped by the country's socialist market economy and multilateralism policies associated with Đổi Mới. The author specifies three main periods of the labour migration policy evolution post-Đổi Mới in 1986. The period from 1986 to 1991 is characterized by 'legalization of labour cooperation as a strategy to sustain multilateral relations with communist countries' (Nguyen 2014, 183). That is, labour migration during this period was mainly in the form of labour exchange with the former Soviet Union and Eastern Bloc countries, Laos and Cambodia. Between 1991 and 1996, labour migration was driven by government policy to diversify 'multilateral relations' with ASEAN countries and integrate into the Asian region. Therefore, the labour dispatch program during this period focused on the export of labour to ASEAN countries. From 1996 to date, labour export is shaped by the country's policies on industrialization, modernization and global integration to facilitate the country's move to a socialist market economy and augment the new distinctive development of the nation after Đổi Mới (Hong Nguyen 2014).

There are a wide range of risks facing Vietnamese migrant workers abroad, especially female workers. According to the Ministry of Labour, Invalids and Social Affairs (MoLISA), Vietnamese female workers, who account for more than 50 per cent of the dispatch workforce, are most vulnerable group as the majority have low levels of formal education, are low-skilled and often work in domestic labour conditions. Language barriers, cultural differences, unfamiliarity with foreign working conditions, a lack of understanding of labour regulations and the policies of the host country, and lack of access to information are key factors that increase their vulnerability.

Furthermore, Vietnamese workers abroad also face risks due to the immaturity and inadequacy of laws and policies aiming to protect their rights outside of Vietnam. Recent reports have also signalled a number of corrupt export companies and agents in Vietnam as well as foreign companies in violation of the host country's labour laws in recruiting and employing Vietnamese labourers (*Viet Nam News* 2011). Female workers being abused by their employers appears to be the most commonly reported violation of rights. Other risks include being forced to work for long hours and carry out work not specified in their contracts or in unsuitable working conditions (*Viet Nam News* 2011).

According to Tran et al. (2014), it is worth noting that while unqualified or low-skilled Vietnamese workers are often well recognized for their hard work and skills in receiving countries, graduates with a Vietnamese qualification are not valued in the Asian region, nor globally. Many Vietnamese graduates would like the opportunity to work overseas but have found it very hard to obtain employment outside Vietnam (Tran et al. 2014). This raises serious concerns about Vietnam's higher education curriculum, which has been described as being out of touch with advances in knowledge and technologies and developments in scientific and social research. It suggests that Vietnamese graduates' skills and knowledge are still a long way from gaining recognition, both in the Asian region and globally (Tran et al. 2014).

Harnessing the Diaspora: What Needs to Be Done?

In 2009 Vietnam joined the World Bank's group of lower-middle income countries, and its gross national income (GNI) per capita reached US$1,030 (World Bank 2012). Within a quarter of a century, Vietnam was transformed from one of the poorest countries in the world in 1986, into an economic success story in 2009 (World Bank 2014). However, there are concerns that recent falls in GDP growth rates in Vietnam might be an early sign that the nation is falling into the 'middle-income trap'. In order to continue on the path of sustained economic growth towards high-income status, Vietnam must tackle corruption and inefficiencies among state-owned firms, strengthen the labour market and develop the skills and knowledge needed for a modern industrialized economy (Berliner et al. 2013).

Some have suggested that the low quality of Vietnam's human resources is creating a bottleneck for the nation's sustainable development. Reports in the local media indicate that local demand for qualified staff is increasing, and that major companies in Vietnam are facing shortages of skilled workers (*Việt Nam News* 2013; *Thanh Nien News* 2013; Montague 2013). Lack of appropriately trained and qualified personnel available domestically suggests that the knowledge and skills of overseas Vietnamese students may well be highly sought after in the near future. It is in the interest of the Vietnamese government to develop and maintain links with current and former overseas students, and to communicate employment opportunities in order to draw on the diaspora's expertise.

Improving transparency and eradicating corruption

Many overseas Vietnamese are reluctant to invest via official channels, preferring to use family connections despite government efforts to cut red tape and facilitate overseas investment (Huynh and Yiu 2012). An Australian study of the Vietnamese diaspora revealed weak business and professional links despite an interest and desire on the part of overseas Vietnamese (Ben-Mosche and Pyke 2012). Barriers to the development of important ties leading to two-way trade and other benefits include antagonisms of the Australian Vietnamese community towards the Vietnamese government as well as Vietnamese bureaucracy. For example, the 'Ease of Doing Business' Report puts Vietnam at 78th out of 183 economies, highlighting that administrative procedures remain the main barriers for investors. (Truong 2013).

According to OneVietnam (http://onevietnam.org/), the largest global online network for the Vietnamese community, mistrust of the government remains the largest obstacle, despite many well-intentioned government initiatives and schemes designed to encourage overseas Việt Kiều to engage with their homeland (James Bao pers. comm.). The challenge for the Vietnamese government is to build trust with the diaspora by addressing concerns over corruption and red tape. Corruption in Vietnam is a major concern and, despite rolling out a series of anti-graft campaigns since 2005, many overseas Vietnamese are frustrated with the government's inability to stamp out corruption. Corruption is considered a major determent for overseas investors and the major reason Vietnam's economy's is struggling to reach its potential (*Businessweek* 2014).

Engaging and tapping the potential contribution of the overseas communities

One of the key tasks for the government is to cultivate and maintain connectedness and a sense of belonging to the motherland for the Vietnamese overseas communities. At the present, Vietnam's efforts concentrate on strategies to encourage the return of diaspora, whereas more investment is needed to foster meaningful engagement with overseas Vietnamese. Advances in communication technologies have made it possible for overseas Vietnamese to contribute to different spectrums of the national development without their having physical residence in Vietnam. Overseas Vietnamese are intimately connected through communication technology and globalized media forms, and the diaspora is now able to remain in closer contact with family and friends at home. Likewise, many overseas Vietnamese are eager to maintain professional connections with Vietnam. They are also keen to remain informed of the changing social and economic conditions. Recent cases of successful Vietnamese academics and business people living abroad, including Jonathan Hanh Nguyen and Alan Phan, who have been actively involved in establishing partnerships with international organizations and foreign countries and providing consultancy, are good examples of how the government might draw on the diaspora community without their physical return to Vietnam. But across the nation activities to engage the diaspora are still fragmented, inconsistent and ad hoc. It is important to have a more coordinated and coherent policy that is based on more nuanced understandings of the diaspora's capabilities and potential contributions across national borders. Also, it is essential for authorities and related organizations to continue efforts to remove the cultural stigma that those who leave Vietnam do not love their motherland.

Providing attractive conditions for returnees and their families

While alleviating the concerns of the older generation of Việt Kiều remains a significant and persistent challenge for the Vietnamese government, the issues concerning overseas Vietnamese students are distinct and remain unaddressed. For Vietnamese students who have often made a considerable financial investment in their overseas education, graduate employment opportunities are a priority. Job availability, appropriate remuneration and working cultures that provide opportunities for Vietnam's international graduates to effectively utilize their skills are factors that are likely to encourage return migration. Conversations with Thu Pham, co-president of VietAbroader (http://portal.vietabroader.org), a student-run, non-profit organization providing study abroad advice to Vietnamese students, suggest that a lack of job opportunities in the STEM (Science, Technology, Engineering, Mathematics) fields is preventing many overseas educated Vietnamese from returning home. The organization reported that while graduates in business and finance are often able to find positions with large multinationals back in Vietnam, opportunities for graduates in the STEM fields were limited, so many chose to remain in the host country (Thu. Pham, pers. comm.).

Interestingly, VietAbroader also reported that while many overseas Vietnamese students felt frustrated by the perceived lack of opportunities for them to utilize skills and knowledge acquired via their international education experience, the organization believes there are significant opportunities for entrepreneurial returnees. VietAbroader has noted a trend for overseas Vietnamese students to return and launch start-up companies in fields ranging from technology to education.

The growing interest in start-up companies is further evidenced in the 2014 launch of Startup Vietnam (http://www.startupvietnam.vn/), a project funded by the US Consulate General with the goal of fostering innovation and entrepreneurship in Vietnam and raising awareness about tech- and non-tech-entrepreneurship in the start-up community. According to the founder and CEO of Startup Vietnam, the start-up environment in Vietnam is in the initial stages of development and lacks the resourcing enjoyed by neighbouring countries, such as Malaysia and Singapore (H. Nguyen, pers. comm.). However, the signs are promising with the Vietnamese government recently establishing the first business accelerator for technology companies: Vietnam Silicon Valley (www.siliconvalley.com.vn). The Vietnam Silicon Valley project provides a four-month intensive start-up acceleration program focusing on entrepreneurs seeking to develop start-ups in online gaming, mobile applications, e-commerce, e-learning, technology applied business and digital media sectors. It will be interesting to see whether initiatives such as the Vietnam Silicon Valley project will alleviate concerns that overseas Vietnamese may have regarding developing professional or business ties with Vietnam.

While economic growth often fuels student mobility, sustained economic development encourages return migration. Creating a favourable social and economic environment for returning Vietnamese students is a central element of Vietnam's long-term plan to reverse any brain drain that may be occurring. As discussed previously, for overseas Vietnamese students who might be considering whether to return home, the availably of suitable jobs is critical. A report from the OECD indicates that newly graduated foreign students in OECD countries are not sufficiently informed of the opportunities available in their countries of origin, in their fields of specialization and in the public and private sectors (OECD 2012). For example, a number of reports indicate that there is a shortage of suitably qualified graduates in key areas such as ICT, suggesting employment opportunities for returning overseas Vietnamese ICT graduates (Einhorn and Kharif 2014) Intel Vietnam, frustrated by the lack of qualified engineers, has resorted to sending local Vietnamese students to the United States to study engineering (Einhorn and Kharif 2014). Providing the right opportunities and conditions for returning students will undoubtedly facilitate future return of overseas students. However, it is also vital that while pursuing broader economic and social reforms, the Vietnamese government maintains ties with its student diaspora in order to keep them abreast of changes taking place at home, as well as informing them of opportunities as they arise. There is clearly the need to establish clear channels of communication so that overseas graduates and other skilled professions are aware of professional opportunities in Vietnam.

Ho et al. (2014) suggest that returnees are looking for more than just high wages. A study on Vietnamese re-expatriation found that for returnee professionals psychological and social factors are more significant motivators for re-expatriating compared with economic or career reasons. The study suggests that if returnees are dissatisfied with opportunities for their family (i.e., children's education, employment opportunities for spouses, housing, etc.) they are more likely to re-expatriate. The implication is that negative re-entry experiences are the most powerful push force affecting intention to re-expatriate. In addition to providing good employment opportunities, there is also the need to recognize the achievements of returnees and to support the returnee's family via repatriation programs that ease the re-entry process (Ho et al. 2014).

Using Social Media to Connect with the Diaspora

In recent decades, rapid development in ICT has provided enormous scope for nations to engage with the diaspora and facilitate their involvement in their home country's development. For a nation like Vietnam, social media provides significant opportunities for the country to both improve its relationship with certain segments of the diaspora while at the same time maintaining contact with the growing number of Vietnamese studying abroad. While diaspora networks are often independent of government and reluctant to engage in activities that may align them with government activities, the Vietnamese diaspora networks such as Vietabroader and One Vietnam, see themselves as providing a trusted channel via which overseas Vietnamese can voice their concerns to the Vietnamese government. In other words, they provide the opportunity for a dialogue to be established between the government and the diaspora. Diaspora networks can feed those concerns back the government.

However, it is ultimately up to the government to deal with concerns around corruption and excessive bureaucracy in order to allay the diaspora's concerns.

Vietnam is clearly aware of the potential of its large and growing diaspora as well as the importance of developing and maintaining positive relationships with overseas Vietnamese. While there are signs that Vietnam is exploring new ways of engaging with the diaspora, including taking advantage of social media tools such as Facebook (Tuoi Tre 2015). An examination of how other nations with large diaspora populations have engaged with their diaspora via social media will provide some important insights into how Vietnam might go about this in the future.

Engaging with Diaspora via Social Media: Examples from Some Asian Countries

South Korea

South Korea has been highly successful in engaging with its diaspora via online networks and social media. In response to demographic decline, continued emigration of the middle class, a rising number of non-Korean residents in the country and a stagnating economy, Korea developed a diaspora strategy aimed at enhancing engagement with the 7 million Koreans living overseas and encourage their contribution to the country's growth. Initiatives included creating dual citizenship and voting rights, education programs and homeland visit programs. Central to the Korean approach was strengthening existing 'imagined communities' of Koreans across the globe via the creation and support of online newspapers and other online portals (Song 2014).

In 1997 the South Korean government established the Overseas Koreans Foundation (OKF), a non-profit organization affiliated with the Ministry of Foreign Affairs and aiming to 'utilise the capabilities of overseas Koreans for national development in line with its globalization policy' (Agunias 2013). One of the most important projects of the OKF has been helping the Korean diaspora to network among themselves and with Koreans in their homeland. The OKF built online networks such as Korean.net (http://www.korean.net) and supported Korean diaspora media such as Dongpo News (http://www.dongponews.net/) and the Overseas *Korean Times* (http://www.oktimes.co.kr/). One focal point of the OKF has been embracing and networking with the younger generations of the Korean diaspora and organizing homeland visits for them. Through these programs, younger overseas Koreans are invited to visit South Korea to learn the traditions, history and language of their ancestral homeland, thus strengthening their sense of Korean identity (Song 2014).

Singapore

Much like the Korean government, the Singaporean government has experimented with ways to better integrate the diaspora into the 'imagined community' of the nation. Importantly, many of the diaspora-engagement strategies discussed below, while serving the purpose of encouraging the return of overseas Singaporeans also are attracting foreign talent. In 1997, then prime minister Goh Chok Tong expressed the fear that 'if Singaporeans are not deeply rooted to Singapore through strong bonds of family, friends, community and nation, the core of our nation will unravel'. (Ziguras and Gribble 2014). The government believed that by strengthening the nation's 'heartware', Singaporeans at home and abroad would be more likely to contribute to the country's economic and social development. Launched in 1997, the Singapore 21 project articulated an officially ordained set of national values with a desire to maintain a 'strong Singapore heartbeat', which would be shared by those living and working abroad (Keong, 2001). The language has changed little in 15 years, with the recent population strategy stating that 'Singaporeans living overseas are an integral part of the Singapore family', who 'continue to contribute actively to Singapore from around the world' (Ziguras and Gribble 2014). However, the enduring aspiration is for these citizens to ultimately return to the homeland: 'We hope that they will return home after their studies or working stints abroad, adding a further dimension to our society' (Singapore Government 2013, 26).

In 2006, the Overseas Singaporean Unit was established to strengthen the diaspora's connection to home and fellow Singaporeans, providing coordination, support and funding for overseas Singaporean communities, including business networks and student societies (Gomes 2010). A key component of the government's diaspora engagement strategy has been the 'Singapore Day' events that have since been held in several key expatriate centres, including New York, Melbourne, Sydney, London and Shanghai. Their purpose was clearly articulated by the deputy prime minister in his speech at the 2007 inaugural event in New York: 'The message we want to send to Overseas Singaporeans is this – even though you are away from home, we remember you and count you among us. Home may not be where you are; it is where your heart resides. Stay connected!' (Seng 2007). These events cleverly use food, nostalgia for Singaporean popular culture, and patriotic messaging to bring together overseas Singaporeans, thereby providing an opportunity to promote return migration by promoting the latest developments in housing, education, infrastructure and employment along with practical advice for potential returnees (Gomes 2010). The Singapore government has successfully used social media platforms such as Facebook, Twitter, Flickr and YouTube as part of a carefully articulated diaspora strategy.

China

China has been highly successful in reversing a brain drain and facilitating return migration and diaspora engagement. While, in the 1980s and early

1990s, the Chinese government was very concerned by the significant student brain drain that was occurring in China, attitudes changed and the Chinese Communist Party began describing the trend of students remaining abroad as 'storing brain power overseas'(Zweig et al. 2008). Over time, market liberalization, the expansion of the private sector and the effects of globalization have made doing business with China and/or returning home attractive options for many overseas Chinese. As a result, China stands to benefit considerably from its diaspora. Central to China's successful approach has been the promotion and strengthening of close relationships between overseas Chinese and the government (Zweig et al. 2008).

China has been very strategic in its dealings with the diaspora. The Chinese consulates have been central to this process. Consular officials, particularly in the education and science sectors, invest considerable time and energy in cultivating ties with talented expatriates and help them to re-establish contact with people in China. Consular officials also organize meetings wherein delegations from China provide information to the diaspora about changing circumstances on the mainland (Zweig et al. 2008). They also help delegations to meet with Chinese student organizations and arrange meetings with important overseas scholars. While the Chinese government does not directly use social media such as Weibo to engage with overseas Chinese students, most of the Chinese Students and Scholars Association (CSSA) use Weibo to connect with overseas Chinese students. As each CSSA needs to be registered through Chinese embassies, it could be viewed as an indirect communication channel between the government and overseas students.

India

In the last decade, India has transformed the way it engages with its diaspora. In 2004 the Ministry of Overseas Indian Affairs was created with the aim of engaging with overseas Indians and facilitating return migration. In 2006, the new Public Diplomacy Division (PDD) was established with the aim of creating a better understanding of India and its foreign-policy concerns. A key area of the PDD is to develop effective social media strategies in order to engage with diverse communities in India and overseas. Notably, the Indian government has boosted investment in communication technology and has heavily utilized social media, opening Twitter, Facebook, YouTube and Flickr accounts. Recognizing that government websites might be the first point of contact for the diaspora looking to engage with India, government sites have been revamped to provide a favourable impression of India in order to facilitate investment, return migration and the development of professional and academic links (Murti and Zaharna 2014).

The election of Prime Minister Narendra Modi has resulted in social media becoming a key method of disseminating information. When Modi took office in 2014, 90 per cent of his ministers had Twitter accounts. Modi has two twitter handles, a personal handle that currently has 10.5 million followers and an official 'Prime Minister' handle that has 5.1 million followers. Connecting with India's expatriate population of around 25 million people is a key focus for Prime Minister Modi, who has also held diaspora events in key locations such as New York and Sydney (Lakshmi 2015).

Engaging via Social Media: Recent Developments

In recent years, the Vietnamese government has shifted its stance dramatically on social media. In 2013 the government introduced laws designed to maintain tight controls on social media (BBC News 2013). The controversial laws permitted personal information to be shared on blogs and social websites but prohibited the dissemination of news articles. The laws proved difficult to enforce and, in January 2015, the Vietnamese government reversed its stance, with the prime minister conceding it was impossible for Vietnam to ban social media and urging officials to embrace websites like Facebook to spread the government's message (*Daily Mail* 2015).

Social media plays an increasingly popular role in influencing the Vietnamese diaspora's connectedness with Vietnam. The most common forms of engagement with Vietnam via social media appear to be the reading of Vietnamese online newspaper, such as VnExpress, the promotion of Vietnam-related programs and events through Facebook, Facebook groups dedicated to specific groups of diaspora, and the blogs of some Việt Kiều. The establishment of the Facebook page Cơm có thịt (Only Rice Is Not Enough) in Australia (https://www.facebook.com/groups/Comcothit.Australia/) is a typical example of how social media is used to connect the Vietnamese diaspora with charity activities based in Vietnam. Cơm có thịt represents the volunteers (mainly Vietnamese overseas students in Australia) of a Vietnam-based charity. According to Bui Thu Thuy, the founder of Cơm có thịt in Australia program and co-founder of its Facebook site, this site taps the potential of social media to reach the Vietnamese diaspora and raise an invaluable amount of money for children from Vietnam's highland regions (Bui Thu Thuy, pers. comm.). Another example in which social media has been used to connect and mobilize the patriotism of the Vietnamese overseas students and expatriates is the establishment of a number of Facebook pages to share relevant information about China's illegal deployment in 2014 of the Haiyang Shiyou 981 oil rig inside Vietnam's Exclusive Economic Zone near Vietnam's Paracel

Islands (Hoàng Sa) (Thayer 2014; Tran et al. 2014). Information about the organization of these protests in 30 cities around the world was frequently updated on these pages during the period of the incursion.

Some successful Việt Kiều connect with their Vietnamese community via personal or professional blogs. For example, one of the most popular blogs by Việt Kiều is *Góc nhìn Alan* (Alan's worldview: http://www.gocnhinalan.com/) which was owned by Alan Phan, a successful Vietnamese businessman residing in the United States. His blog offers critical perspectives on issues ranging from business strategic planning to contemporary Vietnam. Similar to *Góc nhìn Alan* is Tuan's Blog by Nguyen Van Tuan, a well-recognized Vietnamese Australian academic in health science. His blog focuses largely on the research and academic culture in Vietnam and appears to be appealing to different Vietnamese groups. In addition to these blogs, Facebook groups dedicated to specific groups of the diaspora are becoming popular: for example the Vietnamese overseas students in Australia Facebook group Oz Du học (https://www.facebook.com/pages/Oz-Du-h%E1%BB%8Dc/302327569925589), the Vietnamese overseas students in Melbourne group Cộng đồng du học sinh VIỆT NAM tại Melbourne (https://www.facebook.com/groups/Vietnamese.student.in.melbourne/), and the Vietnamese PhD group VietPhD.org (https://www.facebook.com/groups/vietphd/) that connect the Vietnamese who are undertaking or interested in undertaking PhDs all over the world. These groups are loosely connected, and the posts often focus on issues of common concern to their members.

OneVietnam and VietAbroader are two notable examples of diaspora networks that use social media to promote communication between overseas Vietnamese across 30 countries. OneVietnam is a Ford Foundation funded not-for-profit organization based in San Francisco. The organization describes itself as an online hub 'for people passionate about Vietnamese culture to connect, get updates and find opportunities to get involved', offering members the opportunity to 'join a network of start-up founders, chefs, financiers and prolific artists spread over those 30 countries'. OneVietnam has a strong philanthropic focus and connects not-for-profits to a network of 1,200 donors in the Vietnamese community: OneVietnam has 17,817 'likes' on Facebook and 6,132 Twitter followers.

While OneVietnam appears to target overseas Vietnamese professionals, not-for-profits and entrepreneurs, VietAbroader's focus is on overseas Vietnamese students and graduates. VietAbroader is a student-run, not-for-profit organization started by a group of Vietnamese students studying in the United States in 2005. In 2015 the organization had 45,000 registered members and reported a total of 50,000 visits to the website, including 300 members visiting the website on a daily basis. VietAbroader is connected with 118 colleges and universities in the United States, United Kingdom, Singapore and Canada, and in 30 high schools across Vietnam. While the main focus is on providing prospective Vietnamese students with information on study-abroad opportunities, the organization has a growing interest in post-study work opportunities for Vietnamese graduates. In 2012 the organization held its first career conference, with the aim of connecting companies and organizations operating in Vietnam with overseas students and working professionals.

To date, the government's main method of communicating initiatives and opportunities for overseas Vietnamese to work, invest or contribute to Vietnam has been via the local online broadcast media. However, many in the diaspora connecting via Facebook are likely to be wary of government-owned media outlets, and it is unclear to what extent overseas Vietnamese students access Vietnamese news media online. Other forms of social media may be a more effective way of tapping into the younger generation of Vietnamese living abroad. Vietnam is experiencing significant growth in the number of Facebook users and, in 2014, nearly 25 million of the 36 million Internet users in Vietnam had Facebook accounts (VietNamNet Bridge 2014).

While there are signs of a shift in attitude among government officials towards social media and a realization of the critical importance of engaging the younger generation of Việt Kiều, the Vietnamese government maintains tight control over the media, which includes the blocking of websites and surveillance of bloggers and other Internet users. The government's attempts to rein in dissent by enacting laws that restrict online content along with the imprisonment of high-profile bloggers suggests overseas Vietnamese communities will proceed with caution when engaging with the government via social media (Parker 2014).

Conclusion

Vietnamese migrants' connectedness with their home country is a divergent, dynamic and relational process. The forms and effects of Vietnamese migrants' homeland connectedness/disconnectedness are shaped by not only the structural condition, including the home country's policy on diaspora engagement, but also migrants' personal agency, choice and in particular their political and social circumstances. The manner and the extent to which different groups of Vietnamese migrants are motivated to connect and reconnect with Vietnam vary depending on the reasons they left the country and their attitudes towards the Vietnamese government. Therefore, in addition to common policies and programs on facilitating return migration and diaspora engagement, it is important that the government has specific strategies and incentives tailored to strengthen the different diaspora groups' connections to home, addressing their various concerns, experiences and connectedness aspirations.

The Vietnamese government needs to send an important message to overseas Vietnamese. It would benefit Vietnam if overseas Vietnamese were made aware that their knowledge, skills, international qualifications and experience are valued, and that their return or professional engagement is vital to their home country's economic and social development. The Vietnamese government's apparent lack of concern for the student brain drain that is occurring may be sending the wrong message to overseas Vietnamese students. The inadequacy of policies that aim to facilitate the return of overseas Vietnamese students may result in discouraging students from either returning home or maintaining professional links with Vietnam. A study of overseas students in the United States revealed that Chinese students were influenced by their government's efforts to facilitate their return. In contrast, Italian students were conscious that their government had made little attempt to lure students home and were also unaware of any broader policies that the European Union had in place (Szelenyi 2007). According to the InterAcademy Council (2004), a multinational organization of science academies, the importance of attracting, cultivating and retaining the highly skilled overseas students cannot be underestimated because it is self-perpetuating.

It is the highly skilled, highly trained and talented youth with global educational experiences that will go on to become the future leaders required by developing countries. The development of policies that emphasize the important contribution that overseas Vietnamese students and skilled professionals can make to their home country, both by returning home and by engaging from abroad, are vital for Vietnam's future social and economic development.

References

Agunias, Dovelyn R. 2013. 'How to Improve Diaspora Engagement'. *The Guardian*, 21 February.
BBC News. 2013. 'Vietnam Internet Restrictions Come into Effect'. BBC News, 24 November. Online: http://www.bbc.com/news/world-asia-23920541 (accessed 15 December 2014).
———. 2009. 'Vietnam's Diaspora Urged to Return Home'. BBC News. Online: http://news.bbc.co.uk/2/hi/asia-pacific/8373580.stm (accessed 16 January 2015).
Ben-Mosche, Danny, and Joanne Pyke. 2012. *The Vietnamese Diaspora in Australia: Current and Potential Links to the Homeland: Report of an Australian Research Council Linkage Project*. Burwood, Vic.: Centre for Citizenship and Globalisation, Deakin University.
Berliner, Tom, Do Kim Thanh and Adam McCarty. 2013. *Inequality, Poverty Reduction and the Middle-Income Trap in Vietnam*. Hanoi: European Union.
Businessweek. 2014. 'Vietnam Falling Short in Tackling Corruption, Says Party Chief'. *Businessweek*, 6 May.

Chan, Yuk Wah, and Thi Le Thu Tran. 2011. 'Recycling Migration and Changing Nationalisms: The Vietnamese Return Diaspora and Reconstruction of Vietnamese Nationhood'. *Journal of Ethnic and Migration Studies* 37, no. 7: 1101–17.
Clark, Helen. 2015. 'Vietnam Government Turns to Social Media to "Guide Opinion"'. *Asian Correspondent*, 20 January.
Clark, Nick. 2013. 'Vietnam: Trends in International and Domestic Education Asia Pacific International Student Mobility Under the Radar'. *World Education News & Reviews*, 1 June.
Daily Mail. 2015. 'Vietnam PM Says Impossible to Ban Social Media: Report'. Online: http://www.dailymail.co.uk/wires/afp/article-2912858/Vietnam-PM-says-impossible-ban-social-media-report.html (accessed 5 August, 2015).
Dang, Nguyen Anh, Cecilia Tacoli and Xuan Thanh Hoang. 2003. 'Migration in Vietnam: A Review of Information on Current Trends and Patterns, and Their Policy Implications'. Paper presented at the Regional Conference on Migration, Development and Pro-Poor Policy Choices in Asia, 22–24 June, Dhaka. Online: http:/www.livelihoods.org/hot_topics/docs/Dhaka_CP_7.pdf (accessed 10 December, 2015).
Dantri International. 2012. 'Rising Numbers of Vietnamese Study Abroad'. Dantri International, 16 January. Online: http://www.dtinews.vn/en/news/020/20449/rising-numbers-of-vietnamese-study-abroad.html (accessed 10 December 2014).
Docquier, Frédéric, and Hillel Rapoport. 2012. 'Globalization, Brain Drain, and Development'. *Journal of Economic Literature* 50, no. 3: 681–730.
Einhorn, Bruce, and Olga Kharif. 2014. 'Intel's Vietnam Engineering Talent Pipeline'. *Businessweek*, 26 June.
Gribble, Cate. 2008. 'Policy Options for Managing International Student Migration: The Sending Country's Perspective'. *Journal of Higher Education Policy and Management* 30, no. 1: 25–39.
Gomes, Catherine. 2010. 'Keeping Memories Alive: Maintaining Singapore Nationalism Abroad'. *Asia Journal of Global Studies* 3: 37–50.
Ho, Nga Thi Thuy, Pi-Shen Seet and Janice Jones. 2014. 'Understanding Re-Expatriation Intentions among Overseas Returnee Professionals'. Paper read at Academy of Management Proceedings.
Huynh, Jennifer, and Jessica Yiu. 2012. 'Breaking Blocked Transnationalism: Intergeneratio nal Change in Homeland Ties'. Paper read at Conference on Immigrant Transnational Organizations and Development. Center for Migration and Development, Princeton University.
InterAcademy Council. 2004. *Inventing a Better Future: A Strategy for Building Worldwide Capacities in Science and Technology*. Amsterdam: InterAcademy Council.
Keong, Tan Tay. 2001. 'Social Capital and State-Civil Society Relations in Singapore'. IPS Working Papers, no. 9, National University of Singapore.
Lakshmi, Rama. 2015. 'India Wants to Turn 25 million in the Diaspora into Global Ambassadors'. *Washington Post*, 18 February.
Ministry of Foreign Affairs, Vietnam. 2012. 'Review of Vietnamese Migration Abroad'. Ha Noi: Vietnam Government. Online: http://www.moj.gov.vn/vbpq/en/Lists/Vn%20 bn%20php%20lut/View_Detail.aspx?ItemID=4761 (accessed 5 August 2015).
Ministry of Justice, Vietnam. 2000. 'Law on Science and Technology'. http://www.moj.gov.vn/vbpq/en/Lists/Vn%20bn%20php%20lut/View_Detail.aspx?ItemID=4761 (accessed 12 December 2015).
Montague, Alan. 2013. 'Vocational and Skill Shortages in Vietnamese Manufacturing and Service Sectors, and some Plausible Solutions'. *Asia Pacific Journal of Human Resources* 51, no. 2: 208–27.

Murti, Bhattiprolu, and R. S. Zaharna. 2014. 'India's Digital Diaspora Diplomacy: Operationalizing Collaborative Public Diplomacy Strategies for Social Media'. *Public Diplomacy* 5: 3.

Nguyen, Chi Hong. 2013. 'Vietnamese International Student Mobility: Past and Current Trends'. *Asian Education and Development Studies* 2, no. 2: 127–48.

OECD. 2012. 'Better Skills, Better Jobs, Better Lives: A Strategic Approach to Skills Policies'. OECD Publishing. doi: http://dx.doi.org/10.1787/9789264177338-en.

Parker, Emily. 2014. 'Blogging for Freedom in Vietnam.' *The New Yorker*, 1 June.

Pham, Andrew. T. 2010. 'The Returning Diaspora: Analyzing Overseas Vietnamese (Viet Kieu) Contributions toward Vietnam's Economic Growth'. Development and Policies Research Center (DEPOCEN) http://depocenwp.org/upload/pubs/AndrewPham/VK%20contributions%20to%20VN%20growth_APham_DEPOCENWP.pdf (accessed 15 December 2015)

Pham, Hiep. 2011. 'VIETNAM: Young Academic Talent Not Keen to Return'. *University World News*, 24 July. Online: http://www.universityworldnews.com/article.php?story=20110722201850123 (accessed 5 August 2015).

———. 2013. 'Diaspora Talent is Lured Back, but Fails to Stay'. *University World News*, 6 April. Online: http://www.universityworldnews.com/article.php?story=2013040414214828 (accessed 19 January 2015).

Pham, Viet Huong. 2012. 'Overview of Labour Migration of Vietnam'. Paper presented at 2nd ADBI-OECD Roundtable on Labor Migration in Asia: Managing Migration to Support Inclusive and Sustainable Growth, Tokyo, 18–20 January.

Schulmann, Paul. 2014. 'Trends in Vietnamese Academic Mobility'. *World Education News & Reviews*, http://wenr.wes.org/2014/06/trends-in-vietnamese-academic-mobility-opportunities-for-u-s-institutions (accessed 18 January 2015).

Seng, Wong. K. 2007. 'Inaugural Singapore Day Draws Thousands'. In *P.M's. Office*, edited by the Singapore Government. Singapore: Overseas Singaporean.

Singapore Government. 2013. *A Sustainable Population for a Dynamic Singapore* (Population White Paper). National Population and Talent Division, Singapore Government.

Song, Changzoo. 2014. 'Engaging the Diaspora in an Era of Transnationalism.' *IZA World of Labor*. http://wol.iza.org/articles/engaging-the-diaspora-in-an-era-of-transnationalism (accessed 19 January 2015).

Szelényi, Katalin. 2006. 'Students without Borders? Migratory Decision-making among International Graduate Students in the US.' *Knowledge, Technology & Policy* 19, no. 3: 64–86.

Thanh Nien News. 2013. 'Shortage of Skilled Workers Hinders FDI in Vietnam'. *Thanh Nien News*, 23 November.

Thayer, Cathay. 2014. 'China's Oil Rig Gambit: South China Sea Game-Changer?'. *The Diplomat*, 12 May. Online: http://thediplomat.com/2014/05/chinas-oil-rig-gambit-south-china-sea-game-changer/ (accessed 16 December 2014).

Tran, Ly, Simon Marginson, Hoang Do, Quyen Do, Truc Le, Nhai Nguyen, Thao Vu, Thach Pham and Huong Nguyen. 2014. *Higher Education in Vietnam: Flexibility, Mobility and Practicality in the Global Knowledge Economy*. New York: Palgrave Macmillan.

Tran, Ly Thi (2015). Mobility as 'Becoming': A Bourdieuian Analysis of the Factors Shaping International Student Mobility. *British Journal of Sociology of Education*, 1–22. Published online before print: http://www.tandfonline.com/doi/full/10.1080/01425692.2015.1044070

Truong, Le Bach, and Ly Thi Tran (2014). Students' Intercultural Development in Vietnamese Tertiary Education. *Language and Intercultural Communication*. Published online first: DOI: 10.1080/14708477.2013.849717

Truong, Quang. 2013. Vietnam: An Emerging Economy at a Crossroads. Working paper no. 2013/09. Online: http://www.msm.nl/resources/uploads/2014/02/MSM-WP2013-09.pdf (accessed 5 August 2015).

Tuoi Tre News. 2014. Foreign Investors Still Hurt by Red Tape: Forum. Online: http://tuoitrenews.vn/business/24426/foreign-investors-still-hurt-by-vietnams-red-tape-forum (accessed 5 August 2015).

Tuoi Tre News. 2015. Social Media Begin to Have a Voice in Vietnam. Online: http://tuoitrenews.vn/society/27430/social-media-begin-to-have-a-voice-in-vietnam (accessed 5 August 2015).

VietNamNet Bridge. 2014. 'Facebook has 25 million Users in Vietnam'. VietNamNet Bridge, Online: http://english.vietnamnet.vn/fms/science-it/103044/facebook-has-25-million-users-in-vietnam.html (accessed 15 December 2014).

Việt Nam News. 2011. 'Female Workers Abroad Need State Protection'. *Việt Nam News*, 5 December.

———. 2013. 'Hi-tech Firms Face 'Huge Need' for Skilled Workers', *Việt Nam News*, 23 August.

Vietnam Steel Corporation. 2014. Vietnam Steel Corporation (VSC). Online: www.businessportals.com/supplier/vnsteel.html (accessed 13 December 2014).

World Bank. 2015 'Data: Vietnam'. World Bank. Online: http://data.worldbank.org/country/vietnam (accessed 2 March 2015).

———. 2014. 'Vietnam Overview'. World Bank. Online: www.worldbank.org/en/country/vietnam/overview (accessed 2 December 2014).

Ziguras, Christopher, and Cate Gribble. 2014. 'Policy Responses to Address Student "Brain Drain": An Assessment of Measures Intended to Reduce the Emigration of Singaporean International Students'. *Journal of Studies in International Education* 17: 629–47.

Zweig, David, Chung Siu Fung and Donglin Han. 2008. 'Redefining the Brain Drain: China's "Diaspora Option"'. *Science Technology & Society* 13, no. 1: 1–33.

Chapter 4

LIKING IT, NOT LOVING IT: INTERNATIONAL STUDENTS IN SINGAPORE AND THEIR NAVIGATION OF EVERYDAY LIFE IN TRANSIENCE

Catherine Gomes

Introduction

Since the early 2000s, Singapore has been host to international students from all over Asia and beyond who attend both local and foreign-based tertiary institutions.[1] Most of these students are able to blend into Singaporean society, perhaps, because their physical appearance – particularly those with Asian heritage – is similar to the established Chinese, Indian and Malay ethnic groups that form the bedrock of the city-state's multi-ethnic landscape. Some of these students are very familiar and comfortable with Singaporean culture and society, especially those who also spent their formative schooling years in their host nation. Moreover, many international students stay in Singapore after graduation because they are serving out a bond by working with a local company, while others stay due to the increased job opportunities available to them. However, the presence of 'foreign talent' – that is international students at universities and migrant white-collar workers – while being the target of xenophobia among Singaporeans, are also considered by citizens as being a major cause of social tension the city-state. While many

---

1 Different versions of the background sections on international students in Singapore, Singapore as a destination and multiculturalism in Singapore appear in Gomes, Catherine. 2014. 'Xenophobia Online: Unmasking Singaporean Attitudes Towards "Foreign Talent" Migrants'. *Asian Ethnicity* 15, no. 1: 21–40; Gomes, Catherine. 2016. 'Not Quite Fitting In: Asian International Students in Singapore'. In *Global Perspectives and Local Challenges Surrounding International Student Mobility*, edited by Krishna Bista and Charlotte Foster, 281-96. Pennsylvania: IGI Global.

native Singaporeans have not yet engaged in face-to-face abuse of foreign talent, they certainly have expressed their disgust and xenophobia online. Given these factors, I embarked on a journey to uncover how international students in Singapore balance these contradictory factors in their everyday lives in their host nation.

In early 2014 I spent a month in Singapore interviewing 'foreign talent' about their social media practices, social networks/friendship groups, self-perceived identities, their impressions of Singapore, and whether they see a future in their host nation. What I found is that despite the international student participants generally liking Singapore particularly in terms of lifestyle, in general they reported not being (or trying not to be) affected by the anti-foreign sentiments. While a few had local (yet not close) friends and would like to become permanent residents due to the job opportunities available to them, their connections to Singapore appeared superficial. In other words, they had very little emotional investment in Singapore, a country that they see more as a practical place to be in because of good economic prospects. Instead, their more meaningful connections are to their own homelands because of their ability to identify more strongly with nationality and co-nationals while in transience. Hence, these connections are expressed through their self-perceived (national) identities and their host nation (co-national) friendship groups. Like international students in other countries (Sawir et al. 2008), many international students in Singapore make friends with fellow international students from their homeland. Such feelings and bonds towards their home nation are noteworthy since racial harmony and tolerance of different cultures are part of Singapore's national ethos and written into policy and law. I would thus argue that international students in Singapore balance a form of mild integration with indifference, while anchoring their transience in their home-nation-based identity. This they do, as I point out, through their social networks, which are very strongly made up of fellow international student friends from their homelands. For them, having their national identities as their predominant identity provides them with a sense of rootedness while being transient in Singapore – feelings which may well follow those who later stay in city-state post-graduation. Their strong sense of national identity, which is perpetuated by their social networks, takes root despite ethnic and cultural similarities with the main Singaporean ethnic groups.

Research in the area of international students – once the traditional domain of education researchers – is now taking a more sociological, anthropological and cultural-studies turn, with research increasingly looking at the ways in which international students navigate everyday life in the host nation. Work by Collins (2010), Kim (2011), Fong (2011) and Martin and Rizvi (2014) for instance, look at the challenges international students experience while in transience by examining their social relations with cross-cultural encounters, as well as the creative methods they develop to keep connected to their homeland. The disconnection from place is a recurring theme. This disconnection can be to the host country (Collins 2010; Kim 2011) or even to the home nation (Kim 2011). This research, while necessary for understanding broader discussions of contemporary youth and their hyper-mobility, is almost always found in a journey-to-the-West narrative, primarily looking at Asian international students who study in Europe, North America, Australia and New Zealand. The circulation of Asian international students within the Asian region has been less studied. In part, this could be because the export of international education is still in its early stages, with very few Asian countries framing themselves as education hubs. This chapter attempts to start a conversation about the experiences and encounters of international students of similar ethnic and cultural backgrounds as they circulate within the region. Although there is research in this area (e.g., Yang 2014) most have been largely confined to class and labour relations of unskilled workers from developed countries working in more developed Asian nations – for example, the treatment of foreign domestic workers from Indonesia and the Philippines in places such as Singapore, Hong Kong and Malaysia (Constable 1997; Rahman 2005; Ford and Piper 2006; Kaur 2007).

While this chapter features participants from outside the region, most of the students interviewed are from Asia. This chapter also uses international students' social media practices to explore their everyday lives in Singapore, and I use this in partnership with other variables (e.g., friendship groups) in order to create a richer methodological lens. Doing so allows me to make sense of some of the ways in which transient migrants navigate everyday life in Singapore. However, before analysing the data, it is necessary to have a background understanding of international students in multicultural Singapore. As part of the broader foreign talent community in Singapore, international students have an uneasy position in Singaporean society, as they are welcomed by the government with the prospect of job opportunities upon graduation, yet vilified by Singaporeans for the same reasons.

International Students in Singapore

In the early 2000s, the Singapore government began to imagine itself as a global education hub, a host to diverse public and private institutions of higher learning from local and foreign education providers, attracting international students from the region and elsewhere. This was done through the Global Schoolhouse initiative, which led to the establishment of diverse institutions and programs in the nation-state in 2002. The initiative was followed by the launch of the Singapore Education brand in 2003, which was meant to promote Singapore as a 'premier education hub' with the aim of attracting international students (Dessoff 2012, 19). Looking at the current higher-education sector, Singapore has two public universities (National University of Singapore and Nanyang Technological University), three government-supported universities (Singapore Management University, Singapore University of Technology and Design, and the Singapore Institute of Technology), private universities (e.g., Singapore Institute of Management, which administers foreign university degree programs on top of their own) and branch campuses of foreign universities (e.g., James Cook University Singapore). In addition, Singapore has five polytechnics (e.g., Nanyang Polytechnic, Singapore Polytechnic), and other government-affiliated institutions providing industry-specific diploma and degree programmes, for example, the BCA Academy (*The Complete University Guide*, 2014; Ministry of Education, Singapore, 2014a). While this chapter looks at international students attending state-funded universities, it is worth mentioning that the creation of the Global Schoolhouse initiative has served not just international students but also local students. By 2011, Singapore had around 70 registered private higher-education providers with 47,500 full-time and part-time Singaporean students (ICEF Monitor 2012).

Besides making inroads into the lucrative international education market, turning Singapore into a global education hub where Singaporeans and non-Singaporeans benefit from local and foreign institutions is a key strategy the government relies upon to develop a knowledge-based economy, which would see the city-state strengthen its position as a regional services hub and manufacturing base for multinational companies (Sanderson 2002).

In order to attract top international students to its publicly funded universities and polytechnics, the Singapore Ministry of Education administers tuition grants worth about SGD$210 million each year (6% of the 1,700 polytechnic students and 13% of the 2,200 undergraduates at state-funded universities).[2] Upon graduation, these students are then bonded in Singapore for three years to work for local companies (Ministry of Education 2014b). In addition, Singapore also has scholarships, grants and fellowships that are specific to the region, such as the Singapore Government Scholarships for Southeast Asians and the ASEAN Foundation Scholarships in Development, Environment, and IT for ASEAN nationals. International students without scholarships find that the international student fees are not nearly as high as those in other popular education hubs, such as Australia, New Zealand, the United States and the

---

2 In 2013, Singapore's Ministry of Education spent SGD$5.1 million on tertiary education alone (Matthews 2013).

United Kingdom. This is because education in Singapore is heavily subsidized, even for international students. An Arts and Social Science undergraduate degree for new students entering university in 2016/2017, for instance, costs SGD$29,350 per year in Singapore while the equivalent course costs approximately SGD$63,652 per year at a top university in the United States of America.

In 2012 Singapore reported that it had around 86,000 international students (Ministry of Foreign Affairs 2012).[3] At the beginning of 2014, international students made up 18 per cent of university students in Singapore. Unlike other international student hubs such as Australia, the United Kingdom, Canada and the United States, which aim to increase their international student intake since international education is a lucrative market, Singapore is aiming to decrease its international enrolments to 15 per cent by 2015 in order to create more vacancies for local students.[4] Singapore's initial aim of increasing its international student population by almost 100 per cent or to 150,000 by 2015 was reviewed after the 2011 general elections when voters turned against the ruling People's Action Party (PAP), accusing it of favouring international students over local students, who many felt were being denied places in local tertiary institutions. Such sentiments are part of the anti-foreign discourse that has become far too commonplace among Singaporeans, particularly online.

Singapore as a Destination

Singapore is an attractive destination for international students for both economic and lifestyle reasons. Singapore has a wide range of established manufacturing and service industries and other emerging globally competitive businesses areas.[5] The Ministry of Manpower reported that in March 2015, 3,624,200 people were employed. This is 2.9 per cent more than the previous

---

3 Figures for 2014 were not available at the time of writing.
4 In April 2016 the Australian government, for instance, released a National Strategy on International Education in Australia where it aimed to increase international student intake to almost a million students by 2025 as part of its strategy to take Australian international education to the next level of global dominance.
5 The industries Singapore supports are aerospace engineering, alternate energy/clean technology, chemicals industry, consumer business, electronics industry, energy industry, engineering, environmental and water, healthcare, international non-profit organizations, infocomm services and products, logistics and supply-chain management, marine and offshore engineering, media and entertainment, medical technology, pharmaceuticals and biotechnology, precision engineering and professional services. The emerging businesses are automotive, natural resources, lifestyle products and services, safety and security and real-time and space (Singapore Economic Development Board 2014).

year (Ministry of Manpower 2015a). In 2015, the Ministry of Manpower also reported there were 60,700 job openings waiting to be filled. The unemployment rate, at 1.8 per cent at the end of March 2015, is one of the lowest in the world (Ministry of Manpower 2015b).

The Singapore government frequently mentions that the city-state's only resource is its people (e.g., Ministry of Foreign Affairs 2012). In the late 1970s and early 1980s Singapore embarked on ambitious modernization projects that saw a great need for unskilled labourers to help build infrastructure and also domestic workers to replace the rising number of women entering the workforce to meet labour demands. By the late 1980s, however, Singapore realized that it was facing a brain drain where university-educated and skilled Singaporeans were emigrating with little or no intention of returning to the homeland. This situation was made worse by an earlier population-control policy aimed at limiting the birth rate. *Stop at Two* was a prominent media campaign from 1970 to 1976 that promoted no more than two children per family.[6] In order to meet the labour shortage, Singapore started looking overseas as part of its recruitment program to fill an ever-increasing number of jobs available in various industries. While attracting foreign workers to fill skilled positions was one way of addressing the labour shortage, another was by attracting international students. This would mean that international students were also contributing to the economy through the secondary industries (e.g., hospitality). As a result, international students were possibly acculturating and assimilating into Singaporean society and desired permanent residency in order to stay indefinitely in their host nation or at least for a significant number of years.

Since Singapore is rich in job opportunities, international students are able to easily find work locally after graduation. Current immigration policies in Singapore allow them to apply for permanent residence once they are on skilled working visas (S-Pass or E-Pass).[7] The availability of jobs for international student graduates in locally based companies is in contrast to the situation in Western education hub nations where preference is mostly given to citizens and permanent residents.

---

6   This campaign was accompanied by government incentives and disincentives such as tax breaks for those with no more than two children, and large families penalized when it came to public housing, respectively (Library of Congress Library Studies 1989).
7   According to the Ministry of Manpower (2014), the S-Pass (Skilled Pass) 'allows mid-level skilled foreigners who earn a fixed monthly salary of at least $2,200 to work in Singapore' while the E-Pass (Employment Pass) 'allows foreign professionals to work in Singapore. It applies to foreigners who earn a fixed monthly salary of at least $3,300, and have acceptable qualifications'.

Singapore has a high standard of living, a comprehensive education system, an infrastructure that is constantly changing to meet the demands of the nation and a stable government that actively promotes law, order and ethnic harmony among its citizens despite Singaporean hostility to international students and migrants. Singapore also supports a citizenry that is multicultural, multi-ethnic, multi-religious and multilingual. As an Asian nation that supports Asian diversity, Singapore may be highly popular with Asian international students who might feel more at home here while still wanting the overseas experience.

Multiculturalism in Singapore

Singapore prides itself on being a well-maintained multicultural society that has come a long way very quickly from the days of communal politics and violence that dominated the final years of British imperial rule and the difficult years of federation. It is now a nation that has seemingly formed a harmonious society that accommodates ethnic and religious difference (D. P. S. Goh 2008). As stated earlier, Singapore's multicultural identity is primarily made up of three broad ethnic groups – Chinese, Malay and Indian – with the Chinese by far being the largest. Singaporeans have been brought up to believe that Singapore is a successful multicultural nation because there are no obvious signs of racism, as seen in other countries, such as racially motivated violence. The Chinese–Malay–Indian–Others nexus makes up what is known as the CMIO racial categorization in Singapore. While multicultural Singapore puts forward an 'Others' category for Singaporeans of Arabic, Armenian and Eurasian background, they are not as culturally or ethnically recognizable because of their relatively small numbers.

While Singapore's race relations have been critiqued as being complicated and tense (Gomes 2014; Chua 2003; Velayutham 2009), on the surface at least, the different ethnicities of Singapore seem to live and work harmoniously with each other. In the view of the government, the idea of racial harmony not only creates a peaceful space for citizens but national stability for the purpose of foreign investment. There have not been any open communal conflicts or violent ethnic clashes in independent Singapore. The last racially charged incident took place on 21 July 1964, a year before Singapore's independence, when racial tensions between Chinese and Malays exploded on what is known today as the Prophet Muhammad Birthday Riots. A nationally coherent workforce, after all, will be committed to building a wealthy and cosmopolitan Singapore, according to the government.

Since independence, the Singapore government has spared no expense attempting to promote racial harmony among its people. Racial harmony has, for the most part, endured in the independent nation in part because of the strict laws preventing racial incitement. The Singapore Penal Code (Cap 224, 2008 Rev. Ed.), s. 298A states:

Whoever –

(a) by words, either spoken or written, or by signs or by visible representations or otherwise, knowingly promotes or attempts to promote, on grounds of religion or race, disharmony or feelings of enmity, hatred or ill-will between different religious or racial groups; or
(b) commits any act which he knows is prejudicial to the maintenance of harmony between different religious or racial groups and which disturbs or is likely to disturb the public tranquility, shall be punished with imprisonment for a term which may extend to 3 years, or with fine, or with both.

In addition to these laws aimed at preventing racial conflict, Singapore also puts in place soft approaches committed to promoting and fostering racial harmony. Singapore does this through: a national pledge stating unity despite communal differences; the promotion of racial harmony as part of country's tourism campaigns; the establishment of official think tanks such as the Inter-Racial and Religious Confidence Circle (IRCC); and the establishment of racial harmony through the formal education system, in particular in social studies texts. However, many Singaporeans, it would seem, are not fully prepared to accept other ethnicities joining its tapestry of established diversity, including Mainland Chinese and other South Asian nationalities. At this point it is important to note that these laws are in place to police and protect Singaporeans and not foreigners living, working or studying in the city-state.

Singaporeans, since the 2000s have been incredibly critical of new migrants – the overwhelming majority of whom come as workers, while a significant number are made up of international students – entering their country and have been expressing their anger through xenophobic comments online (Gomes 2014; Matthews 2013).[8] Despite strict laws against racial vilification, these comments can be seen in some of the more popular online forums in media and blog sites such as Asiaone.com (http://www.asiaone.com/), The

8 In early 2014, I published an essay in the journal *Asian Ethnicity* discussing the online xenophobia I saw in Singapore in relation to the influx of new migrants and international students. These new migrants were often transient and were more often than not able to convert their status from transient to permanent, since they were training in or occupied in white-collar positions in the city-state. Since the publication of that essay, I have keenly watched the discussions and comments of Singaporeans online (social media and online forums) to see if the xenophobic attitudes I wrote about had changed. While there were voices that condemned such racist behaviour, they were but a few.

Online Citizen: A Community of Singaporeans (http://theonlinecitizen.com/), Sam's Alfresco Haven: Celebrating Singapore's Golden Period! (www.sammyboy.com), and The TR Emeritus (http://www.tremeritus.com/). Unlike the temporary foreign domestic workers and unskilled labourers who have been coming into Singapore since the 1980s, foreign talent migrants – who have been arriving since the 1990s – are educated professionals who often take up permanent residence in their adopted country. The Singapore government sees foreign talent migrants as an investment in Singapore's economic future and argues that it has to open the country's doors to new migrants – because Singaporeans are not reproducing enough to replenish the workforce and because new migrants can help care for an ageing population. With these reasons in mind, in February 2013 the Singapore Parliament endorsed the *Population White Paper: A Sustainable Population for a Dynamic Singapore*, which aims to see the nation's population increase to 6.9 million by 2030, mainly through migration. Some Singaporeans protested against the white paper by organizing social media groups such as 'Referendum on the Population White Paper' and 'Say "No" to an Overpopulated Singapore' on Facebook. By mid-2016, 'Say "No" to an Overpopulated Singapore' had garnered 26,573 'likes'.

An analysis of the online xenophobic comments generally reveals that Singaporeans view foreign talent migrants with great suspicion. In these comments, Singaporeans express their views that the foreign talent migrants are threatening their livelihoods and way of life. Moreover, Singaporeans feel that foreign migrants are unable to integrate into Singapore because they are not fully adopting Singaporean culture (e.g., always speaking Mandarin, rather than English or Singaporean English also known as Singlish). Many Singaporeans express resentment that white-collar transient migrants are able to get permanent residence easily without displaying any form of loyalty to Singapore. Singaporeans state that they want new migrants to disconnect themselves from their homeland (not consider returning to their homeland at any stage) and to not engage in cultural practices of their homeland (Gomes 2014). In 2014, many Singaporean netizens became very angry and took to the Internet to express their rage at a proposed plan for Filipinos to celebrate their national day in the main shopping district of Orchard Road (Palatino 2014). The event was eventually cancelled because of the fear of violence. Moreover, many comments exposed Singaporean displeasure at the ruling PAP, whom they hold responsible for the influx of foreign talent. Here, Singaporeans also noted that they were no longer able to identify with Singapore due to the increasingly overcrowded and changing (permanent and transient migrant) ethnographic landscape, which they blame on government policies.

While face-to-face racial attacks or skirmishes have not been reported as yet, xenophobic protests have unfortunately taken place. On 16 February 2013, around four thousand Singaporeans turned up at an organized protest against the *White Paper on Population*, which had been endorsed in parliament a week earlier. Organized by transitioning.org – an organization that 'cater[s] to the emotional needs of the unemployed' Singaporean – the event was billed as an exclusively 'Singaporean-only' occasion, with foreign talent (including new permanent residents) encouraged not to attend (Goh 2014). Protesters held up placards such as 'Singapore for Singaporeans' and 'Stop Gov Unfairly Treatment Singaporean' (Ramesh 2013; Yahoo! Newsroom 2013).

Methodology: Social Media, Self-Perceived Identity and Social Networks

Increasingly, work in the area of migrants and social media, such as Hjorth and Arnold (2012), have shown that digital technology allows migrants to remain connected to their home cultures and societies by providing virtual networks that allow for direct communication with friends and family, both residing in the homeland and elsewhere. While acknowledging the role played by digital technologies in the migration experience, this project explores how the combined wider field of social networks, self-perceived identities and attitudes towards the host nation, are vital platforms that provide support in the migration experience through self and communal empowerment. In other words, this project views social media as more than a communication tool that enhances trans-connectivity of groups and communities, but one that allows an avenue for further understanding of the migration experience.

With the above in mind, 30 international students studying at Singaporean universities were interviewed as part of a larger qualitative and qualitative study involving the identities of transient migrants (international students and foreign workers) in Singapore and Australia. I also enlisted two research assistants, one of whom was a Singaporean local, to help with participant recruitment and interviews. Participants were recruited through advertising in international student society groups and hostels and via word of mouth. The advertisements requested participants who were international students over the age of 18 who had lived in Singapore for a minimum of 3 months.[9]

As indicated in Table 4.1, the sample included students from a range of countries and from a variety of disciplines. Unsurprisingly, because of

---

9   This project received funding from the Australian Research Council (Ref. DE130100551) and received ethics approval from RMIT University (Application No: CHEAN B-2000903-05/13).

Singapore's status as a regional hub, there were more Asian students who responded to this project.

The participants were interviewed in small groups and as individuals, in addition to completing a short written survey that recorded their demographic information as well as their media use and hobbies. The data in this chapter is reflective of the open-ended questions we asked pertaining to participants' perceived self-identities, social networks, impressions of Singaporean society, plans for the future and social media use. The duration of the interviews ranged from 30 to 60 minutes, depending on the willingness of the respondents to go into more depth. The results revealed that international students are not emotionally invested in their relationship with Singapore through their social media use and their general attitude towards the host nation but they have a more robust connection to the homeland. This connection was demonstrated by their identity as located in the homeland (e.g., identifying themselves according to their nationality) and their social networks consisting of fellow international students from the home nation.

Ordinary Everyday Use of Social Media with Barely Any Mention of Singapore

Perhaps unsurprisingly, social media was part of everyday life for participants. All international students in this study had a social media presence and contributed in some way through passive or active involvement with this communication tool. However complex their social media use may be (e.g., juggling multiple platforms in different languages), their social media practice, as this section will reveal, is unremarkable. By unremarkable I do not mean insignificant but, rather, that they say they do not use social media for activist or political purposes, which are what this medium is often associated with (Castells 2000). While many of the participants had been in Singapore since high school and had the intention of applying for permanent residence, what they told us about their social media activities revealed no meaningful engagement with their host nation – participants did not discuss anything significant about Singapore in the form of posting, commenting, sharing of links, liking and joining, nor did they subscribe to any Singapore-based interest or news groups other than those that were university related.

The international student participants did, however, have a solid yet eclectic social media presence. Participants checked their various social media platforms on a daily basis, often spending free or specific times to check their accounts on their smart phones, laptops or tablets. For instance, some participants may have checked their social media accounts when they were on public transport in order to kill time or before they went to sleep. As Table 4.2

Table 4.1 Demographics of participating international students studying in Singapore.

Gender	F (12)
	M (18)
Age range	18 to 20 (8)
	21 to 25 (15)
	26 to 30 (5)
	31 to 35 (2)
Country of citizenship	Britain (1)
	China (4)
	Indonesia (11)
	India (5)
	Malaysia (3)
	Norway (1)
	Philippines (1)
	South Korea (1)
	USA (1)
	Vietnam (2)
Ethnicity	Batak (1)
	Caucasian (2)
	Chinese (14)
	Chinese–Filipino (1)
	Indian (7)
	Javanese (2)
	Korean (1)
	Vietnamese (2)
Length of stay in Singapore	> 1 year (9)
	1 year to > 2 years (0)
	2 years to > 3 years (2)
	3 years to > 4 years (5)
	4 years to > 5 years (4)
	5 years to > 6 years (7)
	6 years to > 7 years (1)
	< 7 years (2)
Level of current studies	Undergraduate (25)
	Postgraduate (5)
Discipline areas	Arts (4)
	Business and Commerce (8)
	Engineering and Information Systems (4)
	Law (1)
	Science (3)
	Not Specified (10)
Part-time work	Yes (10)
	No (20)

shows, most participants juggled a few social media platforms in dual languages (English and other languages spoken at home). Every participant in this study had a Facebook account, with half (16) of them doubling up as Instagram users, while others used Chinese (e.g., Weibo, WeChat and QQ) or Korean (Kakao Talk) social media platforms. Participants explained that the different language platforms allowed them to keep in touch with different groups of friends (e.g., Facebook for friends made in Singapore, and QQ for Chinese friends in China, Singapore or elsewhere). One participant admitted to using a variety of platforms, which she compartmentalized for different activities (e.g., actively participated on WeChat but quietly looked at what others say on QQ).

Participants told us that their social media activities involved a combination of active and passive communication. For the purpose of this study, I focus on Facebook as a case study since all participants have an account. Moreover, Facebook is the most popular social media platform, with over 1.23 billion users or around a sixth of the global population (Ross 2014). Half were proactive users of Facebook, where they admitted to either commenting on or liking posts and photographs (inclusive of Instagram), while a third would share links or posts with others. Almost half of the participants would communicate their thoughts through status updates, photographs or links, while a third enjoyed using the chat function on Facebook to privately communicate with individuals or small groups of friends. The general activity of participants reflects wider studies done on the social media use of young people in countries such as Australia (Chang 2011; Chang et al. 2012) and North America (Ito et al. 2009; boyd 2014).

Research on social media users generally reveals that consumers are not static in their involvement but participate in a mix of activities such as lurking, liking, linking, posting and commenting (Chang 2011; Lubke 2007; Kaplan and Haenlein 2009). While participants in this study varied in their Facebook presence, the majority admitted that their most common activity was to lurk (Bishop 2007). Here they may have visited the home pages of people in their network or viewed their status updates, photographs and links (e.g., articles and videos). Participants admitted that they enjoyed keeping track of what their friends were up to – particularly those from their homeland, including those who were studying elsewhere overseas. This reveals that participants were more interested in what others similar to them (fellow transients from the homeland) were doing because they were the group participants identified with the most. Social media is a platform for communities to thrive (Castells 2000) and where, more often or not, communities are grounded in virtual friendships based on commonality of experience, as the ongoing Global

Table 4.2 Social media use of participating international students studying in Singapore.

Participant no.	FB	Instagram	Twitter	LinkedIn	QQ	Weibo	WeChat	Blog	YouTube	Snapchat	KakaoTalk
1	Yes		Yes								
2	Yes		Yes								
3	Yes	Yes	Yes								
4	Yes										
5	Yes	Yes	Yes	Yes							
6	Yes	Yes									
7	Yes	Yes	Yes	Yes							
8	Yes	Yes	Yes	Yes				Yes			
9	Yes	Yes	Yes	Yes							
10	Yes									Yes	
11	Yes			Yes							
12	Yes	Yes		Yes							
13	Yes			Yes	Yes	Yes	Yes				
14	Yes			Yes							
15	Yes			Yes							
16	Yes			Yes	Yes	Yes	Yes	Yes			Yes
17	Yes			Yes	Yes	Yes	Yes				
18	Yes										
19	Yes	Yes									
20	Yes	Yes									
21	Yes										
22	Yes	Yes	Yes	Yes				Yes			
23	Yes	Yes		Yes				Yes			
24	Yes	Yes									
25	Yes	Yes									
26	Yes			Yes							
27	Yes			Yes							
28	Yes		Yes								
29	Yes	Yes									
30	Yes	Yes									

Social Media Impact Study (http://www.ucl.ac.uk/global-social-media) led by Daniel Miller is uncovering.

The international students we interviewed let us know that Singapore did not feature in their everyday social media practice. Generally, those participants who posted and shared on Facebook were cautious about what they said, with no participants admitting that they made complaints about others (particularly nationalities such as Singaporeans).[10] They explained that they were not particularly engaged or interested in Singapore, and stated that even news about Singapore from media outlets did not interest them – a trait I also found common in international students in Australia (Gomes 2015). Hence, they did not post any comments or links about Singapore. They suggested that the only Singapore-related subject matter that they discussed on social media outside of their studies related to banal and inoffensive topics, such as the weather and the restaurants they visited. This lack of discussion about Singapore on social media took place despite the international students living in Singapore for anywhere between three to ten years. Participants noted that if they discussed Singapore, they did so in private (e.g., face-to-face or on another, private, communication tool, such as WhatsApp) and not on social media for fear of repercussions from Singaporeans. While it has been noted that international students find it challenging to connect with their host nation in cross-cultural East meets West circumstances (Collins 2010; Kim 2011; Fong 2011; Martin 2014) my conversations with Asian international students reveal that even between ethnically and culturally similar groups, students have difficulty making connections with locals.

Moreover, while there is a lot of online xenophobia in Singapore (Gomes 2014), the international students who participated in this study did not engage with the vitriolic attacks against foreign talent – in fact only a small number of participants admitted that they thought there was resentment towards foreigners in Singapore. They let us know that they did not use social media to retaliate or to question the xenophobia that populates digital media; preferring instead to ignore such postings. This is despite the Singapore government's 'light-touch' approach to Internet content and access. Here, the government, through its Media Development Authority, 'does not restrict or monitor individuals' access to online content'; instead encouraging self-regulation through education and media literacy (Media Development Authority, Singapore

---

10 This admission is quite different to the way Singaporeans use social media and online forums to broadcast their opinions on politics, society and culture in Singapore. Everyday Singaporean netizens who are savvy with online technology have taken to online platforms, particularly social media, to air their grievances about their country and government while doing so anonymously (Gomes 2014).

2014). Perhaps respondents are not interested in having opinions about events and activities in Singapore or, most likely, they do not want to risk their future in the country by being too open or honest about what they do not like in the city-state. This reluctance may not just be their understanding of Singapore's reaction to dissent, but also an attitude they bring with them from their home countries.

Most participants did not explicitly state that they felt or experienced any anti-foreign sentiment in Singapore, least of all on social media. This could perhaps be because many international students do not openly say that they feel tension towards their host nation, for fear – real or imagined – of contravening the conditions of their visa. The Student Pass visa in Singapore comes with strict terms and conditions. Item 9 on the Singapore Immigration and Checkpoints Authority's 'Terms and Conditions of Student's Pass (STP)' clearly state the following: 'You shall not engage in any activity, criminal or otherwise, which is inconsistent with the purpose for which the Student's Pass has been issued.' International students might interpret criminal activity as breaching the strict racial harmony laws prevalent in Singapore and dictated by the Singapore Penal Code as highlighted earlier in this essay.

This possible interpretation of the STP may impact on international students stating that they have never engaged with the anti-foreign sentiments Singaporeans display online or that they generally have not experienced xenophobia. This could be attributed to the politeness of the participants not wanting to offend the researchers, as one of my research assistants and myself are Singaporean by birth. Furthermore, my research assistant is Singapore-based and had just completed an undergraduate degree at one of the local public-funded universities, where a number of participants were enrolled.

In addition, there have been a few high-profile cases of 'foreigners' getting into trouble with locals for online comments made about Singaporeans. British-born Singaporean permanent resident Anton Casey, for instance, was fired from his job at HSBC Singapore and forced into exile with his Singaporean wife and young son after offensive comments he made about Singaporeans using public transport were leaked online.

While the Singapore government has been welcoming to international students as part of its long-term plan at making the city-state a regional education hub, the 2011 general elections made the incumbent PAP rethink the numbers of foreign students it was allowing into its local institutions. During the elections, voter dissatisfaction with the PAP's foreign talent policy resulted in the biggest loss of the popular vote the PAP had ever experienced. Forty per cent of the Singaporean population voted for the opposition. This then resulted in the PAP government responding to voter dissatisfaction by curbing the number of white-collar jobs available to foreigners as well as restricting the number of international students allowed into the country. As mentioned earlier in this chapter, the Singapore government had plans of increasing international student intake in 2015 but, instead, decreased the 2014 number of 86,000 by 15 per cent. It is possible that international students who were interviewed for this project perhaps felt that Singapore was not as welcoming to them as it first had been and, hence, reacted to this situation by not becoming too emotionally connected to the country, despite permanent residence being an economic goal for many of them.

Participants in this project had a paradoxical connection to Singapore. On the one hand they generally liked Singapore for a variety of reasons, including its record as being environmentally aware (clean and efficient), economically attractive (job prospects) and welfare-oriented (low crime). Many of the international students we spoke to were from Asia or had Asian heritage and were able to recognize similarities between Singaporean and their own (ethnic and national) cultures. However, this recognition was limited, with participants stating that they did not really identify with Singaporean society because they saw more cultural differences than similarities. Moreover, while participants liked living in Singapore, with the majority wanting permanent residence, it is their identifying with the homeland that anchors their transience.

Same but Not Really: Chinese Singapore's Cultural Bias

Singapore is a unique international education hub, particularly for many Asian international students. As a host nation, Singapore is unlike other popular destinations for Asian international students such as Australia, New Zealand, North America or the United Kingdom because of cultural proximity and cultural similarities. Paradoxically, while the majority of Asian international students are able to identify with Singapore because it is an Asian nation with a diverse Asian population, this local version of multiculturalism is also problematic. Those who come from Asian cultures, such as the ethnic Chinese from Southeast Asia and Mainland China, explain that while they find Singaporean culture familiar on one level, they are also unable to fully connect with it. They explain that Singaporean culture is 'different' to what they are used to in the homeland. Here, for instance, a few of the respondents from China explained that they felt Chinese Singapore culture is not truly Chinese because of its other ethnic cultural influences.

A few Chinese Malaysian participants expressed that they were unable to identify with Chinese Singaporeans, whom they consider different even though they are ethnically similar. This is so even though Malaysia supports a multiculturalism in a way similar to that of neighbouring Singapore, and both nations have a shared history of British colonial rule. Similarly, Chinese

Indonesians (who make up a significant number of participants in this study) felt disconnected from local Chinese Singaporeans, even though both diasporic groups share similar migrant heritages as descendants of nineteenth- and early-twentieth century Southern Chinese migrants (Owen 2005).

Likewise, Chinese participants revealed that they felt that the Singapore-born ethnic Chinese were both similar yet different from them. Chinese participants admitted that they felt foreign in Singapore even though the island-state is somewhat similar to China because of the strong Chinese Singaporean demographic and because Mandarin is one of the four official languages, is frequently used in the media and among Chinese Singaporeans in general.[11] As the following female undergraduate from China explains:

> I think Singapore is still a foreign country for me even right after I arrived here actually I miss my country. Yeah, I live the past twenty-eight years in China and I don't think China is a great country but since I arrived here I see my country it is really great. Yeah, because of [Singapore's] experience and her achievements and [Singapore] becomes the number two economic country within only thirty years, yeah. And as I have more international friends here so sometimes I practise English more with them because they don't know any Mandarin so sometimes I think this is a foreign country yeah, I don't think it is kind of home to me, yes.

While this student is from China, she finds it challenging living in Singapore because she sees more differences than similarities, even though Singaporean Chinese make up the vast majority of the local population. In particular, she points out that language is a noteworthy issue since Singapore has spared no effort in training Chinese Singaporeans to speak Mandarin, which they learn as a compulsory second language in school (primary to junior college). In addition, Singapore's 'Speak Mandarin Campaign' – a national program to encourage and increase usage of Mandarin over Chinese dialects in the domestic and public spaces – has been in existence since 1979.

Perhaps the regional Chinese diaspora and the Mainland Chinese are unable to totally identify with the Singaporean Chinese as a result of globalization and varied communal and national histories. The diasporic Chinese in Southeast Asia are largely descendants of nineteenth- and twentieth-century migrants whose societies adapted to the national cultures and histories of their homelands. Chinese Indonesians, for instance, speak Bahasa Indonesian

---

11 The four official languages of Singapore are English, Mandarin, Tamil and Malay, while English is the language of choice for government and education.

as their first language and do not carry Chinese family names, a result of anti-Chinese legislation during Sukarno's New Order regime (1965–1998). Moreover, China is not the same ancestral place that was home to the early Chinese migrants, having dramatically changed political systems from imperial to communist and experiencing a cultural rebirth as a result of the Cultural Revolution (1966–1976). For Chinese Singaporeans, their Chinese identity is also dictated by the government.

In *The Singapore Story*, an excellent analysis of the cultural construct of the Singapore government's official narrative of the city-state's history, Hong and Huang (2008) paint a daringly honest picture of a nation whose government has never been shy to express its admiration for the hard-working Chinese migrants of colonial Singapore and of the nationalist diasporic Chinese. Hong and Huang (unsurprisingly) assert that Singapore's history is 'scripted', that the past is distilled to highlight only specific heroes in the story of Singapore. *The Singapore Story* states that besides Lee Kuan Yew (Singapore's first prime minister) and the PAP – whose exploits contributed to freeing Singapore from the clutches of communism and racial unrest and then led the people to enjoy the fruits of capitalism in a nation blessed by racial harmony – the other protagonist of this official narrative is the superhero of the Chinese community, Sun Yat-sen. What Hong and Huang strongly imply is that *The Singapore Story*, while uncomplicated in its choice of national heroes, is ultimately a contrived one that underpins and supports the national values of the state with a strong ethnic Chinese hue. The choice of non-Singaporean Sun Yat-sen as an elevated hero in Singapore supports the strong diasporic Confucian Chinese value system, which Singapore has adopted and adapted for itself. This value system becomes the very tool with which the government controls Singaporean society and dictates national allegiance to both the state and ruling party. Here, the value system of the diasporic Chinese is highlighted as the ideal and necessary framework for the past, present and future economic successes of Singapore, as well as a platform for creating stability.

Hence, even though both the Chinese international students and the Chinese Singaporeans share the same ethnic cultural roots, the development of their cultural identities is based on their differing national experiences. This could explain not only the Chinese international students' inability to find common ground with Chinese Singaporeans, but also (Chinese) Singaporeans' extreme difficulty to find common characteristics with their co-ethnics, thus resulting in online (and offline) displays of xenophobia. So while theoretical studies on diasporic communities and cultures often state that individuals and groups who live outside the geographical boundaries of the country of origin are linked to each other through an imagined cultural community due to the memory of a shared history and culture (e.g., Benedict Anderson's famous

1983 theorization of the 'imagined community'), the relationship between Chinese international students and the Chinese Singaporeans show otherwise.

'Got Used to Here, More or Less'

As discussed elsewhere in this chapter, many of the international students interviewed for this project had been living in Singapore for a number of years.[12] While all participants were enrolled at local universities, a number of international students had also completed their high school (junior college), middle school (secondary) or both in Singapore. Their many years of growing up in Singapore and living among Singaporeans have allowed them the opportunity to form opinions of the society.

While some participants criticized Singaporeans as complaining a lot, are competitive, aggressive and intimidating, are materialistic or lacked humour, these participants also had positive things to say about their host nation and its citizens. A few participants noted that Singapore was well-organized and that it was generally a diverse, open and good country. Moreover, participants commented that Singaporeans were warm and friendly and observed with reserved admiration that Singaporeans worked and studied hard. Participants were able, in other words, to cast a critical eye on their host society and recognize both the good and the not-so-good traits of Singaporeans.

Of the 30 students interviewed for this study, a third of them confidently said that they experienced a sense of belonging in Singapore, even though they were transient, while a few participants stated that although they wanted to feel a sense of belonging in their host nation, such feelings did not exist. The participants provided some reasons that pointed to their ability to identify with Singapore (e.g., Singapore reminds some Chinese students of home because of the ethnic Chinese majority), their positive impressions of the country (e.g., Singapore's efficiency compared to their home nations), the friends they have made with both Singaporeans and non-Singaporeans and the years spent in the host nation. As the following participants explain:

> I have been here for two years and I love Singaporean friends and I am starting to adopt Singaporean cultures and so I just have like some kind of sense of belonging with the society. (Female Indonesian undergraduate)
>
> Well, I guess I've been here for more than ten years, so I think I have gotten used here, more or less. [...] So it's not whether I like it here or not, but it's

---

12 When asked about what he thinks of Singapore, a participant (male undergraduate from Malaysia) replied that because he had been in his host nation for ten years, he had grown used to the place in terms of Singaporean culture and society.

more of a kind of habit I guess. So like I'm – I know how to cope [...] I know that I can meet my friends when I want to, so it's kind of like getting used to the whole environment. (Male Malaysian undergraduate)

Both participants articulated that their length of stay in Singapore had helped them adapt to living there as well as to adopt local traits. While the female Indonesian student was more enthusiastic than the male Malaysian student in terms of feeling a sense of belonging in the host nation, both also admitted that their ability to make a sensible and workable life in transience in Singapore lay in their social networks.

The contribution of social networks to the happiness, well-being, acculturation and social stability of international students is well acknowledged by researchers (Kudo and Simkin 2003; Ying 2002; Gomes and Alzougool 2013; Gomes et al. 2014). The literature has also shown that international students' social networks are strongly made up of other international students (Kashima and Loh 2006; Kashima and Pillai 2011). The literature also notes that while international students form friendships with individuals from their own country, from other countries and from the host country, they often have more friends from their home country.[13] Portes and DeWind (2004), for example, found that international students in the United States formed friendships primarily with other foreigners, citing differences between American and foreign experiences as the reason for their lack of assimilation.

Research has also demonstrated a relationship between having more host country friends with satisfaction, contentment, decreased homesickness and social connectedness. Hendrickson et al. (2011), for instance, analysed the relationships between friendship networks, social connectedness, homesickness and satisfaction levels of international students and explored these relationships through a social network lens by examining friendship network ratios, strength and variability of the friendship groups of 86 international students at the University of Hawai'i. A friendship network grid was developed to assess where international students' friends are from and how strong those friendships are. Contrary to prior research, international students did not report having a higher ratio of individuals from their home country in

---

13   Home country can be country of citizenship or birth country. While all participants are international students, with 12 spending many years in Singapore on previous student visas, only 9 of them identify themselves as students, with another 9 perceiving their identities as international students. In a parallel study I conducted in Australia of 30 international students in Melbourne, all of them identified as international students more so than as their nationalities (Gomes 2013).

their friendship networks. However, international students with a higher ratio of individuals from the host country in their network claimed to be more satisfied and content and less homesick. Furthermore, participants who reported more friendship variability with host country individuals described themselves as more satisfied and content, and more socially connected. This correlates with Sawir et al.'s (2008) earlier Australian study that argued for more social interaction between international students with people from outside the home nation as a more successful way of curbing loneliness. Sawir et al. suggested that international students who formed friendships with nationals from the home nation were more lonely than those who broadened their friendship networks to include others.

During our interviews, participants revealed that they were aware of anti-foreign tension in Singapore and of negative attitudes towards them; however, they seemed to be able to see past this and told us of their admiration for both Singapore and its citizens. What is more, some of the participants empathized with Singaporean attitudes concerning them, noting that they understood the tensions towards them as being 'perfectly normal' (male Indonesian undergraduate). Meanwhile another (male British undergraduate) explained that Singaporean attitudes towards foreigners (especially non-Asians) lay perhaps in their inability to recognize or identify with people outside the Chinese–Malay–Indian (CMI) nexus. He explained that he did not feel a complete sense of belonging in Singapore because he is not one of the CMI races, which he saw as part of the national psyche:

> I think it's natural that within Singaporean society most Singaporeans, they would only consider Asians or their three main races, Malay, Indian, or Chinese to be real Singaporeans. The other races, I think find it difficult to fully nationalize into Singapore[. ...] Well I mean, from young, when people go to school, the – in history, I think in Singapore history they will identify that Indians, Malays and Chinese are the main three races. So, then a lot of time Singaporeans will be told this, so then, naturally they view only those three races as the three races of Singapore.

This participant was perhaps correct in surmising that education played a key role in Singaporean society's attitudes towards foreigners, especially those who did not bear any remote physical cultural resemblance to Singapore-born Chinese, Malays or Indians. While he recognized that he may never really be accepted as a part of Singaporean society because he did not resemble CMIs, he nevertheless stated during the interview that he very much would like to become a permanent resident and make Singapore his long-term home.

In fact, most of the participants we interviewed see a future in Singapore and have had a long-term relationship with this country. Permanent residence was a goal for most of the participants in this study, with two-thirds stating that they intend to actively submit the paperwork for this. Moreover, half the participants had been in Singapore for more than four years, while a third completed their junior college and/or secondary schooling in the city-state, which might indicate a more than cursory connection to Singapore as discussed elsewhere in this chapter. However, an analysis of all participants' social networks and self-perceived identities reveals that these international students situate themselves very strongly with their home nation. It is a strong affiliation with the home nation through nationality, in particular, that dominates international students' self-perceived identity.

Identity Connected to Nationality and Friends from Home

Identifying with the homeland for migrants, permanent or temporary, is not unusual (Gomes 2009; Leong 2012; Guntarik 2013). Permanent migrants for instance connect to the homeland as a way of navigating their everyday life in countries culturally different from their own, while transient migrants often have the intention of eventually going back to the homeland primarily because of the conditions of their visa. Both permanent and transient migrants connect with the homeland in various ways such as by forming/joining communities of people from their home nation who are in similar circumstance (e.g., visa status such as permanent residents, international students and foreign domestic workers), replicating homeland culture through practice (e.g., food, faith, language, the arts and dress) in the private and public spaces and by keeping communication actively open with the homeland (e.g., keeping in touch with friends and family back in the homeland, visiting regularly and consuming news and entertainment media produced by or about the homeland) (Cunningham and Sinclair 2001).

The majority of participants in this study perceive their identities to be strongly affiliated with their home country because of nationality. Of note, respondents stated that they felt that their national identity was stronger in Singapore than in their home countries. As the following participant explains:

> I feel most Indonesian when I am out of Indonesia[...] I am most Indonesian[...] I find friends and Indonesians [...] make me like I am still Indonesian. (Male Indonesian postgraduate)

For this participant, being overseas only reinforced his identity as Indonesian. However, this national identity is not merely a feeling but rather involves an active and committed engagement of specifically looking for fellow (transient) Indonesians to be the primary make-up of his social networks in Singapore. Doing so allows him to navigate an everyday life in transience that is filled with some form of familiarity and camaraderie. Friends, particularly those who are from the home nation and living in Singapore, no doubt are an important part of life in transience.

The participants in this study generally have a vibrant and complex network of friends that they have made in Singapore. While more than half have Singaporean friends, it is the friends from the homeland who dominated these international students' social circles, as they reported that they felt more comfortable with fellow international students rather than with locals. This is despite research on international students and their social networks often pointing out that they feel happier and more of a sense of belonging when they make local friends (Hendrickson et al. 2011). Participants admitted that their friends were fellow foreign students from their respective home nations. Almost all participants made friends with people in close proximity to them (university, accommodation, religious groups/institutions primarily churches, and university clubs). Some participants with Singaporean friends noted that these were long-term friends they made from their earlier school days. They also explained that they found making friends with Singaporeans easier when they were in secondary school and junior college. Participants noted that it was harder to make friends with Singaporeans at university because locals tended to study in their free time and had families to go back home to, whereas the international students tended to spend their after-class hours living and studying with other friends from their country. A female undergraduate from China explains her frustrations:

> I try to make friends with them but I think it would be easier for me to make international friends and I don't know, maybe we have something in common because we are foreigner here, yeah. But making friends with local Singaporean especially the classmates I think it is not as easy as I think about, yeah.

For her and other international students, making friends with international students from the homeland in particular is perhaps seen as practical and beneficial. Having international student friends from the homeland may provide the most comfort and support, not only because of a shared culture but also because of language of communication. Furthermore, international students identify and bond together with other international students from the homeland as a community precisely because of their status as foreigners from their respective nations living and studying in Singapore. Most often, participants make friends with other international students they meet in obvious places, such as while attending their courses. The participants feel that only other international students from their country are able to understand the issues they are going through while living overseas, such as homesickness and the pressure to study long hours, and the practical issues connected with living in Singapore (e.g., finding accommodation). Having other international students from the homeland as friends allows participants to fill the huge gap that has been left because of their separation from their families and their homeland culture. These findings reflect other research on the importance of friendship for overseas students (Kudo and Simkin 2003; Ying 2002; Kashima and Loh 2006; Kashima and Pillai 2011; Gomes and Alzougoo, 2013; Gomes et al. 2014).

Conclusion

Singapore presents a unique yet challenging place for international students. On the one hand, Singapore is an ideal place for (particularly Asian) international students in terms of tuition fees, (seemingly) cultural similarity and familiarity. In addition, for significant numbers of international students, there is the prospect of local jobs at the end of their degrees. On the other hand, however, Singapore is an uneasy and sometimes unwelcoming place for overseas students because of anti-foreign sentiment that has been dominating social media and online forums. Taking into account these contradictory factors, the present study approached 30 international students from state-funded universities in Singapore as part of a broader study of foreigners studying, working and living in Singapore. Participants were interviewed on their social media use, social networks, self-perceived identities and attitudes towards Singapore and Singaporeans. Adopting an approach that queries their everyday life outside study provides a richer and layered understanding of how these subjects navigate their everyday lives as transients. Their answers revealed that they lack an emotional relationship with Singapore (and its people), while anchoring their transience in their home-nation-based identity. Here, they express a form of mild integration with indifference to Singapore through their social-media practice and social networks, even though the majority of them have spent three years or more studying in the city-state and intend to apply for permanent residence. Instead, they expressed a stronger connection to the homeland, particularly through their self-perceived identity, which is strongly rooted in their nationality, and their friendship groups, which largely consisted of fellow international students also from the homeland. This happens despite ethnic cultural similarities between the international students and the main Singaporean racial groups.

If international students and foreign talent in Singapore would like to become permanent residents or even Singapore citizens, the government needs to develop strategies to help with integration. These strategies, however, need to include tenets that acknowledge and appreciate the diversity of people and cultures entering the city-state. Further, these strategies need to include rethinking multiculturalism in Singapore that goes beyond the Chinese–Malay–Indian–Others (CMIO) nexus, thus reassuring Singaporeans that expanding Singapore's multicultural make-up is not a threat to their national culture, society or lifestyle. Rather, the new migrants bring with them an evolving Singapore that enhances rather than hinders local lifestyle and culture. The dual approach of enabling new migrants to practise their (national and ethnic) cultures with rethinking Singaporean multiculturalism to be more inclusive of diversity beyond the CMIO nexus would help new (transient and permanent) migrants have more of a connection to Singapore and a greater sense of identity with Singaporeans.

At the same time, the Singapore government needs to reflect on the cultural disjuncture between transient and new migrants and Singaporean-born nationals. Transient and new migrants from China, Indonesia and India, together with the Chinese and Indian diasporas from elsewhere, may be the ethnic and cultural cousins of the mainly Chinese, Malay and Indian Singaporean ethnicities but as this chapter, along with earlier research I conducted in 2014, has shown, integration and assimilation rarely take place. While the transient migrants in this study do not seem to be bothered much by the xenophobia projected by some Singaporeans, Singapore cannot function in the long term with such rigidly unassimilated societies.

References

Anderson, Benedict. 1988. *Imagined Communities: Reflections on the Origin and Spread of Nationalism*. London and New York: Verso.

Australian Government. 2015. *Draft National Strategy for International Education: For Consultation*. Australian Government. Online: https://internationaleducation.gov.au/International-network/Australia/InternationalStrategy/Documents/Draft%20National%20Strategy%20for%20International%20Education.pdf (accessed 4 June 2015).

Bishop, J. 2007. 'Increasing Participation in Online Communities: A Framework for Human–Computer Interaction'. *Computers in Human Behaviour* 23, no. 4: 1881–93.

boyd, danah. 2014. *It's Complicated: The Social Lives of Networked Teens*. New Haven: Yale University Press.

Castells, Manuel. 2000. *The Rise of the Network Society: The Information Age: Economy, Society and Culture*. New Jersey: John Wiley & Sons.

Chang, Shanton. 2011. 'Facebook and the International Office: Should We or Shouldn't We?'. Conference Proceedings of the 24th ISANA International Education Conference, 29 November – 2 December 2011. Online: http://www.proceedings.com.au/isana/docs/2011/slides_Chang.pdf (accessed 1 July 2014).

Chang, Shanton, Basil Alzougool, Marsha Berry, Catherine Gomes, Sharon Smith and Daniel Reeders. 2012. 'International Students in the Digital Age: Do You Know Where Your Students Go to for Information?' Australian International Education Conference (AIEC), 2–5 October 2012, Melbourne. Online: http://aiec.idp.com/uploads/pdf/2012_chang_fri_1235_212_paper.pdf (accessed 2 July 2014).

Chua, Beng Huat. 2003. 'Multiculturalism in Singapore: An Instrument of Social Control'. *Race and Class* 44, no. 3: 58–77.

Collins, Francis Leo. 2010. 'Negotiating Un/Familiar Embodiments: Investigating the Corporeal Dimensions of South Korean International Student Mobilities in Auckland, New Zealand'. *Population, Space and Place* 16, no. 1: 51–62.

Constable, Nicole. 1997. *Maid to Order in Hong Kong: Stories of Filipino Workers*. New York: Cornell University Press.

Complete University Guide. 2014. 'Studying in Singapore'. The Complete University Guide. Online: http://www.thecompleteuniversityguide.co.uk/international/asia/singapore/ http://www.moe.gov.sg/education/post-secondary/ (accessed 14 April 2014).

Cunningham, Stuart, and John Sinclair (eds). 2001. *Floating Lives: The Media and Asian Diasporas: Negotiating Cultural Identity through Media*. Lanham, MD: Rowman & Littlefield.

Dessoff, Alan. 2012. 'Asia's Burgeoning Education Hubs'. *International Education* (July/August): 16–26. Online: https://www.nafsa.org/_/File/_/ie_julaug12_asia.pdf (accessed 3 April 2014).

Fong, Vanessa L. 2011. *Paradise Redefined: Transnational Chinese Students and the Quest for Flexible Citizenship in the Developed World*. Stanford: Stanford University Press.

Ford, Michelle, and Nicola Piper. 2006. 'Southern Sites of Female Agency: Informal Regimes and Female Migrant Labour Resistance in East and Southeast Asia'. *Southeast Asia Research Centre Working Paper Series* 82: 1–24.

Giddens, Anthony. 1991. *Modernity and Self-Identity: Self and Society in the Late Modern Age*. Cambridge: Polity.

Goh, D. P. S. 2008. 'From Colonial Pluralism to Postcolonial Multiculturalism: Race, State Formation and the Question of Cultural Diversity in Malaysia and Singapore'. *Sociology Compass* 2, no. 1: 232–52.

Goh, Gilbert. 2014. 'About'. *Transitioning.Org*. Online: http://www.transitioning.org/about-2/ (accessed 30 April 2014).

Gomes, Catherine. 2014. 'Xenophobia Online: Unmasking Singaporean Attitudes Towards "Foreign Talent" Migrants'. *Asian Ethnicity* 15, no. 1: 21–40.

Gomes, Catherine, and Basil Alzougool. 2013. 'Transnational Citizens and Identities: International Students' Self-Perceived Identities, Their Social Networks and Their Consumption of Entertainment Media in Australia'. Proceedings of the 24th ISANA International Education Conference, 3–6 December 2013, 1–15. Online: http://proceedings.com.au/isana/docs/2013/Gomes_Catherine.pdf (accessed 13 March 2014).

Gomes, Catherine, Marsha Berry, Basil Alzougool and Shanton Chang. 2014. 'Home Away from Home: International Students and Their Identity-Based Social Networks in Australia'. *Journal of International Students* 4, no. 1: 2–15.

Guntarik, Olivia. 2013. 'Literary Fictions: Asian Australian Writers and the Literary Imagination'. *Creative Industries Journal* 6, no. 1: 5–16.

Hendrickson, B., D. Rosen and R. K. Aune. 2011. 'An Analysis of Friendship Networks, Social Connectedness, Homesickness, and Satisfaction Levels of International Students'. *International Journal of Intercultural Relations* 35, no. 3: 281–95.

Hjorth, Larissa, and Michael Arnold. 2012. *Online@AsiaPacific: Networked Sociality. Creativity and Politics in the Asia–Pacific Region*. New York: Routledge.

Hong, Lysa, and Huang Jianli. 2008. *The Scripting of a National History: Singapore and Its Pasts*. Singapore: NUS Press.

ICEF Monitor. 2012. 'Singapore's "Carefully Calibrated" Expansion Plans'. ICEF Monitor, 4 September. Online: http://monitor.icef.com/2012/09/singapores-carefully-calibrated-expansion-plans/http://monitor.icef.com/2012/09/singapores-carefully-calibrated-expansion-plans/ (accessed 14 April 2014).

Immigration and Checkpoints Authority. 2013. 'Terms & Conditions of Student's Pass (STP)'. Immigration and Checkpoints Authority, Singapore. April. Online: http://www.ica.gov.sg/data/resources/docs/Visitor%20Services/Terms_and_Conditions_STP.pdf (accessed 4 July 2014).

Ito, Mimi, et al. 2009. *Hanging Out, Messing Around, and Geeking Out*. Cambridge, MA.: The MIT Press.

Kaplan, Andreas, and Michael Haenlein. 2009. 'Users of the World, Unite! The Challenges and Opportunities of Social Media'. *Business Horizons* 53, no. 1: 59–68.

Kashima, E. S., and E. Loh, 2006. '"IS" acculturation: Effects of International, Conational, and Local Ties and Need for Closure'. *International Journal of Intercultural Relations* 30, no. 4: 471–85.

Kashima, E., and D. Pillai. 2011. 'Identity Development in Cultural Transition: The Role of Need for Closure'. *Journal of Cross-Cultural Psychology* 45, no. 5: 725–39.

Kaur, Amarjit. 2007. 'International Labour Migration in Southeast Asia: Governance of Migration and Women Domestic Workers'. *Intersections* 15. Online: http://wwwsshe.murdoch.edu.au/intersections/issue15/kaur.htm (accessed 2 July 2007).

Kim, Youna. 2011. *Transnational Migration, Media and Identity of Asian Women: Diasporic Daughters*. New York and Oxford: Routledge.

Kudo, K., and K. A. Simkin. 2003. 'Intercultural Friendship Formation: The Case of Japanese Students at an Australian University'. *Journal of Intercultural Studies* 24, 2: 91–114.

Leong, Susan, and Qian Gong. 2012. 'Provincialising Perth?: Satellite Television and the Chinese in Perth'. In *Cultures in Refuge: Seeking Sanctuary in Modern Australia*, edited by Devleena Ghosh, Robert Mason and Anna Haye, 133–49. Burlington, VT: Ashgate.

Library of Congress Library Studies. 1989. 'Singapore Population Control Policies'. Online: http://www.photius.com/countries/singapore/society/singapore_society_population_control_p~11008.html (accessed 6 October 2014).

Lim, Catherine. 2011. 'How GE 2011 Proved Me–Oh, So Wonderfully!–Wrong', *Catherinelim.Sg: Political Commentaries on Singapore* (blog), 5 August. Online: http://catherinelim.sg/2011/05/09/how-ge-2011-proved-me-oh-so-wonderfully-wrong/#more-999 (accessed 20 May 2012).

Lubke, Jennifer. 2007. 'Lurking and Linking: How I Built My Virtual Learning Network'. Supervised Readings 594 – Dr Ed Counts, The University of Tennessee. December 3. Online: http://web.utk.edu/~jlubke/TECH575/eportfolio/PDFs/vln_essay.pdf (accessed 5 July 2014).

Martin, Fran and Fazal Rizvi. 2014. 'Making Melbourne: Digital Connectivity and International Students' Experience of Locality'. *Media, Culture & Society* 36, no. 7: 1016–31.

Matthews, David. 2013. 'Singapore: No Sleep for the Lion City's Universities'. *Times Higher Education*, 21 November. Online: http://www.timeshighereducation.co.uk/features/no-sleep-for-singapores-universities/2009064.fullarticle (accessed 24 April 2014).

Media Development Authority, Singapore. 2014. 'Internet'. Online: http://www.mda.gov.sg/RegulationsAndLicensing/ContentStandardsAndClassification/Pages/Internet.aspx.

Ministry of Education, Singapore. 2014a. 'Post-Secondary Education'. Ministry of Education. Online: http://www.moe.gov.sg/education/post-secondary/ (accessed 4 April 2014).

———, Singapore. 2014b. 'TG Online'. Ministry of Education. Online: https://tgonline.moe.gov.sg/tgis/normal/index.action (accessed 21 April 2014).

Ministry of Foreign Affairs, Singapore. 2012. 'Education in Singapore'. Ministry of Foreign Affairs. Online: http://www.mfa.gov.sg/content/mfa/overseasmission/washington/about_singapore/education_in_singapore.html (accessed 5 April 2014).

Ministry of Manpower, Singapore. 2013. 'Labour Market Statistical Information'. Ministry of Manpower. Online: http://stats.mom.gov.sg/Pages/Home.aspx (accessed 24 April 2014).

———. 2014. 'Passes and Visas'. Ministry of Manpower. Online: http://www.mom.gov.sg/foreign-manpower/passes-visas/Pages/default.aspx#sthash.X8CJOYRl.dpuf (accessed 22 April 2014).

———. 2015a. 'Unemployment'. Ministry of Manpower. Online: http://stats.mom.gov.sg/Pages/Unemployment-Summary-Table.aspx (accessed 4 June 2015).

———. 2015b. 'Unemployment Situation, First Quarter 2015'. Ministry of Manpower. Online: http://stats.mom.gov.sg/iMAS_PdfLibrary/mrsd-ES-Q1-2015.pdf#page=8 (accessed 4 June 2015).

Owen, Norman. 2005. 'Singapore'. In *The Emergence of Modern Southeast Asia: A New History*, edited by Norman Owen, 459–70. Honolulu: University of Hawai'i Press.

Palatino, Mong. 2014. 'Xenophobia and Public Discontent in Singapore'. *The Diplomat*, 8 May. Online: http://thediplomat.com/2014/05/xenophobia-and-public-discontent-in-singapore/ (accessed 4 July 2014).

Portes, A., and J. DeWind. 2004. 'A Cross-Atlantic Dialogue: The Progress of Research and Theory in the Study of International Migration'. *The International Migration Review* 38, no. 3: 828–51.

Rahman, Noor Abdul. 2005.'Shaping the Migrant Institution: The Agency of Indonesian Domestic Workers in Singapore'. In *The Agency of Women in Asia*, edited by Lynn Parker, 182–216. Singapore: Marshall Cavendish Academic.

Ramesh, S. 2013. 'Singaporeans Hold Protest against White Paper on Population'. If Only Singaporeans Stopped to Think (blog). Online: http://ifonlysingaporeans.blogspot.com.au/2013/02/sporeans-hold-protest-against-white.html (accessed 30 April 2014).

Ross, Monique. 2014. 'Facebook Turns 10: The World's Largest Social Network in Numbers'. ABC News, 4 February. Online: http://www.abc.net.au/news/2014-02-04/facebook-turns-10-the-social-network-in-numbers/5237128 (accessed 4 July 2014).

Sanderson, Gavin. 2002. 'International Education Developments in Singapore'. *International Education Journal* 3, no. 2: 85–103. Online: http://dspace.flinders.edu.au/xmlui/bitstream/handle/2328/3142/SANDERSON.pdf?sequence=1 (accessed 1 July 2014).

Sawir, E., S. Marginson, A. Deumert, C. Nyland, and G. Ramia. 2008. 'Loneliness and International Students: An Australian Study. *Journal of Studies in International Education* 12: 148–80.

Singapore Economic Development Board. 2014. 'Industries'. Future Ready Singapore. Online: http://www.edb.gov.sg/content/edb/en/industries.html (accessed 1 July 2014).

Singapore Penal Code. (Cap 224, 2008 Rev. Ed.), s. 298A.

Velayutham, Selvaraj. 2009. 'Everyday Racism in Singapore'. In *Everyday Multiculturalism*, edited by Amanda Wise and S. Velayutham, 255–73. New York: Palgrave Macmillan.

Yahoo! News. 2013. '4,000 Turn up at Speakers' Corner for Population White Paper Protest'. *Yahoo! News Singapore*, 16 February Online: https://sg.news.yahoo.com/huge-turnout-at-speakers--corner-for-population-white-paper-protest-101051153.html (accessed 30 April 2014).

Yang, Peidong. 2014. 'Foreign Talent': Desire and Singapore's China Scholars. PhD thesis. Oxford: St. Cross College.

Ying, Y. W. 2002. 'Formation of Cross-Cultural Relationships of Taiwanese International Students in the United States'. *Journal of Community Psychology* 30, no. 1: 45–55.

Part 2
SOCIAL MEDIA AND EXISTING MULTICULTURAL RELATIONSHIPS IN A CONTROLLED COMMUNICATION ENVIRONMENT

Chapter 5

IS 'ALLAH JUST FOR MUSLIMS'? RELIGION, INDIGENIZATION AND BOUNDARIES IN MALAYSIA

Susan Leong

Introduction

On 2 January 2014, members of the Selangor Islamic Affairs Department (JAIS Jabatan Agama Islam Selangor) confiscated 321 Malay- and Iban-language Bibles from the premises of the Bible Society of Malaysia (Gomez 2014). The raid follows on from the Court of Appeal ruling a few months earlier in October 2013 that the 'usage of the word Allah is not integral to the Christian faith' (Anbalagan 2014). It was reasoned that allowing the use of 'Allah' to denote God in the Bahasa Malaysia (Malay) section of the Catholic publication, *Herald*, would 'cause confusion in the community', and the court upheld the home minister's original 2007 ban by a majority of four to three (Shadbolt 2013). Armed with this ruling, JAIS sought to enforce and extend the remit of the ban. Despite being chided later for not first informing the Selangor State Government, and the court ordering the return of the seized Bibles (*Mail Malay* Online 2014a), JAIS succeeded in emphatically asserting Islamic privilege in Malaysia. Through the bellicose enactment of their insistence that Allah is the sole reserve of Muslims, JAIS's raid infringed on the right of indigenous, Malay-speaking and Christian compatriots to freely practise their religion as they see fit (Figure 5.1). The legal strength of JAIS's position was reinforced when the Federal Court dismissed the Catholic Church's application to reverse the ruling later in the year (Mail Malay Online 2014a). In Malaysia, it seems, 'Allah [is] just for Muslim[s]'.

The term *Allah* is widely accepted as being a contraction of the Hebrew *al ilāh* or the Syriac *alāh* (the god) (Thomas 2006, 171). According to Thomas,

Figure 5.1 Protester outside Malaysia's Federal Court. Courtesy of *Malaysiakini* and H. T. Lim©2014.

the term has been used in translations of the Bible written in languages common among 'majority Muslim communities in the Middle East, Africa and most of Asia [...] includ[ing] Arabic, Turkish and Azerbaijani in the Middle East; Bambara, Fulfulde, Hausa, and Mankinka (sic) in Africa; and Malay, Indonesian, Javanese, Madurese and Sundanese in Asia' (2006, 172). Malay translations of the Bible go back to the sixteenth century and, outside of Europe and the Middle East, Malay is the first language the Bible was translated into because it was the lingua franca of trade in the region (Hunt 1989, 35). Early translations were the work of the Protestant Dutch colonials who were motivated to win over the locals converted to Catholicism by the Portuguese, a rival colonial power in the region at the time (35). Various individuals and committees undertook the task of translation at different stages and, even then, there was much dispute over the proper and consistent representation of Malay, as it was a language learnt, spoken and written differently in different places by various translators (37). Consequently, many words were borrowed from the Persian and Arabic languages to explain what were understandably alien concepts (37). Muslim Malay-language teacher (*munshi*) and translator, Abdullah bin Abdul Kadir, or Munshi Abdullah, is generally acknowledged as one of the first translators with a 'long and continuous exposure to the Malay language', and one who played a major role in the production of an idiomatically accurate Malay translation of the Bible (40).

Given the mix of influences of Persian, Arabic, Indonesian and Dutch that came to bear on the Malay-language translations of the Bible, and the accepted social practice of using Allah to denote God in the region over centuries, how did matters come to such an impasse in Malaysia in the twenty-first century, and what brought about this change in attitude? In *New Media and the Nation in Malaysia*, I define a social imaginary as 'the loosely co-ordinated body of significations that enable our social acts and practices by making sense of them' (Leong 2014, 16). The social imaginary framework can be understood as a process whereby ideas and concepts – I call them 'significations' after Castoriadis (1997) – from one society are introduced into another where, if found to be relevant and typical of the new realm, they filter through to be adopted into the second social imaginary. Conversely, if the signification is deemed irrelevant or atypical of a society, it is discarded (Leong 2014, 26). At the same time, a signification can sometimes take on traits that are characteristic of the receiving social imaginary. In other words, borrowed significations are indigenized as they filter through into social imaginaries. Here, the social imaginary framework explains how Islam in Malaysia has arrived at its current manifestation.

To further untangle the complexities of what is at stake here, the discussion in this chapter will briefly trace the twists and turns in Malaysian history and politics that have led to the primacy of Muslim rights in the country. It will then look at a few social media spaces that illustrate the ongoing tussle over related issues, namely, the proposal to implement *Hudud* (the Islamic penal code) in the state of Kelantan, as well as the nation's angst over the place and position of Islamic law within Malaysia. The social media spaces discussed include the Facebook groups, 'I support Hudud in Kelantan'[1] and 'Save Malaysia, No Hudud'[2] as well as a pair of online petitions 'Petisyen Menyokong Hudud' (Petition Supporting Hudud)[3] and 'I am #26'.[4] In doing so, the chapter asks what difference social media has made to how agency, representation and anxieties are played out within Malaysia's multilingual, multicultural social imaginary. Overall, the chapter argues that erecting boundaries around who has the right to use the term Allah, and where, is tantamount to tearing apart the lived experience that is Malaysia. Before going further, it is necessary to clarify here that although the terms 'new media', 'alternative media' and social media denote different sets of media technologies, in Malaysia they are used interchangeably to refer collectively to Internet-enabled platforms like blogs, social networking sites like Facebook and Twitter,

1 https://www.facebook.com/isupporthududinkelantan
2 https://www.facebook.com/save.malaysia.no.hudud
3 http://www.petitionbuzz.com/petitions/hudud4malaysia
4 https://www.change.org/p/the-prime-minister-of-malaysia-i-am-26-saya-26

video sites like YouTube, and instant messaging apps like WhatsApp. For the purposes of this chapter the fluidity of these terms is retained, although the main term used is *social media*.

The Imbrications of Race, Religion and Politics in Malaysia

As a whole, Islam is 'far from monolithic' but, rather, 'pluralistic in its interpretations [with] a rich diversity [...] united by common beliefs and practices and the spiritual bonds inherent in the idea of the global "Muhammadan" community (*ummah*)' (Bakar 2010, 669). Islam arrived in Malaysia courtesy of Indian (and later, Chinese) traders and missionaries passing through the Southeast Asian region (SarDesai 2003; Houben 2003). Writing of 'the specific characteristics of Islam in Southeast Asia', Houben explains that

> the development of the religion in the region has to be seen in the context of processes that influenced the community of Muslims as a whole but also those that were specific to Southeast Asia itself. Islam in Southeast Asia is pluralist, [and] has been modified by local cultures. (2003, 167)

The divergence from orthodox Islam is a result of multiple processes, from its mode of arrival and how 'pre-Islamic ritual practices' were enfolded into understandings of the religion when common people were converted, to the strengthening of official Islam that occurred as part of the 'power-sharing arrangement between the Sultans and the colonisers' (Houben 2003, 154–56). This absorption of Islam into local social practices was very much a part of the general tendency within Southeast Asia then, for the 'selective borrowing of cultural elements from the outside' (157). Such accommodation remains possible largely because Islam, as practised and understood by Muslims in Malaysia and most of Southeast Asia for the past eight centuries, is of the Sunni branch and follows the Shafi'i school of law or jurisprudence (Bakar 2010, 668; Yusuf n.d.). As Irshan (2002, 68) observes, the various schools of Islamic law survive 'because they are rooted in the tradition of the societies in which their philosophy is prevalent'. The Shafi'i school is one of four schools of law or jurisprudence (*mazhabs*) within Sunni Islam that also includes Hanafi, Maliki and Hanbali (Yaran 2007, 16). Although all the schools belong under the umbrella of the Sunni branch of Islam, the methodologies they employ in resolving questions of Islamic law differ and distinguish them from each other (Irshad 2002, 67–68; Yaran 2007, 16). While the Hanafi school is considered the more tolerant and progressive and the Hanbali school the most conservative and literalist, the Maliki and Shafi'i schools occupy the centrist position. Unlike the Hanbali school, which eschews human reason and personal opinion for strict adherence to scripture and *hadith* (a record of the Prophet Muhammad's sayings), the Shafi'i school allows for the use of *ijma* (consensus) and *qiyā* (deductive analogy) whenever scripture and *hadith* do not prescribe solutions (Hughes 2013, 148; Abdal-Haqq 2002, 71).

Malaysia is a constitutional monarchy and federation comprising 3 federal territories and 13 states (Department of Statistics 2010, 2). It is this federated model of government that allows the regulation of Islam to be a state rather than federal responsibility in the nation. Each state manages the balance between the various religions and races according to its own dictates. Apostasy from Islam, for example, is a criminal offence in some states (Pahang, Perak, Malacca, Sabah and Terengganu) and only converts in the state of Negeri Sembilan have the right to legal recourse (Camilleri 2013, 231). This system of religious authority is one of the main reasons the 'Malay version of Islam is [...] intensely localised, with its own parochial lines of authority, practices and social relationships' (Barr and Govindasamy 2010, 296). Given that 61.3 per cent of 28.3 million Malaysians identify as Muslim and just 9.2 per cent as Christians, Christianity is very much a minority religion in the country (Department of Statistics 2011, 5, 9). According to the 2010 population census, there were 2,392,823 Christians in Malaysia, with the highest concentration residing in the states of Sarawak and Sabah (Department of Statistics 2011, 82, 91, 92). Slightly more than half of Christians in Malaysia (1,239,164) are indigenous people from the tribes of Kadazan-Dusun, Bajau and Murut in Sabah and the Iban, Bidayuh and Melanau in Sarawak (Department of Statistics 2011, 82, 91, 92). Apart from Islam and Christianity, the two other major religions practised in Malaysia are Hinduism and Buddhism.

The population is divided into the four main race categories of *Bumiputera* (literally 'sons of the soil', mostly comprising ethnic Malays but can include the aboriginal people of Sabah and Sarawak), Chinese, Indian and Others, with the last being a catch-all category for Eurasians and those of other descent (Department of Statistics 2011). All Malays in the country are Bumiputeras though not all Bumiputeras are Malays as the indigenous tribes such as the Dayaks, Bidayuh and Ibans of Borneo Malaysia are non-Malay Bumiputeras. Where matters become especially complicated in Malaysia is in the historical imbrication between race and religion, springing from the Malay Reservations Act of 1913 that has been retained to the present day. Essentially, the act linked the definition of a Malay person inextricably to the practice of Islam and the use of Malaysian languages (Andaya and Andaya 2001, 183). This definition of a Malay person as someone 'who professes the religion of Islam, habitually speaks the Malay language and conforms to Malay custom' and was born in, or has parents who were domiciled in, the Malaysian Federation or Singapore was adopted into the Malaysian Constitution as Article 160 in 1957 (Commissioner of Law Revision 2006). It is this rigid articulation of the relationship between race and religion that continues to separate the Malay–Muslims from the rest of Malaysian society. In other words, while all Malaysians are identified by the categories of race and religion, only Malays are bound by virtue of their race to the religion of Islam.

The 'Bible incident' referred to at the beginning of this chapter started in 2007 when the Home Ministry barred the Catholic *Herald* from using the term Allah. This was contested and overruled in 2009, reinstated by the Court of Appeal in 2013, and upheld by the highest court in the land in 2014 (Anbalagan 2014; *Mail Malay* Online 2014). The controversy has seen much impassioned protests for and against the various rulings at different stages. Rash and damaging incidents span the seven-year period and include the vandalism of churches, Sikh temples and Muslim prayer rooms (Hookway 2010). In the interim, Prime Minister Najib Razak put forward a ten-point resolution in 2011 intended to clarify: (1) that no conditions attach to the printing and importation of Bibles of any language into Sabah and Sarawak (East Malaysia) and; (2) that in 'the interest of the larger Muslim community, for Peninsula Malaysia, Bibles in Bahasa Malaysia/Indonesia, imported or printed, must have the words "Christian Publication" and the cross sign printed on the front covers' (Aliran 2014). Although these conditions were complied with, the subsequent ban and JAIS's seizure of the Bibles has cast great doubt on the validity of the resolution. All the Bibles seized have since been returned to the Association of Churches in Sarawak, along with an admonition to respect the 'sensitivities of Muslims' (Malaysiakini 2014) but no other national solution acceptable to all concerned parties is in sight, leaving Malay-speaking Christians little choice even as the incident further sours strained relations between the races.

Scholars of Malaysia commonly trace the deterioration of relations between the races to the New Economic Policy (NEP) enacted after the 1969 racial riots and the affirmative action policies in favour of Bumiputeras in the areas of education, employment, business and housing implemented afterwards (Chin 2009). Another school of thought reaches back further to argue that the delineations between the races established by the colonial administration were perpetuated by the founders of the new nation-state through their adoption of Article 160, and point to the racialized enactment of nationhood as the root of the niggling disaffection between the diverse peoples of Malaysia (Sani 2010, 24). Together with the continuation of the NEP's pro-Bumiputera affirmative action policies, the deep entwinement of Malay identity with Islam has hardened the boundaries between the races, effectively belying much of the syncretism that is life in Malaysia. Still others point to the late 1980s and 'the rapid escalation of the Islamization race between UMNO

[United Malays National Organisation] and PAS [Parti Islam Se-Malaysia, Pan Malaysian Islamic Party]' (Noor 2005, 212).[5] From this perspective, the attempts by PAS and UMNO to 'out-Islam' each other are motivated as much by political as religious reasons (Whiting and Majoribanks 2013, 85, 94). In the face of competition against the PAS drawing on the same majority Malay–Muslim pool of support, UMNO recast itself as the party of modern and moderate Islam, poised to take the Malays into better economic times, and at the same time portrayed its competitor as the party of conservative, backward and militant Islam (Noor 2005; Case 2010).

Regardless of its start point, the Islamization of Malaysian society was further entrenched in 1988 when Prime Minister Mohamad Mahathir amended Article 121 of the Federal Constitution so that the civil courts 'would have no jurisdiction in respect of any matter within the jurisdiction of the Syariah courts' (Commissioner of Law Revision 2006, 112). This amendment, now known as Article 121A, brought into being 'two parallel [...] jurisdictional realms between civil and *syariah* law' in the one nation of Malaysia (Yeoh 2011, 96). It was also under Mahathir's watch in 1996 that the central body of Islamic Affairs, Pusat Islam, was 'elevated into the Department of Islamic Development of Malaysia or JAKIM (Jabatan Kemajuan Islam Malaysia) [... and] empowered to draft, streamline, evaluate and coordinate Islamic laws, which included the power to determine what constitutes correct and what constitutes deviant Islamic practices' (Goh 2012, 126). Hence, not only is the form of Islam practised in Malaysia dictated to by the government, the interpretations and enactments of Islam's teachings in everyday social practice are also imposed upon Muslim citizens.

Barr and Govindasamy (2010, 307) contend there is a systematic attempt 'to assimilate non-Malays and non-Muslims into Malaysian society on terms dictated by the hegemonic core national group: Malay–Muslims'. It is certainly true that during a relatively short-lived term (2003–2009), Prime Minister Abdullah Badawi was very keen to promote the idea of *Islam Hadhari* (civilizational Islam) as a 'progressive and inclusive' alternative to PAS's 'reactionary and exclusive' form of Islam (Khalid 2007, 145). Although framed as a national ideology it is hard to imagine how this revised 'vision of Malaysia as the product of a glorious 1,400-year-old Islamic civilization' could have found room to include non-Muslims or any other histories (Barr and Govindasamy 2010, 299). Hopes were high for Badawi's successor, Najib Razak, who started his first term with a more inclusive embracing of diversity

---

5   PAS is today a part of the opposition coalition, Pakatan Rakyat (People's Alliance), while UMNO remains the majority partner in the ruling coalition, Barisan Nasional (National Front).

under the '1Malaysia concept' that encompassed all races and religions. They were further raised in 2011 when Razak fulfilled an election promise to repeal the infamous Internal Security Act (ISA), which allowed indefinite detention without trial in Malaysia (Lim 2012). However, any gains these moves might have brought about for civil liberties were soon eroded by the equally flawed Peaceful Assembly Act (2011a) and the Security Offences (Special Measures) Act (2012a). In fact, with the latest addition of the Prevention of Terrorism Act (POTA) 2015 the state has regained the power to detain individuals without trial for up to 60 days if deemed by the authorities to be 'engaged in the commission or support of terrorist acts involving listed terrorist organisations in a foreign country or any part of a foreign country' (Thiru 2015).

As the leader of the major party (UMNO) in the ruling coalition, Prime Minister Razak has also yet to take a stance on opposition party PAS's intention to introduce Hudud (Islamic penal code) in the state of Kelantan. Provided the burden of 'stringent evidentiary requirements' is met, the Islamic penal code imposes much more severe penalties for 'stealing, robbery, fornication, bearing false witness, consuming liquor and apostasy' than currently permitted in Malaysia (Seda-Poulin 1993, 225). Passed by the PAS-dominated State Legislative Assembly of Kelantan in March 2015, the Kelantan Syariah Criminal Code II (1993) 2015 (KSCC) has yet to be tabled for debate in Parliament (*Star* Online 2015). PAS has been in power in Kelantan since the 1990s and the implementation of Hudud in the state has been part of its agenda from the beginning. However, as the other Malay–Muslim party and major partner in the ruling federal coalition, UMNO has shifted its ground several times over the years on PAS's ambitions to implement Islamic codes of behaviour in the state of Kelantan (Seda-Poulin 1993, 224). Should the amendments proposed by PAS be eventually passed by Parliament, religion and race would be even more firmly imbricated in Malaysian political and social life.

Social Space, Social Media and Social Imaginary

Alongside the permeation of Islamic mores into broader society discussed above, ethno-religious minorities in Malaysia have also been incrementally edged out of social spaces through both individual and communal gestures. Documented examples of this include: a group of Muslims that led a protest using a cow's head at the re-siting of a Hindu temple in District 23 of Shah Alam (Leong 2012); bodies taken from bereaved families and claimed for Islamic burial by the Penang Islamic authorities who alleged conversion of the deceased before death; and brides removed from weddings for marrying outside the faith (Looi 2014; *Malay Mail* Online 2014b). Despite non-Muslim bodies being unquestionably a part of public space and society in Malaysia, their needs, wants and preferences have repeatedly been abrogated in favour of those of the majority.

Such was undoubtedly the experience of two Malaysian Indian mothers, Shamala and Subashini, whose former spouses unilaterally converted their children to Islam after their marriages broke down and obtained custody of their children courtesy of the deference showed to the syariah court by the civil courts in 2003–2004 and 2007 respectively (Steiner 2013). Even in interfaith custody battles such as the 2014 Indira Gandhi case, where the civil courts ruled in favour of the non-Muslim party, their rulings carry little weight so long as the police force remains reluctant to recognize and enforce the authority of the civil court over that of the syariah court (Yatim 2014). As Nadarajah writing of the plight of minority Malaysian Indians puts it:

> Malaysia's cultural and ethnic diversity is strained as a Malay nationalism that defines the Malaysian 'national project' sees this diversity as a nuisance, an interruption and an affront to an immanent Malay historical destiny. In such a culturally contested terrain, the quest for belonging [...] remains distant, subjugated and demoralized. (2010, 152)

The cordoning of social space described above has taken place alongside the withdrawal of Malaysian Muslims from the hybrid spaces and activities where they have in the past freely socialized with fellow citizens and contributed much to the experience of a distinctly Malaysian way of life. Indeed, extant multicultural spaces are being depleted of the richness of diversity through the narrowing and policing of what is acceptable social practice for Muslims. These constraints commonly start out as a means of defining acceptable mundane social practices for the Islamic faithful, such as declaring yoga to be *haram* (forbidden) (Malaysiakini 2008b) but inevitably end up affecting the broader Malaysian society. Another somewhat more bizarre example is the Home Ministry's ban on Malay-language versions of comics featuring Japanese superhero, Ultraman, based on the reasoning that using Allah to denote Ultraman King was likely to confuse young readers (Lim 2014). Such protections are a tacit infantilization of Muslims. The Islamization of Malaysia is not only about the perceived need to safeguard Islam from Christianity's encroachment or vice versa but, more broadly and importantly, it concerns the overarching issue of who belongs in the nation, what is acceptable social practice within Malaysian society and, thus, what shape the social imaginary will take in the future: multi-ethnic and multi-religious as it has been to-date, or predominantly monocultural and Islamic?

There is a foundational principle, which has been incrementally diminished over the past three decades or so, of inter-Muslim rivalry and the sidelining of minorities. That principle rests on two articles contained within the Constitution of Malaysia: Article 3, which stipulates Islam to be the national religion; and Article 11, which upholds the right of those of different faiths to practise their religions in 'peace and harmony in any part of the Federation' (Commissioner of Law Revision 2006, 20, 26). Originally formulated by the founders of the newly formed nation to ensure that the diversity of cultures and religions that made Malaysia home would be able to coexist side by side in peace, the intention of these two articles has been severely undermined since. Incidents, both trivial and profound – such as the banning of the sale of beer in Malay-majority parts of the state of Selangor in 2009 and the 'Bible incident' discussed previously – have seen non-Muslims increasingly squeezed out of the centre and forced towards the periphery of Malaysian society.

A rare but important exception in recent times has been the surprise results of the 2008 general elections, in which the opposition coalition won government in five states in Malaysia. That win has allowed the minor parties and the multifarious constituencies they represent to retain a foothold in the heart of Malaysia's political landscape. Both sides of the political divide have credited the 'political tsunami' (Lim 2008) to the role of social media – such as YouTube, online news portals and blogs – in keeping the public informed of the opposition's rallies, policies and movements during the election campaign (Malaysiakini 2008a). However, as Weiss (2013, 609) points out, the pivotal role of social media during the 2008 elections was as much a consequence of mainstream media's failure to properly cover opposition parties' campaigns as it was a consequence of social media's characteristics. Social media and other Internet communications in Malaysia have so far been effective alternative sources of information to mainstream media because the Mahathir administration promised in 1998 to 'ensure no censorship of the Internet' (MSC Malaysia 2008). Made primarily to facilitate the participation of and investment from international firms into the then-new Multimedia Super Corridor mega project, the promise of non-censorship remains a key part of the Bill of Guarantees (*Business Times* 1996; MSC Malaysia 2008). The latitude the promise opened up for online expression has been crucial to how social media has developed as both a tool and a space for more open dialogue and civic participation by Malaysians.

To date the number of Internet users in Malaysia stands at 18.6 million or 63.5 per cent of the population (Malaysia Communications and Multimedia Commission 2013, 8). Overall, patterns of Internet usage in Malaysia follow global trends that see male users (56.4%) outnumbering female (43.6%) and users younger than 35 years of age forming 72.1 per cent of the user group (2013, 12–13). Facebook is also the most popular social media platform (84.2%), followed by Twitter and Google + (2013, 19). On the whole, the computer literacy rate for Malaysian citizens aged 5 to 69 years is more than 45 per cent in every state. There is also no doubting the ubiquity of mobile phones in Malaysia, as the lowest penetration rates is 87 per cent in Sarawak and the highest is 203.5 per cent in the federal territory of Kuala Lumpur. Malaysians have taken to mobile phones, with many possessing more than one (2013, 14). At the same time, smart phone usage is rising steeply so that estimates doubled between 2011 and 2012 (2013, 17), with close to 70 per cent of mobile phone users accessing the Internet through their smart phones (2013, 19). Even so, 74 per cent of the mobile phone usage continues via feature phones, indicating there to be a substantial gap between those who can afford to use smart phones and those unwilling or without the means to do so (2013, 19).

During the 2013 general election, social media's value for the opposition waned slightly as a ruling coalition, mindful of the cost of their former negligence in the lead-up to the 2008 election, belatedly devoted a whole host of resources to the task of the creation and maintenance of content across multiple social media platforms addressed to various constituencies (Darwis 2012; Hopkins 2014). As Vee (2011, 56) points out, by virtue of being in power the government of the day will always be better resourced to use social media for the provision of counter-information and vying for the attention of the citizenry. The current prime minister's much-followed Twitter account (@ Najib Razak), Facebook page, Instagram account and blogs written by various members of the ruling polity are prime examples. The PM even has a second Mandarin Facebook account (Ah Jib Gor, Brother Ah Jib) aimed at reaching out to ethnic Chinese voters.

Nonetheless, as demonstrated by the recent arrests of Facebook users for alleged acts of sedition (Malaysiakini 2014b) and by the case brought by Najib Razak against subscription-based online news portal, Malaysiakini, for defamation (Human Rights Watch 2014), the existence of social media as a space and tool for the expression of alternate views and critiques precludes neither the state nor individuals from silencing dissent by other means. Indeed, the array of measures available was further expanded when revisions to the Sedition Act were passed on 10 April 2015. Amongst other things, the augmented Sedition Act now allows a Sessions Court judge to 'compel a publisher of online material deemed seditious' to stop 'using any electronic devices' as well as 'censor online seditious material put up by anonymous sources' (Kamarulzaman 2015). In addition, the Sedition Act now also stipulates it is an offence to excite 'ill will, hostility or hatred' on grounds of religion and race, punishable with a maximum sentence of

20 years (Kamarulzaman 2015; Yin 2015). As the Home Minister explains it, the Act has been amended specifically to deal with 'threats carried out on social media' (Yee 2015).

Since the 2015 revision, no less than 91 cases have been brought against individuals on the grounds of sedition; they include law professor Azmi Sharom, lawyer Eric Paulsen, journalist Susan Loone, politician Rafizi Ramli, student activist Khalid Ismath and political cartoonist, Zulkiflee Anwar Ulhaque, commonly known as Zunar (Amnesty International 2016, 4–9). Whereas in 2010 there were just 5 cases brought under the Sedition Act, the number of arrests has been steadily rising, from 7 in 2011 and 9 in 2012 to 18 in 2013 and 41 in 2014 (Yin 2015, 5). And, at 91, the number of investigations in 2015 alone was nearly 5 times as many as had been brought in the first 50 years since the Act's 1948 adoption (Amnesty International 2016, 3). Small wonder the overall effect of the revised Sedition Act and its application has been described as 'chilling' (Amnesty International 2016). The charges against academic Azmi Sharom have been dropped (*Malay Mail* 2016) but many of the other cases are still pending. The spate of arrests for sedition and the government's boosted powers to regulate with impunity what might be said on and offline have produced some of the desired effect, with sociopolitical websites like *Fake Malaysia News* taking the precaution to 'tone down' on satirical content (Zachariah 2015). Others, like artist Fahmi Reza, continue to push the boundaries with campaigns and memes like 'Kami Semua Penghasut' ('We are All Seditious'), which features clownish caricatures of Prime Minister Najib Razak (Advox 2016).

To be sure, the popularization of social media is not confined to any one side of the ethno-religious and political divide in Malaysia. As Lim (2010, 178) finds, information and communication technologies have also promoted 'a greater Ummah consciousness, a heightened sense of belonging to a global community of believers' and 'awakened a consciousness among Muslims all over the world to unite and stand up for themselves'. Yet, it is important to recognize that this pan-Islamic consciousness is strongly influenced by Wahhabi Islam, a sectarian movement emerging out of the Sunni branch of Islam, who follow the Hanbali school of law (Bakar 2010, 668). In Malaysia, the arrival of Saudi Arabian Wahhabi *dakwah* (preachers) in recent times has led to a shift towards Sunni orthodoxy even as it has awakened the sense of a pan-Islamic global community (Yusuf n.d.). Wahhabi Islam is different to the Islam that developed in Southeast Asia, which occurred under very different circumstances and is dominated by the Shafi'i School (Rabasa 2003, 13). It needs to be said, too, that the ease with which Wahhabi Islam has come to influence Muslims in Malaysia in recent years is due to precisely the same flexibility that saw the Bible translated into Malay in earlier centuries and accommodated the numerous minor and major differences in how Islam was practised in previous decades.

Still, a major distinction of the Islamic sense of community now in the Malaysian social imaginary is the understanding that there is no need to separate the religious from the political, as with the separation of church and state, a principle that grounds Western secularism (Hashemi 2014, 443). This was reinforced in a survey of 38,000 Muslims across 39 countries in Europe, Africa, Asia and the Middle East, who expressed a desire for 'their teachings to shape not only their personal lives but also their societies and politics' (440). The same view appears to be gaining currency in Malaysia, where a recent public opinion survey by Merdeka Center (2014) revealed that 71 per cent of the Malays polled supported Hudud, even if 58 per cent of the same population thought Malaysia was not yet ready to implement it. That the neighbouring kingdom of Brunei has since 2014 begun to implement Hudud in three stages is evidence that adoption of orthodox Islam is not impossible in Southeast Asia (Adam 2014). Consequently, PAS's intention to implement Hudud in Kelantan is causing much alarm amongst non-Muslims (Zurairi 2012; 2014). Given the erosion of shared social space that has already occurred, questions are rife over what, how and to whom Hudud would apply once it is in place in Kelantan.

Examples of how social media facilitates the sense of ummah consciousness can be found in Facebook pages and groups promoting Hudud, such as 'I support Hudud in Kelantan'. The group's main message reads, 'Only hudud can guarantee the happiness and success of Kelantan in this world and in the afterlife. For both our interests, support HUDUD in Kelantan',[6] and has well over 43,000 likes. Members of this Facebook page repeatedly cite the effectiveness of Hudud in other parts of the Islamic world, such as Brunei and Saudi Arabia, as reason for implementing the same in Kelantan. For example, two of the more popular posts involve much rejoicing at a 50 per cent drop in crime rates in Brunei after the advent of Hudud, and another details how severe punishment is meted out to all offenders including a Saudi prince. Perhaps the overall sentiment of such groups and others like it is best summed up through the emphatic statement made in one post: 'The ONLY Way TO Curb The Escalating Social ILLS is the implementation of HUDUD'. Another Facebook group, 'Save Malaysia, No Hudud', argues against the implementation of the Islamic penal code, declaring that Hudud will take Malaysia back to 'the dark ages'. Started by a minor partner in the ruling coalition, Parti Gerakan Rakyat Malaysia (Malaysian People's Movement Party),

---

6   My translation from Malay.

the smaller group (just over 9,000 likes) argues that the proposed implementation of Hudud is an issue of national concern, and not one that only affects Muslims and the Kelantanese. Indeed, their declared mission is to 'protect and defend the Federal Constitution – stop any intention to implement Hudud Law'. For these dissenters the push for Hudud is politically motivated, and they contend non-Muslims should fear and resist having the Islamic penal code foisted on all of Malaysian society.

As mentioned earlier, PAS's push to implement Hudud goes back to the early 1990s, so it predates Malaysians' widespread access to the Internet. Over the years advocates and detractors of the proposal have tapped into many kinds of social media. Towards the end of 2014, for example, a group made up of 25 prominent Malays who were also retired senior civil servants wrote an open letter to the people of Malaysia urging for open debate and rational discourse on the 'continuing unresolved disputes on the position and application of Islamic laws' in the country (Star Online 2014). This led to the setup of an online petition 'I am #26' echoing the group's concern and supporting the call for open and safe discussion. Up until recently the petition has garnered signatures from close to 6,000 individuals who share a belief in the value of rational debate on Islamic law in Malaysia. An earlier petition, 'Petisyen Menyokong Hudud' (Petition Supporting Hudud) started in May 2014 appears to have fared better gathering close to 22,500 signatures. What is of interest is how each petition attempts to win support through the use of international social media platforms. There are no user figures available for Petitionbuzz.com but Change.org on which 'I am #26' is hosted claims to have 70 million users in 196 countries. Yet while the 'I am #26' petition aims to address a broad Malaysian audience in Malay and English, the other petition is available only in Malay, its author seemingly having decided only Malay readers would support their cause. Additionally, although both petitioners understand Malaysia to be the primary arena of their tussle, they also reach out globally, albeit to substantially different constituents. The pleas of 'I am #26' as well as the letter that prompted the petition itself are founded on democratic principles and the rule of law, hence in addition to moderate Muslims and Malaysians its global constituency is the international family of democratic nations. The first intended audience of the petition 'Petisyen Menyokong Hudud' is obviously Malaysian Muslims but even so the petition eschews the non-Muslim others in the nation to draw instead on the discourse and sodality of the pan-Islamic community.

The examples described above are one part of the answer to the earlier question of what social media has added to how agency, representation and anxieties are played out within Malaysia's multilingual, multicultural mediasphere. As a simple search on any online search engine reveals, social media has given sustained space for discussion, information and consideration from multiple points of view to all who care to engage with the issues radiating from the ban of Allah in Malay-language Bibles. There are also staccato exchanges facilitated by platforms such as Twitter, Facebook and WhatsApp, which draw on, extend and circulate the web of textual, visual and aural material created. From the programs put together by Al Jazeera, the Qatar-based media corporation, discussing the issue and vox populi compiled by Malaysiakini.tv, to local radio station BFM's ('Battle for Malaysia') podcast dissecting the complexities of the issue, there is a rich and deep store of expert opinion, rhetoric and plain-speech conversations building on social media.[7] Another case in point is the social media advocacy group, Projek Dialog,[8] which styles itself as a 'social discourse space' concerned with social issues in Malaysia. A collective of interested individuals and organizations, Projek Dialog employs a mix of English and Malay content, using a web portal and social media platforms Facebook, YouTube and Twitter to promote and disseminate healthy debate and public discourse on some of contemporary Malaysia's thorniest issues. Working in partnership with UK-based NGO, Article 19,[9] which champions freedom of expression, Projek Dialog uses a combination of textual, photographic and video elements to tackle topics as diverse as the rise of the Islamic state (ISIS), religious freedom and human rights in the social media era, the practice and understanding of *halal* and Hudud, and questions such as 'What is a Malaysian?'.

Still, there is no way of ensuring that any content thus generated is always reasonable, polite or conclusive. After all, passions can run high when issues matter most. It would, however, be wrong to dismiss these exchanges as white noise and the product of the chattering classes. I contend them to be much preferred to the silence of apathy, the surrender of the cowed or the hegemony of authoritarianism. Dialogues such as these, which now find room in social media, are not just a part of how significations (ideas and concepts) are inserted and adapted into social imaginaries. They are also vital to the animated practice of the 'habits of critique, engagement and mobilization' that are the lifeblood of robust democracies (Leong 2014, 126). As for how Malaysian netizens will respond to the looming threat posed by the amended Sedition Act, the immediate effect is likely to be inhibitive, but there is no

---

7   See https://www.youtube.com/watch?v=_B9N5Ck9zgs, https://www.youtube.com/watch?v=zDac5GXjLMo, https://www.youtube.com/watch?v=vfkiyDdoASw, https://www.youtube.com/watch?v=cV89G-wrgDQ, http://www.bfm.my/battleformalaysia-the-politics-of-religion.html
8   http://www.projekdialog.com
9   http://www.article19.org

reason to believe that Malaysians' willingness to partake of the democratic process would be vanquished by the punitive act. After all, Malaysians' participation in sociopolitical life of the nation pre-dates social media, even if social media technologies have proved to be a timely and welcome boon (Leong 2014, 96). It is equally possible that, over the longer term, the necessity for caution under the circumstances could render Malaysian social media users even more adept at reading between the lines and temper their online interactions with greater sobriety.

Conclusion

More than a dozen years after the Mahathir administration promised not to censor the Internet, Malaysians reportedly spend an average of 8.2 hours online each day, of which 3.5 hours are occupied with social media use alone (Kemp 2015). In other words, Malaysians are by and large well placed and skilled in their usage of social media. Early adopters of social media, ranging from ordinary citizens and minorities to civil society, have had substantial advantages over the media and political establishment, particularly in the years leading up to 2008. Although in the period since, latecomers to these platforms and the powers-that-be have caught up such that, as the analysis of the social media spaces here show, the odds are now fairly even on all sides. Still, Malaysians' facility with social media has introduced a readiness and immediacy to how the various interest groups are able to link their causes, borrow authority and seek support from, and be global advocates for discourses on Christianity, human rights, democracy and Islam. Correspondingly, ideas and concepts from the world over have also swiftly and easily filtered through into the Malaysian social imaginary by the same means. In a sense the contestation over the appropriateness of using the term, Allah, to denote God for non-Muslims is part of the continued development of the Malaysian social imaginary, magnified and amplified by social media. Understanding these developments through the social imaginary framework allows us to see that such disputes are part of how societies come to define themselves, and that no one resolution lasts forever, because significations are constantly subject to new stimuli. How, then, will the situation be resolved?

Writing of the impasse between Islamists and progressives, Goh (2012, 132) suggests that one way out of it is to 'look to history to recover the moral and civic dimensions of ethnic interchange as potential for the politics of respect, incorporation and unity'. The remnants of 'the suppressed narratives of inter-ethnic conviviality and mutuality forged from a long history of cultural diversity, common experience and struggle that made up the modern nation-state', Goh (2012, 135) urges, have important lessons for the present.

Lessons such as those contained in the words of Malaysia's first prime minister, Abdul Rahman, who in 1959 declared unequivocally: 'Our country has many races and unless we are prepared to drown every non-Malay, we can never think of an Islamic Administration' (cited in Camilleri 2013, 227). The erection of increasingly rigid boundaries around the delineations between Muslim and others denies how the history of Islam was introduced into Malaysia and the layers of indigenization of customs, ideas, linguistic and multiple other influences that have left a vital imprint on Malaysian society and its practice of Islam (Winstedt 1966, 38–39). In the same way as the local culture and social practices embedded within are intrinsic to what constitutes Islam in Southeast Asia, the Islamic practices embedded within local culture are crucial to Malaysian culture. Rather than confuse Muslims, the 'use of Allah in translations of the Bible has served as a bridge between Christians and Muslims for understanding each other' (Thomas 2006, 172). As such, the Malaysian Muslims who now expect the term Allah to be neatly and quickly excised from Malay- and Iban-language Bibles are seeking to remove a vital part of Malaysian culture, including Malaysian Islam. An episode of the online satire program *The Effing Show*, entitled '*Allah, Apa Lagi?*' (2013) (Allah, What Else?),[10] makes light-hearted work of demonstrating the futility and limits of disentangling the intricately interwoven nature of Malaysian culture, language and customs. What the producers so effectively wrap up in humour is how destructive it would be to compel the extrication of a particular signification from the syncretic Malaysian social imaginary.

In closing, it is the contention here that the Allah ban issue is not only about the vexed contestation over whether Allah is the sole reserve of Muslims, but also concerns how people can, as cultural studies scholar Stuart Hall says, 'live together in difference' (cited in Yuval-Davis et al. 2006, 6). According to Hall, the

> multicultural question is whether it is possible for groups of people from different cultural, religious, linguistic, historical backgrounds, to occupy the same social space[. ...] What are the terms on which they can live with one another without either one group [the less powerful group] having to become the imitative version of the dominant one – i.e. an assimilation, or on the other hand, the two groups hating one another, or projecting images of degradation. (2006, 6)

It is precisely because Islam is a way of life 'that encompasses all areas of human activity, private and public, ranging from the theological to the political'

---

10 https://www.youtube.com/watch?v=vT0O80tuPAA

(Houben 2003, 149) that the practices and lived experience of its believers have never been apart from the non-Muslim others that share Malaysia. Put differently, in a nation where Islam is the national religion and Malay the national language, the ideas and the words of Islam cannot fail to be a part of the social imaginary. The question is: what is to be gained by removing the traces of each other embedded and enfolded within Islam in non-Malays and outside influences in Malay-Muslim life, and what is lost when the sum total of the nation's shared histories and common experiences are forcibly eradicated piecemeal from its social imaginary?

Acknowledgements

I am grateful to the anonymous reviewer for their close reading and insightful feedback on the draft version of this chapter. I am responsible for any errors in translation.

References

ABC News. 2014. 'Malaysia's Highest Court Dismisses Divisive "Allah" Case'. ABC News, 25 June. Online: http://www.abc.net.au/news/2014-06-23/top-malaysian-court-dismisses-divisive-religious-case/5544324 (accessed 13 September 2014).

Abdal-Haqq, I. 2002. 'Islamic Law: An Overview of Its Origins and Elements'. *Journal of Islamic Law and Culture* 7: 27–165.

Adam, S. 2014. 'Brunei Imposes Islamic Criminal Law after UN Criticism'. Bloomberg, 30 April. Online: http://www.bloomberg.com/news/2014-04-30/brunei-imposes-islamic-criminal-law-after-un-criticism.html (accessed 12 September 2014).

Advox 2016. 'Malaysian Police Threaten Internet Users for Sharing Clown Memes of Prime Minister'. Advox, 13 February. Online: https://advox.globalvoices.org/2016/02/13/malaysian-police-threaten-internet-users-for-sharing-clown-memes-of-prime-minister/ (accessed 23 February 2016).

Aliran. 2014. 'Bahasa Malaysia Bibles: The Cabinet's 10-point Solution'. Aliran, 25 January. Online: http://aliran.com/web-specials/bahasa-malaysia-bibles-10-point-solution/ (accessed 12 September 2014).

Amnesty International. 2016. 'Critical Crackdown: Freedom of Expression under Threat in Malaysia'. Online: http://amnesty.my/sites/default/files/Malaysia_Critical_Crackdown_2.PDF (accessed 21 February 2016).

Anbalagan, V. 2014. 'Resolve "Allah" Issue Quickly, Former AG Urges Federal Court'. *The Malaysian Insider*, 7 January. Online: http://www.themalaysianinsider.com/malaysia/article/resolve-allah-issue-quickly-former-ag-urges-federal-court (accessed 14 January 2014).

Andaya, B. W., and L. Y. Andaya. 2001. *A History of Malaysia*. Basingstoke: Palgrave.

AsiaOne. 2012. 'End to Malaysia's ISA'. AsiaOne, 22 April. Online: http://news.asiaone.com/News/AsiaOne%2BNews/Malaysia/Story/A1Story20120422-341230.html (accessed 12 December 2012).

Bakar, O. 2010. 'Islam and the Three Waves of Globalisation: The Southeast Asian Experience.' *Islam and Civilisational Renewal* 1, no. 4: 666–84.
Barr, M. D., and A. R. Govindasamy. 2010. 'The Islamisation of Malaysia: Religious Nationalism in the Service of Ethnonationalism'. *Australian Journal of International Affairs* 64, no. 3: 293–311.
Business Times, 1996. Bill to ensure best deal for investors. Online: Factiva Database (accessed 29 November 2012).
Camilleri, R. 2013. 'Religious Pluralism in Malaysia: The Journey of Three Prime Ministers'. *Islam and Christian-Muslim Relations* 24, no. 2: 225–40.
Case, W. 2010. 'Political Legitimacy in Malaysia: Historical Roots and Contemporary Deficits'. *Politics & Policy* 38, no. 3: 497–522.
Castoriadis, C. 1997. 'The Social Imaginary and the Institution'. In *The Castoriadis Reader*, edited by D. A. Curtis, 196–217. Cambridge, MA: Blackwell.
Chin, J. 2009. 'The Malaysian Chinese Dilemma: The Never Ending Policy (NEP)'. *Chinese Southern Diaspora Studies* 3: 167–82.
The Commissioner of Law Revision, Malaysia. 2006. Federal Constitution (as of 1 November 2010). The Commissioner of Law Revision. Online: http://www.agc.gov.my/images/Personalisation/Buss/pdf/Federal%20Consti%20(BI%20text).pdf (accessed 26 August 2014).
Darwis, M. F. 2012. 'Saifuddin: Cybertroopers, Social Media Key to BN's GE13 Success'. *The Mayalasian Insider*, 14 October. Online: http://www.themalaysianinsider.com/malaysia/article/saifuddin-cybertroopers-social-media-key-to-bns-ge13-success (accessed 18 October 2012).
Department of Statistics, Malaysia. 2010. 'Population Distribution and Basic Demographic Characteristic Report 2010'. Department of Statistics, Malaysia. Online: https://www.statistics.gov.my/ (accessed 8 September 2014).
———. 2011. 'Population Distribution and Basic Demographic Characteristics'. Online: https://www.statistics.gov.my/ (accessed 17 October 2011).
———. 2013. 'Report on Education and Social Characteristics of the Population 2010'. Online: https://www.statistics.gov.my/ (accessed 8 September 2014).
Goh, B. L. 2012. 'Dilemma of Progressive Politics in Malaysia: Islamic Orthodoxy Versus Human Rights'. In *Questioning Modernity in Indonesia and Malaysia*, edited by W. Mee and J. S. Kahn, 115–44. Singapore: NUS Press.
Gomez, J. 2014. 'Selangor Islamic Authorities Raid Bible Society of Malaysia, 300 Copies of Alkitab Seized'. *The Mayalasian Insider*, 2 January. Online: http://www.themalaysianinsider.com/malaysia/article/selangor-religious-authorities-raid-bible-society-of-malaysia-chairman-held (accessed 10 January 2014).
Hashemi, N. 2014. Rethinking Religion and Political Legitimacy across the Islam–West Divide. *Philosophy and Social Criticism* 40, no. 4: 439–47.
Hookway, J. 2010. 'Vandals Strike at Malaysia Mosques with Boar Heads'. *The Wall Street Journal*, 28 January. Online: http://online.wsj.com/article/SB10001424052748703906204575028040817874812.html (accessed 2 March 2011).
Hopkins, J. 2014. 'Cybertroopers and Tea Parties: Government Use of the Internet in Malaysia'. *Asian Journal of Communication* 24, no. 1: 5–24.
Houben, V. J. H. 2003. 'Southeast Asia and Islam'. *The Annals of the American Academy of Political and Social Science*, 588: 149–70.
Hughes, A. W. 2013. *Muslim Identities: An Introduction to Islam*. New York: Columbia University Press.

Human Rights Watch. 2014. 'Malaysia: Premier Threatens Outspoken Website'. Human Rights Watch, 28 May. Online: http://www.hrw.org/news/2014/05/28/malaysia-premier-threatens-outspoken-website (accessed 12 August 2014).

Hunt, R. A. 1989. 'The History of the Translation of the Bible into Bahasa Malaysia'. *Journal of the Malaysian Branch of the Royal Asiatic Society* 62: 35–56.

Kamarulzaman, Z. 2015. 'Sedition Act Amendments Passed in Wee Hours'. Malaysiakini, 10 April. Online: http://www.malaysiakini.com/news/294832 (accessed 10 April 2015).

Kemp, Simon. 2015. 'Digital, Social & Mobile Worldwide in 2015'. *We Are Social* (blog), 21 January. Online: http://wearesocial.net/blog/2015/01/digital-social-mobile-worldwide-2015/ (accessed 21 January 2015).

Khalid, K. M. 2007. 'Voting for Change? Islam and Personalised Politics in the 2004 General Elections'. In *Politics in Malaysia: The Malay Dimension*, edited by E. T. Gomez, 138–55. Hoboken, NJ: Routledge.

Leong, S. 2012. 'Sacred Cows and Crashing Boars: Ethno-Religious Minorities and the Politics of Online Representation in Malaysia'. *Critical Asian Studies* 44, no. 1: 31–56.

———. 2014. *New Media and the Nation in Malaysia: Malaysianet*. London: Routledge.

Lim, C. W. 2012. 'Repeal of ISA is Commendable, but Provisions in New Law that Depart from Ordinary Principles Must Be Reviewed'. The Malaysain Bar, 10 April. Online: http://www.malaysianbar.org.my/press_statements/press_release_repeal_of_isa_is_commendable_but_provisions_in_new_law_that_depart_from_ordinary_principles_must_be_reviewed.html (accessed 12 April 2012).

Lim, I. 2014. 'Ultraman Book Ban: Reference to Allah May Confuse Muslims, Says Official'. *The Malay Mail* Online, 7 March. Online: http://www.themalaymailonline.com/malaysia/article/ultraman-book-ban-reference-to-allah-may-confuse-muslims-says-official (accessed 13 September 2014).

Lim, K. S. 2008. 'Political Tsunami in General Election'. Lim Kit Siang for Malaysia (blog), 8 March. Online: http://blog.limkitsiang.com/2008/03/08/political-tsunami-in-general-election/ (accessed 21 July 2011).

Lim, M. 2010. 'Muslim Voices in the Blogosphere: Mosaics of Local-Global Discourses'. In *Internationalising Internet Studies: Beyond Anglophone Paradigms*, edited by G. Goggin and M. McLelland, 178–95. Hoboken, NJ: Taylor and Francis.

Looi, S.-C. 2014. 'Body of Muslim Convert Taken Away During Chinese Funeral Ceremony'. *The Malaysian Insider*, 9 June. Online: http://www.themalaysianinsider.com/malaysia/article/body-of-muslim-convert-taken-away-during-chinese-funeral-ceremony (accessed 12 September 2014).

Malay Mail Online. 2014a. 'Jais Concedes to New SOP, but Insists on Keeping Seized Bibles'. *Malay Mail* Online, 13 January. Online: http://www.themalaymailonline.com/malaysia/article/jais-concedes-to-new-sop-but-insists-on-keeping-seized-bibles (accessed 14 Janaury 2014).

———. 2014b. 'With Jais on the Loose, DAP MP Fears Non-Muslims "Under Siege"'. *Malay Mail* Online, 5 June. Online: http://www.themalaymailonline.com/malaysia/article/with-jais-on-the-loose-dap-mp-fears-non-muslims-under-siege (accessed 12 September 2014).

———. 2016. 'AG Drops Sedition Case against Azmi Sharom'. *Malay Mail* Online, 12 February. Online: http://www.themalaymailonline.com/malaysia/article/ag-drops-sedition-case-against-azmi-sharom (accessed 23 February 2016).

Malaysia Communications and Multimedia Commission. 2012. *Hand Phone Users Survey 2012*. Malaysia Communications and Multimedia Commission. Online: http://www.skmm.gov.my/skmmgovmy/media/General/pdf/130717_HPUS2012.pdf (accessed 12 August 2014).

———. 2013. *Internet Users Survey 2012*. Malaysia Communications and Multimeida Commission. Online: http://www.skmm.gov.my/skmmgovmy/media/General/pdf/InternetUsersSurvey2012.pdf (accessed 15 August 2014).

Malaysiakini. 2008a. 'Abdullah: Big Mistake to Ignore Cyber-campaign'. Malaysiakini, 25 March. Online: http://www.malaysiakini.com/news/80354 (accessed 18 October 2012).

———. 2008b. 'Yoga Declared "Haram" for Muslims'. Malaysiakini, 22 November. Online: http://www.malaysiakini.com/news/93564 (accessed 25 November 2009).

———. 2011. 'Najib Announces Repeal of ISA'. Malaysiakini, 15 September. Online: http://www.malaysiakini.com/news/175949 (accessed 21 September 2011).

———. 2014a. 'Bible Returned, but with Strict Conditions'. Malaysiakini, 14 November. Online: http://www.malaysiakini.com/news/280507 (accessed 9 April 2015).

———. 2014b. 'FB User Nabbed for Anti-Sultan, Islam Post'. Malaysiakini, 12 February. Online: http://www.malaysiakini.com/news/254177 (accessed 12 September 2014).

Merdeka Center. 2014. 'Public Opinion Survey 2014: Peninsular Malaysia Voter Survey: Public Opinion on Hudud Implementation: 12th – 21st April 2014'. Merdeka Center. Online: http://merdeka.org/v4/index.php/downloads/category/2-researches?download=143:04b-national-poll-2014-hudud-law-v14-july-2014 (accessed 31 July 2014).

MSC Malaysia. 2008. 'MSC Malaysia 10 Point Bill of Guarantees'. MSC Malaysia. Online: http://www.mscmalaysia.my/bogs (accessed 28 July 2011).

Nadarajah, Y. 2010. 'Abiding by Malaysia: Mediating Belonging through Cultural Contestations'. In *Migration, Belonging and the Nation-State*, edited by A. Babacan and S. Singh, 133–55. Newcastle-upon-Tyne: Cambridge Scholars.

Noor, F. A. 2005. *From Majapahit to Putrajaya*. Kuala Lumpur: Silverfish.

Rabasa, A. M. 2003. *Political Islam in Southeast Asia*. New York: Routledge.

Sani, M. A. M. 2010. 'Constitutional and Legislation Practices in Protecting Ethnic Relations in Malaysia: Restrict Hate Speech, Not Legitimate Political Speech'. In *Dynamic of Ethnic Relations in Southeast Asia*, edited by M. A. M. Sani, R. Nakamura and T. L. Shamsuddin, 9–39. Newcastle-upon-Tyne: Cambridge Scholars.

Sardesai, D. R. 2003. *Southeast Asia: Past & Present*. Los Angeles: Westview Press.

Seda-Poulin, M. L. 1993. 'Islamization and Legal Reform in Malaysia: The Hudud Controversy of 1992.' *Southeast Asian Affairs*: 224–42.

Shadbolt, P. 2013. 'Christian Churches in Borneo Vow to Continue Using the Word "Allah"'. CNN, 15 October. Online: http://edition.cnn.com/2013/10/15/world/asia/malaysia-allah/ (accessed 14 January 2014).

The Star Online. 2009. 'Selangor PAS Wants Beer Included in Ban, Liu to Be Removed'. *The Star* Online, 4 August. Online: http://www.thestar.com.my/story/?file=%2f2009%2f8%2f4%2fnation%2f20090804144354&sec=nation (accessed 13 September 2014).

———. 2014. 'Group of Prominent Malays Calls for Rational Dialogue on Position of Islam in Malaysia'. *The Star* Online, 12 July. Online: http://www.thestar.com.my/News/Nation/2014/12/07/Group-prominent-malays-calls-for-moderation/ (accessed 13 April 2015).

———. 2015. 'May Tabling for Hudud Bill'. *The Star* Online, 10 April. Online: http://www.thestar.com.my/News/Nation/2015/04/10/May-tabling-for-hudud-Bill-PAS-Private-Members-Bill-did-not-make-it-for-yesterdays-debate/ (accessed 15 April 2015).

Steiner, K. 2013. 'The Case Continues? The High Courts in Malaysia and Unilateral Conversion of a Child to Islam by One Parent'. *Australian Journal of Asian Law* 14, no. 2: 1–15.

Thiru, S. 2015. 'Prevention of Terrorism Bill 2015 Violates Malaysia's Domestic and International Commitments, Is an Affront to the Rule of Law and Is Abhorrent to Natural Justice'. Malaysian Bar, 5 April. Online: http://www.malaysianbar.org.my/press_statements/press_release_|_prevention_of_terrorism_bill_2015_violates_malaysias_domestic_and_international_commitments_is_an_affront_to_the_rule_of_law_and_is_abhorrent_to_natural_justice.html (accessed 10 April 2015).

Thomas, K. J. 2006. 'Allah in Translations of the Bible'. *International Journal of Frontier Missions* 23, no. 4: 171–74.

Vee, V. T. 2011. 'The Struggle for Digital Freedom of Speech: The Malaysian Sociopolitical Blogsphere's Experience'. In *Access Contested: Security, Identity, and Resistance in Asian Cyberspace*, edited by R. Deibert, J. Palfrey, R. Rohosinski and J. Zittrain. Cambridge, MA: The MIT Press. Online: http://access.opennet.net/wp-content/uploads/2011/12/accesscontested-chapter-03.pdf (accessed 12 August 2014).

Weiss, M. L. 2013. 'Parsing the Power of "New Media" in Malaysia'. *Journal of Contemporary Asia* 43, no. 4: 591–612.

Whiting, A. and T. Majoribanks. 2013. 'Media Professionals' Perceptions of Defamation and Other Constraints Upon News Reporting in Malaysia and Singapore'. In *Democracy, Media and Law in Malaysia and Singapore*, edited by A. T. Kenyon, T. Majoribanks and A. Whiting, 129–56. Abingdon: Taylor and Francis.

Winstedt, R. 1966. *Malaya and Its History*. London: Hutchinson University Library.

Yaran, C. S. 2007. *Understanding Islam*. Edinburgh: Dunedin Academic Press.

Yatim, H. 2014. 'IGP Ordered to Get Child Back or Answer to Court'. Malaysiakini, 10 September. Online: http://www.malaysiakini.com/news/274203 (accessed 12 September 2014).

Yee, X. Y. 2015. 'Zahid: Sedition Act Amendments Necessary, Especially against Threats on Social Media'. *The Star* Online, 11 April. Online: http://www.thestar.com.my/News/Nation/2015/04/11/Zahid-Sedition-Act-amendments/ (accessed 12 April 2015).

Yeoh, S. G. 2011. 'In Defence of the Secular? Islamisation, Christians and (New) Politics in Urbane Malaysia'. *Asian Studies Review* 35, no. 1: 83–103.

Yin, S. L. 2015. *The Sedition (Amendment) Bill 2015: Context & Implications*. Petaling Jaya: Institut Rakyat.

Yusuf, I. n.d. 'The Middle East and Muslim Southeast Asia: Implications of the Arab Spring'. Oxford Islamic Studies Online. Online: http://www.oxfordislamicstudies.com/Public/focus/essay1009_southeast_asia.html (accessed 11 December 2014).

Yuval-Davis, N., K. Kannabiran, and U. Vieten (eds). 2006. *The Situated Politics of Belonging*. London: Sage.

Zacahariah, E. 2016. 'Toning Down Satire, Humour after Amendments to Sedition Act'. *The Malaysian Insider*, 23 April. Online: http://www.themalaysianinsider.com/malaysia/article/toning-down-satire-humour-after-amendments-to-sedition-act (accessed 23 February 2016).

Zurairi, A. R. 2012. 'PAS Dials Down on Hudud, Concedes It Can't Rule Alone'. *The Malaysian Insider*, 18 November. Online: http://www.themalaysianinsider.com/malaysia/article/pas-dials-down-on-hudud-concedes-it-cant-rule-alone (accessed 12 December 2012).

———. 2014. 'Hudud Should Apply to All Malaysians, Jakim Paper Suggests'. The *Malay Mail* Online, 5 June. Online: http://www.themalaymailonline.com/malaysia/article/hudud-should-apply-to-all-malaysians-jakim-paper-suggests (accessed 12 September 2014).

Chapter 6

ETHNIC MINORITIES AND MULTI-ETHNIC HERITAGE IN MELAKA: RECONSTRUCTING DUTCH EURASIAN AND CHITTY MELAKA IDENTITIES THROUGH FACEBOOK

Loo Hong Chuang and Floris Müller

On 7 July 2008, the historical centre of Melaka City,[1] the capital of the state of Melaka, and Georgetown, the capital of the state of Penang, were both officially recognized as 'World Heritage Sites' by the United Nations Educational, Scientific and Cultural Organization (UNESCO). UNESCO (2008) describes these historic cities as 'unique architectural and cultural townscape[s] without parallel anywhere in East and Southeast Asia'. Such official recognition of the country's national heritage bodes well for the Malaysian tourism sector, which celebrates diversity and thrives on its multicultural inheritance. In reality, however, the hegemonic role of the Malaysian government led by the ethnocentric United Malays National Organization (UMNO) is to strive to construct a national identity and heritage based solely on the Malay majority, which often leads to the further marginalization of ethnic minorities in multi-ethnic Malaysia (Cheah 2002; Reid 1997).

Official national heritage sites have come to be regarded with scepticism and disdain among many academics and social critics (King 2012). Heritage sites have been accused of functioning as political tools for manufacturing and maintaining hegemonic power. Such sites may be constructed in ways that give authenticity to the notion that 'the nation' has, since its formation, been a singular ethnic group with original and exclusive rights to the

---

[1] Melaka is the third-smallest state in the Federation of Malaysia. The capital of the state is known as Melaka City. In this chapter, we prefer the Bahasa Malaysia spelling of Melaka over the English Malacca.

national territory. Naturalizing the nation-state's privileging of a single ethnic group, the heritage site reinforces the political status quo, which allows for the marginalization, discrimination and exploitation of minorities and indigenous peoples living within its territory (Hitchcock et al. 2009, 2010; Wood 1997).

In this chapter, we argue that having a *multicultural* world heritage site in Melaka is positive for the ethnic minorities who are marginalized in the state-constructed narrative and heritage of the city. Using the world heritage site of Melaka as a case study, we suggest that in a multicultural, globalizing and digitizing society, traditionally conceived heritage sites may inadvertently be promoting and deepening democratic processes rather than vitiating them. Using materials from Facebook groups[2] frequented by marginalized ethnic groups, we argue that the reworking of Melaka as a world heritage site has created a discursive space in which national and ethnic identity in Malaysia can be rearticulated in more inclusive ways. Moreover, the artificiality of the government's restyling of Melaka's inner city as a Disneyesque theme park may actually have spurred ethnic groups to enter this discursive space through social media and begin the recuperation of their own often-forgotten traditions. In the following pages, we will first discuss the conditions of Dutch Eurasians and Chitty Melaka, two ethnic minorities in Malaysia who trace their origins back to Melaka. Next we will demonstrate how developments in heritage conservation and tourism in Malaysia and by UNESCO have come together to reproduce Melaka as a specifically multicultural world heritage site. Then we will turn to the ways in which the Dutch Eurasians and the Chitty Melaka have taken to the Internet to rework their ethnic identities and traditions. In our analysis, we aim to demonstrate how their activities are not only predicated on the possibilities of social media technologies but also react to and function within the discourses surrounding Melaka as the birthplace of the national multicultural heritage.

Dutch Eurasians and Chitty Melaka in Multi-ethnic Malaysia

In many modern nation states, the establishment of majority and minority communities within a territorial national border is determined by the changing political conditions, which in turn define who is incorporated in the imagined community and who remains the internal Other (Anderson 2006; Eriksen

---

2 We have approval from the page administrators for full access to all materials available on the Facebook pages 'Chetti (or Chitty) Melaka a.k.a. Peranakan Indian' (https://www.facebook.com/groups/24323821523/) and 'Malaysian Dutch Descendants Project' (https://www.facebook.com/groups/114801754712/).

2002; Ohnuki-Tierney 1998). Malaysia is no exception. Formed in 1963, the Federation of Malaysia comprises 13 states: 11 states from the Malay Peninsula, and Sabah and Sarawak in North Borneo. It also brings together diverse ethnic communities from all these states.[3] The Malaysian government officially recognizes three major ethnic categories: Malays, Chinese and Indians (King 2009; Ting 2009). According to the 2010 census,[4] Malaysian citizens consist of the ethnic groups of the Bumiputera[5] (67.4%), Chinese (24.6%), Indians (7.3%) and Others (0.7%) (Department of Statistics 2011). Bumiputera is said to be a term introduced in the pan-Malaysia census 'to accommodate the emergence of a large variety of indigenous communities after the creation of Malaysia in 1963' (Saw 2006, 13). It includes the Malays, the Kadazans, the Bajans and the Muruts from Sabah, as well as the Ibans, the Bidayuhs and the Melanaus in Sarawak.

Constituting less than 1 per cent of the total population and being classified as 'Others', the Dutch Eurasians and other ethnic minorities such as the Chitty Melaka have been rendered politically insignificant compared to the Malays and other Bumiputeras, the Chinese and the Indians (Daniels 2005; Means 1976; Milne and Mauzy 1986). Because the Dutch Eurasians and the Chitty Melaka are not officially recognized by the Malaysian government, there are no designated official groupings for either hybrid community in Malaysia. As a result, both Dutch Eurasians and Chitty Melaka are not only marginalized from the discourses of multiculturalism, but are excluded from accessing the power of the nation in multi-ethnic Malaysia. This displacement has profoundly affected the two communities, their identities and cultures.

---

3 The Federation of Malaya came into being in 1948, uniting the 11 states in the Malay Peninsula. In 1957, Malaya became an independent country under a multi-ethnic Alliance government led by Tunku Abdul Rahman, the first prime minister of Malaysia (Milne and Mauzy 1986; Means 1976). Brunei withdrew from the Federation in July 1963 over issues around sharing oil revenues and the status of the sultan. From 1963 to 1965, Singapore was a part of Malaysia. It was argued that political differences between Lee Kuan Yew's PAP party and the Alliance party led by Tunku Abdul Rahman that resulted the Tunku announcement of the separation of Singapore from the Federation of Malaysia (Milne and Mauzy 1986; Quah 2000).

4 Ethnic compositions from the Malaysia 2000 census were presented as the Malays constituting 53% of the population with the rest of the population as: 26% Chinese, 8% Indians, 12% other *Bumiputera* ('sons of the soil'), and 1% Others. In the 2010 census, the Malay and other Bumiputeras were collapsed into the ethnic group Bumiputera.

5 However, the indigenous groups of the Malay Peninsula, the *Orang Asli* (a Malay term that means 'original people'), are not considered Bumiputera. They are excluded from the special status granted to the Malays and other Bumiputeras (Ong 2009).

The Malaysian Dutch Descendants

'Eurasian' is a complex term used to describe a heterogeneous community of people with mixed European and Asian ancestry. The Dutch Eurasians are descendants of the residents of Melaka and the Dutch colonial settlers who first arrived in Melaka in 1641. With an estimated population of 2,000 now living in Malaysia, they are 'a minority within an ethnic minority' (De Witt 2011, 224). This is because under the rubric of Eurasian, the community is often subsumed within the Portuguese Eurasians, who constitute the majority of Eurasians living in Malaysia (Sibert 2002; Williams 2007). According to Daniels (2005 67), *Serani*[6] is sometimes used interchangeably with the category of Eurasian and they are believed to be the descendants of 'European men, Portuguese or Dutch, who intermarried with Asian women'. Until early 2000, many Malaysians had not heard of Dutch Eurasians or as De Witt (2011, 228) puts it, 'it was presumed that the people had long ceased to exist in Malaysia'. The invisibility of Dutch Eurasians is generally in stark contrast to the prominence of the Dutch presence in the 'heritage core' of the city of Melaka. These include two colonial buildings in the central tourist area in Melaka – the Dutch Stadthuys (built in1650) and the Christ Church (built in 1753) (Worden 2010). Yet compared to the Portuguese Eurasians, the modern culture and heritage of the Dutch Eurasians are absent from Malaysia's national narratives and tourism materials. As a result, the Dutch Eurasian community remained relatively invisible until 2002 when a small group of them founded the Malaysian Dutch Descendants Project (MDDP), 'dedicated to the minority and forgotten community of Dutch descendants[7] living in Malaysia' (Dutchmalaysia.net 2002).

In 2004, nearly 150 people of Dutch descent from around the world, including Melaka, Indonesia, Sri Lanka and South Africa, attended the first ever 'International Gathering of Dutch Descendants', organized by the MDDP in Melaka (De Silva 2007). Through Dutchmalaysia.net – the official website of the MDDP, launched in 2002 – the MDDP also began to conduct a 'Eurasians at the Grassroots' project 'to record lesser-known stories and aspects regarding the Dutch Eurasians' in order 'to gather a collection of stories about the background, history, culture and heritage of the average Eurasian family' (Dutchmalaysia.net 2002). In addition, the MDDP has

---

6   The Portuguese Eurasians were given a partial Bumiputera status in the early 1990s. For a detailed discussion, please see Fernandis (2000, 2003).
7   We use Dutch Eurasians as a term to refer to all Eurasians with Dutch ancestry living in Malaysia. Malaysian Dutch Descendants is used specifically for Malaysian citizens who identify themselves as a distinct ethnic group.

a Facebook group for their community. As of December 2014, there were 432 members in this Facebook group. Launched in 2009, membership to this group remains open, comprising individuals from the Dutch Eurasian community living in Malaysia and beyond, as well as local and international non-Dutch Eurasian members.

The Chitty Melaka

The Chitty (*Chetty*, *Chetti*, also referred to as Straits-born Indians) are descendants of Indian settlers and local inhabitants of Melaka. The community now prefers to be referred to as the Chitty Melaka to emphasize their Melakan origin. They are said to be the oldest surviving hybrid *peranakan* community in Malaysia (Dhoraisingham 2006). The Malay term *peranakan* carries multiple and evolving meanings that reflect the ways in which local communities have responded to the sociocultural changes in the Malay Archipelago from the era prior to European colonization to the formation of modern nation-states in Southeast Asia until today. According to Pue and Shamsul (2012, 40), the term peranakan begins as a reference to 'individuals who are local born progeny of a native with a foreigner. An individual is perceived to be a foreigner if he or she comes from somewhere outside the local community, regardless of race or ethnicity'. In the nineteenth century, the Peranakan community was a heterogeneous community. Pue and Shamsul (2012, 41) contend that 'the concept of *peranakan* subsequently become Peranakan, an ethnic group that is "neither foreign, yet neither indigenous"'. This change was attributed to the influx of Chinese and Indian immigrants to Melaka in the mid-1900s during the period of British colonial rule that prompted the emergence of a distinctive peranakan identity originating in Melaka[8] (Pue and Shamsul 2012; Worden 2010). Despite being a socially constructed term referring to a heterogeneous community, peranakan remains a contested concept and is often mistakenly perceived to be an exclusive reference to Peranakan Chinese. One possible explanation of this is the socio-economic status of Peranakan Chinese relative to other peranakan communities. As Ravichandran (2009, 2) puts it, the Chitty Melaka is lesser known because the 'community has not been prominent in business and politics, unlike their *peranakan* cousins, the Baba and the Nyonyas'[9]. In addition, the Chitty Melaka are often classified as Indian in

---

8 Ravichandran (2009) makes a similar claim that it was during British colonialism that some of the Chitty Melaka relocated to Penang and Singapore, and that the community was eventually outnumbered by Indian migrants.
9 Baba and Nyonyas are two other terms that are used to refer to the *Peranakan* Chinese. Both terms are gendered with *baba* referring to the males, and *nyonyas* to the females.

Malaysia's rigid ethnic categorizations despite their mixed ancestry, thus making them another 'minority within an ethnic minority'.

The Chitty Melaka community see themselves as having a close affinity with Peranakan Chinese for two reasons. First, the Chitty Melaka community is believed to have assimilated the indigenous Malays' socio-cultural fabric in a unique way. They speak Malay, wear the *kebaya* (traditional dress), and adopt food culture and other aspects of general social conduct, in a manner similar to Peranakan Chinese (Ravichandran 2009). Unlike the Dutch Eurasians, who are subsumed into a wider category of Eurasians, Chitty Melaka's affinity with the Peranakan Chinese gives them a stronger sense of self and community. According to Ravichandran (2009, 13), the Chitty Melaka see 'themselves as non-Indian'. He continues:

> Despite their interactions with the larger Hindu Indian [community in Malaysia] through religious activities and intermarriages, the community still perceives themselves as distinct from their Hindu cousins. They find greater affinity with the Baba and Nyonyas of Melaka and appreciate their traditional interactions with them. (13)

The second reason is related to the decision made by the Association of Chetti Melaka (Peranakan Indian) in Singapore to revitalize the Chitty Melaka community in Malaysia and Singapore. According to David Bok[10] from the Association of Chetti Melaka in Singapore, in earlier days the community was called 'the Straits-born Indian, meaning Indians who were born in the Straits Settlements of Penang, Malacca and Singapore. But this was unsatisfactory because not all Indians born in the Straits Settlements are Chetti Melaka'. Bok states that when the Association of Chetti Melaka in Singapore was formed in 2007, the term peranakan was included into the name of the association in order to leverage 'on the intellectual and social capital that has been invested in it by other *peranakan* communities, eminently the Chinese *peranakan*' and to gain visibility in Singapore and Malaysia. As briefly discussed earlier, this is a different situation from the Malaysian Dutch Descendants, who want to be distinguished from the Portuguese Eurasians.

Even though the Chitty Melaka community is briefly mentioned in some anthropological accounts of Melaka (see Daniels 2005; Sarkissian 1997), and the *Kampung Chitty* (the Chitty Village) in Gajah Berang is listed as one of the historical sites of Melaka (Melaka Historic City Council, 2014), the

---

10 The conversations between the authors and David Bok began at the first Chitty Symposium on 4 October 2014 and subsequently in follow-up emails.

community's contributions to the much-celebrated multicultural heritage of Melaka are often sidelined. In the predominantly multicultural settlement of Melaka's heritage landscape, the Chitty Melaka receive little attention compared to other ethnic groups. As Worden (2010, 143) puts it, 'lacking both an invented tradition which could be adapted for tourism and also claims to Bumiputera status, they are almost absent in Melakan heritage representations and are struggling to maintain a distinct identity'. Modern Chitty Melaka are not only Hindu: there are those who are Muslim or Christian because of intermarriage. Urban migration, English-language education and other processes of modernization create internal diversity in the community (Ravichandran 2009). The present-day Kampung Chitty in Gajah Berang, gazetted as a heritage village in July 2002, has about 300 residents from 30 Chitty families (Uthaya Sankar 2014).

In late 2013, news about Kampung Chitty's being threatened by a development project of two 22-storey condominium blocks, a 12-storey hotel annex and a six-storey car park, revived concerns about the survival of the Chitty community in Melaka among members of the Chitty Melaka Facebook group (Murali 2014). This development prompted the Association of Chitty Melaka in Singapore to organize in October 2014 the first-ever Chitty Symposium, entitled, 'The Lost Tribe of Chetti Melaka – Who Are We?', and held at the Asian Civilization Museum in Singapore. The one-day symposium not only brought together invited guest speakers from various Peranakan groups from Malaysia and Singapore, such as the Jawi Peranakan and the Peranakan Chinese, to collectively address the issues faced by the Chitty Melaka community, but also proposed the concept that 'A Chitty Melaka becomes a Chitty Melaka by birth, adoption or marriage because only these processes get him into the family and the community' (David Bok, pers. comm.).

The re-emergence of the two hybrid communities of the Malaysian Dutch Descendants and the Chitty Melaka to assert their identities is not merely an expression of the much-celebrated character of the region as one 'where many religions and cultures met and coexisted' (UNESCO 2008), but rather a desire by both communities to be seen as distinct ethnic groups with respective cultures, traditions, and heritages.

Tourism Developments and Heritage Conversation in Malaysia

Neglected by the Malaysian government, ethnic minorities such as the Dutch Eurasians and the Chitty Melaka were further marginalized and displaced when tourism development in Melaka was incorporated into a government tourism project that emphasized Malay ethnicity and a Malay-centred

Malaysian nationhood. Tourism in Malaysia began during the colonial years and was mainly a leisure activity for the colonial officers and the European community. After independence in 1957, it was the role of both the federal and state governments to develop tourism into an industry. Still, early tourism development mainly focused on attracting international tourists to major cities such as Kuala Lumpur and Penang (Worden 2010). The Malaysian government began to see the significance of tourism in the 1980s and the government's involvement gradually diversified the focus of the tourism industry. Capitalizing on the growth of regional tourism in Southeast Asia, a campaign called 'Visit Malaysia Year' was launched in 1990 with the theme 'Fascinating Malaysia: Year of Festivals'. This attracted 7.4 million tourist arrivals compared to 4.8 million in 1989 (Visit Malaysia Year, 2014). The second Visit Malaysia campaign was launched in 1994 with an added focus on nature and ecotourism. By now all 13 states in the Federation of Malaysia had a department to manage and promote tourism. Some of these state governments have since replicated the nationwide Visit Malaysia campaigns, for example, 'Visit Sabah 2000' and 'Visit Perak Year 2012' (Yamashita 2009). It was not until the early 2000s that domestic tourism played 'a larger role in tourism development nationwide'[11] (Jenkin 2010, 154). Campaigns initiated by the federal and state governments to develop the tourism industry were successful, with tremendous economic returns. For example, the third Visit Malaysia campaign in 2007 recorded a total of 20.97 million tourist arrivals and generated RM$46.1 billion in tourist receipts (Visit Malaysia Year 2014). By 2013, the tourism industry had become the second-largest foreign exchange earner after manufactured goods, and with tourist receipts up to RM$65.44 billion (about US$20.25 billion) it was the sixth-largest contributor to the Malaysian economy (*The Malaysian Insider* 2014). The fourth Visit Malaysia campaign in 2014 attracted approximately 27.5 million foreign tourists (Tourism Malaysia 2014).

Overall, these campaigns have collectively cultivated an official image of Malaysia as a country rich in 'diversity' for international and domestic tourists. Tourism Malaysia's website proudly states that 'multiculturalism has made Malaysia a gastronomical paradise' with 'a bubbling, bustling melting pot of races and religions where Malays, Indians, Chinese and many other ethnic groups live together in peace and harmony' (Tourism Malaysia 2014). As King (2009, 65) summarizes, 'the image promoted by the Malaysian official agencies is therefore one of unity in diversity, a combination of the three major ethnic categories in a colourful, vibrant, interconnected and

---

11 In early 2000s, the government changed the working week of civil servants from six to five days. Increases in disposable income were also another contributing factor.

harmonious cultural tourism package'. Therefore, with the World Heritage Site status granted to Melaka, UNESCO actually endorses the conservation of 'diversity' in Malaysia. In reality, however, the existence of diverse ethnic communities has been the main source of ongoing tensions, conflicts and discontent in multi-ethnic Malaysia, especially in the early history of independent Malaysia (Cheah 2002).

Political discontent in the early 1960s culminated in communal riots on 13 May 1969. As a result of the riots, in 1971 the government implemented the New Economic Policy (NEP) for a period of 20 years. The NEP was designed to 'reduce and eventually eradicate poverty, by raising income levels and increasing employment opportunities for all Malaysians, irrespective of race', as well as to 'correct economic imbalance, so as to reduce and eventually eliminate the identification of race with economic function' (Means 1991, 24). Under the NEP, the representation of multi-ethnic Malaysia was also limited through the formulation of the National Cultural Policy (NCP) in order to engineer a cohesive national culture. Zawawi (2003) describes the NCP as a blueprint to modulate 'unregulated multiculturalism' by emphasizing Malay culture over the cultural practices of other ethnic communities in Malaysia. Zawawi (2003, 146) writes that the policy was conceptualized 'to transcend the heterogeneity of multiculturalism and provide an overarching national identity, which integrates all the different ethnic/cultural communities into a Malaysian nation-state'. In practice, the NCP also preferred a homogenous and cohesive construction of the Malay community and identity to the formerly pluralistic Malay community, which existed prior to the 1970s. In other words, managing unregulated multiculturalism in Malaysia also meant moulding each internally heterogeneous ethnic community into a distinctive multicultural entity. This means that the policy tried to impose boundaries upon the various ethnic communities. Nair (1999, 73) argues that 'post-1969 representations of ethnic identity and interests suggest a highly problematic construction of the nation in political discourse, one which is simultaneously inclusionary and exclusionary'. Commenting on the contradictions in the construction of a Malaysian nation, Verma (2002, 41) suggests that 'whereas society was plural or multi-ethnic, the state was mono-ethnic; in other words, it came to be identified predominantly with the Malay community'.

These multiple processes of inclusion and exclusion, together with the implementation of the NEP since the 1970s by the United Malays National Organization (UMNO), led government to create a mindset that reinforces and legitimizes 'Malay political primacy justified on the basis of indigeneity' (Ting 2009, 31). As Ting puts it, by asserting the superior position of Malay cultural (and religious) heritage in the national polity, as was done for instance through the proclamation of the National Culture Policy in 1971, the cultural and religious practices of other less empowered ethnic groups are accorded an 'informal' and lesser status. (2009, 32)

Transforming Melaka from an Ethno-centric to a Multiculturalist World Heritage Site

Like nationhood and history, heritage sites are usually considered to be a tool for nation building and therefore eyed with much suspicion among critical scholars. As King and Parnwell put it,

in newly independent or postcolonial developing states this is an even more urgent task and the need, in Benedict Anderson's terms, to 'imagine' the nation leads to the selection and deployment of archaeological finds and innovation, often in the context of an 'imagined' golden or glorious age of endeavour and achievement which was subsequently eclipsed by colonialism. (2010, 3–4)

In an increasing ethno-centric nationalist environment since the 1970s, focusing predominantly on a constructed Malay heritage, Melaka was subsequently reimagined as the cradle of Malay culture and identity (Khoo 2006; Nair 1999). For instance, as part of its tourism project the Melakan state government built a replica of a fifteenth-century wooden palace of the Melaka Sultanate and transformed many colonial buildings into museums to reclaim solely the Malay heritage in multicultural Melaka. This is a classic example of using heritage sites as political tools to reconstruct 'the nation' by reinforcing the status quo of a singular ethnic group at the expense of other minorities. As Worden (2010, 135) puts it, 'the absence of buildings and artefacts from the pre-colonial Malay era means that the indigenous past has been materially as well as metaphorically reconstructed'. In addition, tourism materials promoting Melaka selectively celebrate the cultural practices and heritages of the two Malay-ized Melakan inhabitants, the Portuguese Eurasians and the hybrid Peranakan Chinese, but only because of their exoticized identities and touristic value (Worden 2010). All these processes are, in the words of Worden (2010, 134), 'some skilful reordering of Melaka's history and heritage landscapes' in 'the creation of Malay cultural heritage in a predominantly European, Chinese and multicultural settlement'. A heritage site like Melaka is therefore no more than an 'imaginative construct', as the selection and conservation of its heritage reflects an ideological construct of how a country represents and emphasizes its national cohesiveness and historical continuity (King and Parnwell 2010).

For about 30 years, this situation has pushed marginal ethnic minorities in Malaysia further into marginality.

The ethno-nationalist attempt to mobilize a narrowly constructed heritage of Melaka in the nation-building project backfired when UNESCO rejected two applications for Melaka to be enlisted as a World Heritage Site. In the late 1980s, the rejection was 'on the grounds that too much of the original city centre had been destroyed' because of land reclamations, while a second attempt in the late 1990s was 'met with UNESCO criticism that local communities, notably Chinese residents, were being neglected' (Worden 2010, 143). Therefore, it could be argued that it was only after careful navigation of the paradoxes between a mono- and multi-ethnic heritage that the city of Melaka received UNESCO's approval.

Rejecting the ethnocentric national narrative and construction of heritage in Melaka, the UNESCO inscription broadens the definition of heritage in Malaysia. This is evidenced in the following quote:

> [Melaka] bears testimony to a living multi-cultural heritage and tradition of Asia, where the many religions and cultures met and coexisted. They reflect the coming together of cultural elements from the Malay Archipelago, India and China with those of Europe, to create a unique architecture, culture and townscape. (UNESCO 2008)

The UNESCO World Heritage Site status[12] has given a boost to cultural tourism in Melaka specifically and in Malaysia in general. The total number of tourist arrivals in Melaka increased to 13.5 million in 2013 and the Melakan government was expecting 15 million arrivals in 2014 (*The Star* 2014). As part of the tourism activities together with the museums, festivals and other theme park-like tourist attractions, Melaka now annually commemorates on 7 July the gaining of the UNESCO imprimatur by means of World Heritage City Celebration, featuring 'scores of traditional and cultural activities, local food and highlights of its historical significance through the conservation' (Visit Malaysia Year 2014). To attract more tourists after the success of the 2014 Visit Malaysia Year campaign, 2015 was branded the 'Malaysia Year of Festivals 2015', and attracted 25.7 million tourist arrivals in a country with only 30 million inhabitants (Visit Malaysia Year 2014; Tourism Malaysia 2016).

---

12 The site is now placed under the responsibility of the Ministry of Tourism and the Ministry of Culture, Arts and Heritage. The former is responsible for developing the tourism industry and the latter is 'in charge of preserving and developing Malaysian heritage as well as regulating, promoting, and developing heritage tourism' (Worden 2010, 131).

In response to the UNESCO recognition of Melaka as a World Heritage Site, the Malaysian government has intensified the process of restyling the old inner city of Melaka to suit the needs of both the tourism industry and the nation-building project (Kahn 1997; Wood 1997; Worden 2010). The result is strikingly reminiscent of Disney theme parks, with little attempt made to produce an air of historical authenticity. The former Dutch city hall ('Stadthuys') has been turned into an 'ethnographic museum' in which every ethnicity deemed relevant to the nation's birth is accorded its own room. Each ethnic group is represented by mannequins wearing traditional attire. For the indigenous groups, replicas of their traditional houses are also placed in the rooms. Opposite the Stadthuys, there is a Dutch-style replica of a windmill. Historically, there never was a windmill during the Dutch colonization of Melaka, but it was placed there to emphasize the 'Dutchness' of the area. About a hundred meters away a life-size replica of a Portuguese wooden ship from colonial times dominates the surroundings. The ship functions as an additional tourist attraction and can only be entered after paying a fee. A little further down the river, a large Arabic waterwheel has been placed on the shore. Such a waterwheel was historically never found in Melaka or anywhere in Malaysia; nonetheless, it stands amongst the other tourist attractions, representing yet another ethnic group that makes up Malaysia's 'multicultural heritage'. These Disneyesque theme park characteristics of the Melaka World Heritage Site reflect both the economic and political ambitions of the Malaysian government. In economic terms the picture-perfect Portuguese vessel and the Dutch windmill are lucrative tourist attractions. In terms of political ambitions, the emphasis on separately representing each ethnic group of the nation seems to present an artificial, sterilized version of ethnic communities living together in harmony.

In postcolonial Malaysia, the question of heritage in the development of tourism in Melaka complicates our contemporary understanding of the meaning of heritage sites in a globalizing multicultural society. As briefly discussed above, UNESCO has rejected the ethno-nationalist construction of the culture and heritage of Melaka. Even though the Malaysian government continues to play an important role in the selection and definition of national heritage sites, there are other powerful actors in the context of the transformation of heritage sites in a globalizing world. As Hitchcock et al. point out,

> heritage is also contested and transformed not only by representatives of the state but also by global actors, including representatives of international organisations such as the United Nations Educational, Scientific and Cultural Organization (UNESCO), researchers and foreign tourists, as well as domestic tourists, local communities and their neighbours. (2010, 3)

In the case of Melaka, the Malaysian government is forced to acknowledge cultural diversity in the construction of national heritage sites. In short, tourism developments and heritage conservation in Malaysia have come together with UNESCO to reproduce Melaka as a *multiculturalist* world heritage site.

Reconstructing Dutch Descendants and Chitty Melaka Identities

In modern times, most human beings are perceived to belong to respective nations and all could also be ethnically identified (Eriksen 2002). This is a problematic concept for both the Dutch Eurasians and the Chitty Melaka, who have been excluded from the discourse of belonging to multi-ethnic Malaysia. Like heritage, nations and ethnic communities are neither 'natural' nor pre-existing because both communities emerge not from a shared past or a shared culture, but from 'present-day *constructions* of the past' (Eriksen 2002, 73). While boundaries of ethnicity and national identity are never absolute and static, having an identity does allow communities to think about themselves in relation to others or, as Anderson (2006, 6) puts it, 'by the style in which they are imagined'. This is evident in the Facebook page of the Malaysian Dutch Descendants Project (MDDP), where the administrator wrote to inform its members that 'an attempt is being made to bring this community together and to protect their heritage, to make their existence known and to help the community regain its identity'. On the descriptions of the Chitty Melaka Facebook group, the administrator invites all the Chitty Melaka brothers and sisters to 'get together to revive our rich culture heritage. Let us do it NOW before we completely disappear in the next few generations'. All responses to revive or to regain the ethnic identity of these communities are best illustrated in the posting of a new member of the MDDP Facebook group. She wrote:

> Looking at all these posts, I feel very lost. My father was a Burgher, married a Eurasian and lived in Malaysia. I was born in KL, married a local Chinese and migrated to Australia. Right here and now, I feel I have lost a whole lot of heritage because little was spoken of about the Burghers before the days of computers and Facebook! Back then we were all Eurasians and that was that. In fact in school I was termed 'others' and looked upon as different and somewhat of an outcast. Did not help with my existing inferiority complex. Therefore I grew up in the shadows, so to speak. Thank you Facebook! (16 November 2014)

A post like this is common on the walls of Facebook pages, and such posts reveal that neither ethnic minority constitutes a socioculturally cohesive community, especially since many individuals have only recently connected with each other. Being invisible for years, these communities are struggling to maintain their distinct cultural practices and identities. Social media platforms such as Facebook are therefore a blessing for the Dutch Eurasians and the Chitty Melaka. With members of both communities now widely dispersed in different parts of Malaysia and globally, Facebook pages become the virtual sites where these communities, who trace their origins to Melaka, can meet and communicate. These sites also provide opportunities to revive their cultures, identities and heritages because for many members these Facebook pages are the first opportunity they have had to come into contact with these communities and to then construct a collective past as a community.

Engaging with (in)authenticity

All heritage sites are constructed and, as a result, the question of authenticity is a crucial and lingering concern in tourism studies. It was once imagined that tourist activities would destroy the authenticity of local cultures. In reality, tourism has 'made local residents self-conscious about a thing they possess called culture' (Pichard, cited in King 2009, 48). Still, the Dutch Descendants and the Chitty Melaka have different views about tourism developments in Melaka in relation to the question of authenticity, primarily because of both communities' presence in Melaka's multicultural heritage. Active members of the MDDP Facebook page often express their concerns about the overdevelopment of tourism in Melaka, especially the planning around the heritage sites. They are critical of not only the lack of authenticity in tourism activities promoted by the state, but of the mismanagement of the heritage sites. For example, when responding to a photograph of a road collapse beside the river bank near the Stadthuys, posted on 2 June 2013, a member wrote, ironically, 'They can use the Malacca mini windmill to drain out the water in the ground'. In a 7 July 2013, a post about a news story on the tourism development and commercial appeal of Melaka, in which the owner of a guest house claimed that 'the exterior is original because we are not allowed to change the design of the building' (Tiong 2013), a MDDP member responded, 'Looking at the picture of the Galileo Guesthouse attached to this article on NST [*New Straits Times*], I am sure that, especially the ground floor, never, at any point in time, looked like this!'

Being surrounded by 'staged', touristic and mismanaged heritage sites has made the Dutch Descendants more reflective about their cultural identity and heritage in multi-ethnic Malaysia. Mismanagement of the heritage sites frustrates the MDDP members, especially those who are protective of the Dutch heritage buildings. After posting a picture of a plaque installed at St. Paul's Church, a MDDP member wrote:

> If you thought the airco[n]s at the Stadthuys were bad [...] you might have spotted some of these plaques. If you thought the recent increase in signboards was ridiculous, these are not on a separate stand in front of the monument, but actually built in! Can you imagine, defacing a centuries old monument for something as retarded as this plaque? The pic included is the one on the St. Pauls Church, but the old gate also has it[; ...] have not been to the Stadthuys recently, but would not surprise that it also has one somewhere. I think this started with the replica of the Middleburgh bastion, that one had one from the beginning. The retard that came up with this should be shot (name: see plaque)! They are clearly trying to push the boundaries of their UNESCO status. I have never seen so much construction going on, especially in Heeren Street. For me though, the plaques are worse than anything else[. ...] UNESCO can and should take Melaka's heritage site status away because of this alone! The word 'retards' just doesn't cover it! (15 February 2014)

Damage done to the heritage sites is not only seen as a threat to the heritage buildings left behind by the Dutch in Melaka but is perceived as an attempt by the Malaysian government to dismiss the Dutch influences on the multicultural heritage of Melaka. It is within this context of staginess, inauthenticity and governmental mismanagement of cultural heritage that the increased activity of the Dutch Descendants' community online and offline needs to be understood.

Unlike the Dutch Eurasians in Melaka, the Chitty Melaka cannot lay claim to any eye-catching heritage buildings in the city centre. Despite being a very small, dispersed and fragmented community, as well as lacking a prominent presence in Melaka, the Chitty Melaka are still forthright when discussing the ways in which the city has been transformed into a tourist attraction. Like the Dutch Eurasians, they use social media in order to express their discontent. For example, the fact that the Kampung Chitty has been branded as a 'heritage village' is discussed on the page. The discussion is started by the posting of a photograph of the commemorative plaque that reads as follows:

> The Chettis have been around since the reign of Parameswara. Back then, most of them belong to the group of traders who were living in Kampung Kling and Kampung Belanda. They originated from the Coromandel Coast, Kalingapatnam, South India and Tamil Nadu. In the earlier days, there were

Chettis holding high posts in the government administration such as that of the Prime Minister. However, things began to change during the Dutch colonisation. The Chettis were imposed strict supervision in their trading which eventually caused them to move to more remote areas, such as Gajah Berang and Tengkera. As a result of the incident, many Chettis decided to switch their profession from trading to agriculture. (6 August 2014)

This text offers a narrative in which the Chitty Melaka are described as early and influential inhabitants of Melaka. Suggesting that before the Dutch colonization, Chitty once had 'high posts in the government administration such as that of the Prime Minister', it expresses the current marginalization of the Chitty identity in the Melakan power hierarchy. As such, the heritage status of Kampung Chitty offers members of the Facebook page discursive tools to rework their identity in relation to a national narrative that has traditionally only recognized Malays, Chinese and Indian groups.

After a slow start in 2008, the Chitty Melaka Facebook page began attracting Chitty from different generations to form an online community, especially those who no longer lived in Kampung Chitty. The page frequently receives open questions from individuals trying to find out more about the Chitty Melaka community. Some are university students researching about ethnic minorities, and others simply have an interest in the Chitty. It was these postings that triggered an exchange among the younger members in the Chitty Melaka community in order to reassess their culture and identity. For example, responding to Philip Chia, who wanted to know about the history of the Chitty in Melaka, how they came to be in Singapore and about the distinctions between the Chitty and the Chettiars (posted on 24 August 2011). A group member replied:

To add on a few here [...] let me tell u roughly about the history of chettis (p.s: pls correct me if I'm wrong) [...] one of the most significant difference between chettis and chettiars that will differentiate between these two is the history behind them [...] chettis came down to Tanah Melayu (Malaysia) during the Dutch occupation somewhere around the year 1700s [...] i would like to highlight that our ancestors are basically MERCHANTS or TRADERS from kalingapatnam, india which was once a well known port [...] basically, if they were to sail to china, they will have to drop by tanah melayu (malaysia) for approximately 6 months or more in order to wait for the change of the 'angin monsoon' [...] hence, within this period of time, some of our ancestors will settle down with the locals here [...] and this is how chetti melaka are born [...] this is where inter-marriage between the indians and the malays begin.

> Unlike chettis, chettiars came down to tanah melayu (malaysia) during the british occupation...they were brought down here by the british...basically the chettiars are MONEY LENDERS [...] therefore,i would like to emphasize here that there are no connection between chettis and chettiar. (posted on 12 October 2011)

The younger Chitty Melaka are enthusiastic about sharing what they know about their community and are not shy to admit their lack of knowledge about their ethnic culture. Explaining about their community on the Facebook page requires help to reaffirm their identity. For example, a Chitty member added:

> I can't tell much about the chetti's although im one of them cause im still learning about chettis [...] but one thing for sure, chettis and chettiars are way too different [...] chettiars are money lenders form india [...] but we chettis, our ancestors whom are traders form kalinga sailed here, married the locals and settled [sic] down [...] thus forming a peranakan group known as the chettis [...] for [m]ore info, you may visit our village [...] including our museum. (posted on 13 October 2011)

Responding to online inquiries like these also revealed that the younger generations know very little about their culture and identity. However, when in doubt or when there were concerns about authenticity or for verification, these information seekers were asked to visit Kampung Chitty and the Chitty Museum in Melaka. In a response to an inquiry about Chitty Melaka wedding culture a member on the Chitty Facebook page replied:

> I would advice u to come to Kampung Budaya Chetti Melaka at Gajah Berang Melaka [...] As we have museum and all the Chetti community is friendly and able to provide you with the real information [...] (posted on 29 September 2011)

Unlike the Dutch Descendants' critical view of the newly revamped colonial buildings and the mismanagement of heritage sites in the city centre of Melaka tourist district, the Chitty Melaka see their museum and their village as two sites that contain 'the real information' about their community and that are perhaps less contaminated by tourism development.

In tourism studies, there is a growing concern about an increasing 'interpenetration of tourism and ethnicity' (Hitchcock et al. 2009, 15) because international tourism is not only having profound influences on ethnicity but is becoming an integral part of the formation and transformation of ethnic identity. Social anthropologist Thomas H. Eriksen writes that cultural difference between two groups is not the decisive feature of ethnicity [. ...] For ethnicity to come about, the groups must have a minimum of contact with each other, and they must entertain ideas of each other as being culturally different from themselves. If these conditions are not fulfilled, there is no ethnicity, for ethnicity is essentially an aspect of a relationship, not a property of a group. (2002, 12)

As illustrated in our analyses, tourism and social media have an equally transformative effect on this 'aspect of a relationship' not only because of increasing contacts but because 'being culturally different' has become essential for identity formation. Tourism, therefore, 'provides a way to understand what has been happening to ethnicity' (Wood 1997, viii) because 'ethnicity is also increasingly recognized as shaped by contemporary global processes, rather than by residue from parochial pasts' (Wood 1997, 2). For both ethnic minorities, which are less socio-culturally cohesive, responding to tourism in Melaka is becoming the contemporary global process that could help to reshape their ethnic identities.

Repositioning the community

Like all forms of identity, ethnic identity is conceived as always in process. Historians, sociologists, political scientists and anthropologists have also acknowledged that the formation, maintenance and reproduction of a collective identity involves a dual process which, in the words of Schlesinger (1991, 300), consists of 'one of inclusion that provides a boundary around "us", and one of exclusion that distinguishes "us" from "them"'. This provides ethnic communities with various ways to position themselves in relation to other communities, whether to distinguish themselves from them or to gain affinity with them. Dutch Descendants and Chitty Melaka are no exception.

For the Dutch Descendants, distinguishing themselves from the Portuguese Eurasians in Malaysia requires a conscious effort. Furthermore, the lack of recognition of their modern culture and heritage in Melaka was often juxtaposed with the inauthentic Portuguese Eurasians' tourist activities endorsed by the Melakan government. For example, after posting a news story on 18 November 2011 about a four-day celebration at the Portuguese Settlement in Ujong Pasir, Melaka, to commemorate the 500th year of the arrival of the former European naval power in Melaka, the administrator of the MDDP Facebook page, commented thus:

> I'm all for traditions and celebrations, however, most of the time it feels like the Portuguese community (or what's left of it) receives attention only because of

their commercial value to the State. The Portuguese were the destroyers of the Melaka Sultanate, plundered the place, let its fabled trade position fade away and were not on best terms with the local population (or anyone else for that matter) for a number of reasons. How ironic is it when 5 centuries later they are showcased on a regular basis by the local media (read Tourism Malaysia), doing their dances, boasting about a dying language, etc[. ...] It makes one wonder whether their current position/status is a blessing or a punishment. (posted on 18 November 2011)

He added:

[I]t's ironic that the Portuguese, considering their negative history, receive so much attention today whereby every event is milked for all its worth. This is not the case for the Dutch or even the British. So where's the difference, what do the Portuguese have that the Dutch do not have or cannot regain? Don't speak Dutch? Follow a language class! Learn about a couple of Dutch traditions and re-introduce them into family life! Like the Portuguese, they used to celebrate the taking of Malacca, why not remember it today? You can even learn a Dutch dance or chanty and dress like they did so many years ago! Cook something Dutch once in a while. Relatively simple things that can bring the Dutch descendants on par with the Portuguese descendants. Why doesn't it happen? Why do the Dutch choose to be sidelined? And why do the Portuguese descendants, who vent their complaints about their situation at least once a year, keep clinging to the past? (posted on 18 November 2011)

This post on the MDDP Facebook page has received the most comments. The conversation of 53 comments quickly turned from being about the lack of recognition of Dutch Eurasians in Malaysia, to a long discussion between MDDP members about repositioning Dutch Descendants in Melaka, especially in relation to the Portuguese Eurasians. Responding to the post, a MDDP member wrote:

Also interesting in your example here is that the celebration 'attracted tourists and foreign media', this is what I mentioned in my first comment, that the Portuguese community (if you can still call it that) only receives attention because of their commercial value. They are being milked for all they are worth! They are a tolerated resource more than anything else. How long would the attention last if they stopped dancing and singing for the tourists? I'm guessing they would disappear almost overnight. (posted on 25 November 2011)

Being 'on par with the Portuguese descendants' here should not be read solely as a rejection or resentment of the Portuguese Eurasians in Malaysia simply because the Dutch Descendants' consciously want to be distinguished from them. Rather, members of the MDDP see the touristic culture of the Portuguese Eurasians as a trade-off. As one MDDP member puts it:

> Indeed, anything for a tourist dollar, and Tourism Malaysia is known for juggling fact and fiction. The deal here imho [sic], quid pro quo, you get your village if you dance for us? Hence my remark in my first post, about the position of the Portuguese being a blessing or a punishment. As for the Dutch, there's nothing wrong by reclaiming what was once theirs, and as far as I know they do not have any demands so there is no need to sell out to Tourism Malaysia. (posted on 26 November 2011)

These series of conversations reveal not only a consciousness among the MDDP members of their frustrated intention to be distinguished from the Portuguese Eurasians, but the ways in which they see themselves and their newly rediscovered Malaysian Dutch identity. Responding to exhortations to keep up with the Dutch 'customs', a member exclaims:

> How Dutch are we today? It's not easy for us to keeping Dutch culture, language (as most of the Malaysian Dutch descendant don't speak the Dutch! nor do I) etiquette, customs, manners and protocol (What a pity that most of us don't practice! Furthermore, we don't understand what are all these customs)!! (posted on 25 November 2011)

Online interactions among the MDDP Facebook page members to construct a common heritage and to reconnect the diverse Dutch Eurasian community in and beyond Malaysia are complex and involve a great number of negotiations. This is because, despite various MDDP attempts to re-establish the community's collective identity, this newly constructed Dutch Descendants' identity is 'neither foreign, yet neither indigenous'. As De Witt puts it:

> Although Malaysian Dutch descendants exist as a minority within a minority and the community has long remained invisible and forgotten, they persist to be proud of their European roots which are reflected in their surnames and their Dutch heritage. Nevertheless, Malaysian Dutch descendants are quintessentially Malaysian in every other way and represent a tiny but unique part of Malaysia. (2008)

For the Chitty Melaka Facebook group members, who are aware of their hybrid identity, the topic that received the most comments was about the Bumiputera status and was intensely discussed in three separate posts in 2012.

On 26 February 2012, a member posted a news story from a local daily that the prime minister of Malaysia had assured the Thai minority of their entitlement to Bumiputera benefits and privileges. The post generated a total of 46 comments, with the younger Chitty members deciding to form a committee to renew the claim for the Bumiputera status. A member wrote in response to several enthusiastic comments:

> I personally think that the younger generation with greater ability and capacity able to drive this in a team whereby all of us deserve the status […] everyone shall put away the past and non-productive agenda to meet this objective that is Bumi status. (posted on 26 February 2012)

From 26 February to 17 March 2012, discussions on this thread turned into action plans, with the younger Chitty Melaka trying to recruit other members to renew the quest to be recognized as Bumiputera.

> Best to find out more from the Portuguese community on how they obtained bumi privileges. The Chitty community deserves Bumi status and privileges 200%! (posted on 26 February 2012)
> Glad Sumi Pillay I want to build a SOLID Task Force U will be the Admin then! (posted on 26 February2012)
>   As a kick off mayb[e] family tree would be great, den [sic] the memorandum t[h]at was submitted to Melaka government years back would be a great baseline. This task force need to h[a]v[e] skills in presentation, documentation, interview and etc. (posted on 17 March 2012)

On 10 April 2012, a post about the chief minister of Melaka being positive to the prime minister regarding the suggestion to grant Bumiputera status to the Peranakan Chinese also received some favourable responses from the Chitty community:

> [L]et's clean up our house first […] ie: remove all ill feelings amongst the community […] lets begin to speak in one voice. (posted on 12 April 2012) U got it right bro. There's a lot of things we need to address b4 we can sit and speak as one voice. (posted on 13 April 2012)

From these brief accounts of the Facebook activities among the Chitty Melaka, it is evident that 'lacking both an invented tradition which could be adapted for tourism and also claims to Bumiputera status' (Worden 2010, 143) does not deter the Chitty Melaka from utilizing the online interactive medium to revive their culture and heritage in order to reposition their community in multi-ethnic Malaysia. The Facebook discussion about the

Bumiputera status, especially, is a positive first step for the Chitty Melaka, who constitute not only an ethnic group struggling to maintain their distinct identity, but a community without any strong and organized community associations to campaign for and champion their culture and heritage, much like the Malaysian Dutch Descendants Project.

Becoming prominent on social media, both the Malaysian Dutch Descendants and the Chitty Melaka are exploiting the interactive and global reach of their separate Facebook groups to reshape the debate about national belonging within the national discourse surrounding Melaka as the birthplace of the national heritage sites. This allows them to demand a new and inclusive national narrative within the multicultural heritage of Melaka. The intersection of tourism and social media has also stimulated the development of new narratives of belonging through the quest for Bumiputera status among the Chitty Melaka.

Conclusion

After years under authoritarian rule, Malaysia is known to have a media system that serves the interests of the governing state. Until today, the media is closely controlled through direct and indirect ownership, censorship, or strict rules and regulations (Zaharom Nain and Wong 2004). Despite a no-censorship guarantee for the Internet in the mid-1990, media organizations, news editors, journalists, activists, politicians, academics and netizens have been selectively targeted more frequently in recent years (*Malay Mail* Online 2016). The increased cases of Internet censorship to curb freedom of expression and information in Malaysia also limit the democratizing potential of social media. Fortunately, the Dutch Eurasians and the Chitty Melaka are not direct targets because both groups are politically less significant to the authority and, most importantly, their demands for social recognition are not seen as anti-government.

With the growing importance of social media platforms, there is a shift in media studies from an underlying assumption that modern mass media is a crucial instrument for the formation and maintenance of collective identities, including national and ethnic identity (Anderson 2006), to considering social media as the space to construct, consolidate, strengthen and define collective identities (Postill and Pink 2012; Eriksen 2007). Unlike traditional mass media that make thinking and talking about a collective identity plausible, activities on social media allow members to participate directly in the making of culture, identity and heritage. As a result, the global reach of the Internet and social media platforms also contribute to creating new conditions for the formation and maintenance of collective identity, especially among formerly invisible ethnic minorities.

The reworking of Melaka as a World Heritage Site has created a discursive space in which national and ethnic identity in Malaysia can be rearticulated in more inclusive ways. In our globalizing world, heritage sites do not necessarily ossify national identity. They may instead create new spaces of negotiation, and produce sufficient leverage to re-authenticate local identities that were previously excluded from the national narrative. The lack of authenticity in the national narrative may also have a positive effect on opening up space to construct alternative narratives of belonging for ethnic minority groups and to contest dominant and exclusive representations of national identity. Rearticulating their identities, the Malaysian Dutch Descendants and the Chitty Melaka are also reclaiming and defining their positions in the mosaic of a multi-ethnic Melaka in opposition to an ethno-centric construction of this national heritage site.

References

Anderson, Benedict. 2006. *Imagined Communities: Reflections on the Origin and Spread of Nationalism*, 2nd ed. London: Verso.
Cheah, Boon Kheng. 2002. *Malaysia: The Making of a Nation*. Singapore: Institute of Southeast Asian Studies.
Daniels, Timothy P. 2005. *Building Cultural Nationalism in Malaysia: Identity, Representations, and Citizenship*. New York: Routledge.
Department of Statistics Malaysia. 2011. 'Population Distribution and Basic Demographic Characteristics Report 2010'. Department of Statistics Malaysia, 5 August. Online: http://www.statistics.gov.my/ (accessed 30 November 2014).
De Witt, Dennis. 2008. 'History of the Dutch and Dutch–Eurasians in Malaysia'. Dutchmalaysia.net, 27 May. Online: http://www.dutchmalaysia.net/lang_en/press/paper_20080527_history_of_the_dutch_and_dutch_eurasians_in_malaysia.html (accessed 16 February 2015).
———. 2011. *History of the Dutch in Malaysia*. Selangor: Nutmeg Publishing.
De Silva, Rina. 2007. 'Malaysian Potpourri (The Dutch Community): Surnames Clue to Dutch Roots'. The Malaysian Bar, 7 August. Online: http://www.malaysianbar.org.my/echoes_of_the_past/malaysian_potpourri_the_dutch_community_surnames_clue_to_dutch_roots.html (accessed 17 November 2014).
Dhoraisingam, Samuel S. 2006. *Peranakan Indians of Singapore and Melaka: Indian Babas and Nyonyas Chitty Melaka*. Singapore: ISEAS.
Dutchmalaysia.net. 2002. Official website of the Malaysian Dutch Descendants Project. Online: http://www.dutchmalaysia.net/lang_en/ (accessed 20 November 2014).
Eriksen, Thomas H. 2002. *Ethnicity and Nationalism*. 2nd ed. London: Pluto Press.
———. 2007. 'Nationalism and the Internet'. *Nation and Nationalism* 13, no. 1: 1–17.
Fernandis, Gerard. 2000. 'The Portuguese Eurasians in Malaysia: *Bumiquest*, a Search for Self Identity'. *Lusotopie*: 261–68.

———. 2003. 'The Portuguese Community at the Periphery: A Minority Report on the Portuguese Quest for Bumiputera Status'. *Kajian Malaysia* XXI, nos. 1 & 2: 285–301.

Hitchcock, Michael, Victor T. King, and Michael Parnwell (eds). 2009. *Tourism in Southeast Asia: Challenges and New Directions*. Copenhagen: NIAS Press.

———. 2010. *Heritage Tourism in Southeast Asia*. Copenhagen: NIAS Press.

Jenkin, Gwynn. 2010. 'Interpreters of Space, Place, and Cultural Practice: Processes of Change through Tourism, Conservation, and Development in George Town, Penang Malaysia'. In *Heritage Tourism in Southeast Asia*, edited by M. Hitchcock, V. T. King and M. Parnwell, 147–72. Copenhagen: NIAS Press.

Kahn, Joel S. 1997. 'Culturalizing Malaysia: Globalism, Tourism, Heritage, and the City in Georgetown'. In *Tourism, Ethnicity and the State in Asian and Pacific Societies*, edited by M. Picard and R. E. Wood, 99–127. Honolulu: University of Hawaii Press.

Khoo, Gaik Cheng. 2006. *Reclaiming Adat: Contemporary Malaysian Film and Literature*. Vancouver: UBC Press.

King, Victor T. 2009. 'Anthropology and Tourism in Southeast Asia: Comparative Studies, Cultural Differentiation and Agency'. In *Tourism in Southeast Asia: Challenges and New Directions*, edited by M. Hitchcock, V. T. King and M. Parnwell, 43–68. Copenhagen: NIAS Press.

———. 2012. 'Culture, Heritage and Tourism in Southeast Asia'. *Pertanika Journal of Social Sciences & Humanities* 20, no. 1: i–vii.

King, Victor T. and Michael Parnwell. 2010. 'Heritage Tourism in Southeast Asia'. In *Heritage Tourism in Southeast Asia*, edited by M. Hitchcock, V.T. King and M. Parnwell, 1–27. Copenhagen: NIAS Press.

Malay Mail Online. 2016. 'Expect walls to close in further on freedom of expression and information — Centre for Independent Journalism'. *The Malay Mail* Online, 27 February. Online: http://www.themalaymailonline.com/what-you-think/article/expect-walls-to-close-in-further-on-freedom-of-expression-and-information-c#sthash.fw3o15x4.dpuf (accessed 29 February 2016).

Malaysian Insider. 2014. 'Tourism Contributed RM 51.5 Billion to GNI Last Year'. *The Malaysian Insider*, 8 April. Online: http://www.themalaysianinsider.com/malaysia/article/tourism-contributed-rm51.5-billion-to-gni-last-year-bernama#sthash.pWX5T6pm.dpuf (accessed 17 November 2014).

Mandal, Sumit K. 2003. 'Transethnic Solidarities in a Racialized Context'. *Journal of Contemporary Asia* 33, no. 1: 50–68.

Means, Gordon P. 1976. *Malaysian Politics*, 2nd ed. London: Hodder and Stoughton.

———. 1991. *Malaysian Politics: The Second Generation*. London: Oxford University Press.

Melaka Historic City Council. 2014. 'Chitty Village'. Melaka Historic City Council. Online: http://www.mbmb.gov.my/en/chitty-village (accessed 25 November 2014).

Milne, R. S. and Diane K. Mauzy. 1986. *Malaysia: Tradition, Modernity, and Islam*. Boulder: Westview Press.

Murali, R. S. N. 2014. 'Malacca CM Steps in to Solve Chitty Village Row'. *The Star*, 1 January. Online: http://www.thestar.com.my/News/Nation/2014/01/01/CM-steps-in-to-solve-Chitty-village-row-Idris-orders-probe-into-approval-of-highrise-condominium-pro/ (accessed 25 November 2014).

Nair, Sheila. 1999. 'Colonial "Others" and Nationalist Politics in Malaysia'. *Akademika* 54: 55–79.

Ohnuki-Tierney, Emiko. 1998. 'A Conceptual Model for the Historical Relationship between the Self and the Internal and External Others'. In *Making Majorities: Constituting*

the nation in Japan, Korea, China, Malaysia, Fiji, Turkey, and the United States, edited by D. C. Gladney, 31–51. Stanford: Stanford University Press.
Ong, Puay Liu. 2009. 'Identity Matters: Ethnic Perceptions and Concerns'. In *Multiethnic Malaysia: Past, Present and Future*, edited by T. G. Lim, A. Gomes and Azly Rahman, 463–82. Petaling Jaya: The Strategic Information and Research Development Centre.
Postill, John and Sarah Pink. 2012. 'Social Media Ethnography: The Digital Researcher in a Messy Web'. *Media International Australia*. Online: http://blogs.bournemouth.ac.uk/research/files/2013/04/Postill-Pink-socialmedia-ethnography.pdf (accessed on 17 November 2014).
Pue, Giok Hun and A. B. Shamsul. 2012. *Peranakan as a Social Concept*. Bangi: UKM Press.
Quah, Jon S. T. 2000. 'Globalization and Singapore's Search for Nationhood'. In *Nationalism and Globalization: East and West*, edited by L. Suryadinata, 71–101, Singapore: Institute of Southeast Asian Studies.
Ravichandran, Moorthy. 2009. 'The Evolution of the Chitty Community of Melaka'. *Jebat* 36: 1–15.
Reid, Anthony. 1997. 'Endangered Identity: Kadazan or Dusun in Sabah (East Malaysia)'. *Journal of Southeast Asian Studies* 28, no. 1: 120–36.
———. 2001. 'Understanding Melayu (Malay) as a Source of Diverse Modern Identities'. *Journal of Southeast Asian Studies* 32, no. 3: 295–313.
Sarkissian, Margaret. 1997. 'Cultural Chameleons – Portuguese Eurasian Strategies for Survival in Post-Colonial Malaysia'. *Journal of Southeast Asian Studies* 28, no. 2: 249–62.
Saw, Swee-Hock. 2006. 'Population Trends and Patterns in Multiracial Malaysia'. In *Malaysia: Recent Trends and Challenges*, edited by S. H. Saw and K. Kesavapany, 1–25. Singapore: Institute of Southeast Asian Studies.
Schlesinger, Philip. 1991. 'Media, the Political Order and National Identity'. *Media, Culture and Society* 13: 297–308.
Sibert, Anthony E. 2002. 'The History of Penang Eurasians'. The Penang Story. Online: http://penangstory.net.my/mino-content-paperanthony.html (accessed 25 November 2014).
Star, The. 2014. '15 Million Tourists Expected in Malacca'. *The Star*, 19 January. Online: http://www.thestar.com.my/News/Nation/2014/01/19/15-million-tourists-expected-in-Malacca/ (accessed 16 November 2014).
Ting, Helen. 2009. 'The Politics of National Identity in West Malaysia: Continued Mutation or Critical Transition?' *Southeast Asian Studies* 47, no. 1: 31–51.
Tiong, John. 2013. 'Commercial Appeal'. *New Straits Times*, 7 July. Online: http://www2.nst.com.my/life-times/sunday-life-times/commercial-appeal-1.314281 (accessed 30 November 2014).
Tourism Malaysia. 2014. 'About Malaysia'. Tourism Malaysia. Online: http://www.tourism.gov.my/en/my/about-malaysia (accessed 16 November 2014).
Tourism Malaysia. 2016. 'Malaysia Tourism Statistics in Brief'. Tourism Malaysia. Online: http://www.tourism.gov.my/statistics (accessed 16 August 2016).
UNESCO. 2008. 'Melaka and George Town, Historic Cities of the Straits of Malacca'. UNESCO World Heritage List. Online: http://whc.unesco.org/en/list/1223/ (accessed 16 November 2014).
Uthaya Sankar, S. B. 2014. 'Saksikan Kemusnahan Kampung Chetti' ['Witnessing the Demolition of Chitty Village']. Projek Dialog, 21 November. Online: http://www.projekdialog.com/featured/saksikan-kemusnahan-kampung-chetti/ (accessed 21 November 2014).

Verma, Vidhu. 2002. *Malaysia: State and Civil Society in Transition*. Boulder, CO: Lynne Rienner.

Visit Malaysia Year. 2014. 'History of Visit Malaysia Year'. Visit Malaysia Year. Online: http://www.vmy2014.com/about-vmy2014/history-of-visit-malaysia-year (accessed 17 November 2014).

Williams, Regina. 2007. 'Eurasians' Rich Heritage'. The Malaysian Bar, 6 August. Online: http://www.malaysianbar.org.my/echoes_of_the_past/eurasians_rich_heritage.html?date=2009-10-01 (accessed 25 November 2014).

Wood, Robert. E. 1997. 'Tourism and the State: Ethnic Options and Constructions of Otherness'. In *Tourism, Ethnicity and the State in Asian and Pacific Society*, edited by M. Picard and R. Wood, 1–34. Honolulu: University of Hawaii Press.

Worden, Nigel. 2010. 'National Identity and Heritage Tourism in Melaka'. In *Heritage Tourism in Southeast Asia*, edited by M. Hitchcock, V. T. King and M. Parnwell, 130–46. Copenhagen: NIAS Press.

Yamashita, Shinji. 2009. 'Southeast Asian Tourism from a Japanese Perspective'. In *Tourism in Southeast Asia: Challenges and New Directions*, edited by M. Hitchcock, V. T. King and M. Parnwell, 189–206. Copenhagen: NIAS Press.

Zaharom, Nain and Lay Kim Wang. 2004. 'Ownership, control and the Malaysian media'. In *Who Owns The Media: Global Trends And Local Resistances*, edited by P. N. Thomas and Z. Nain, 249–67. Penang, Malaysia: Southbound Sdn. Bhd.

Zawawi, Ibrahim. 2003. 'The Search for a "New Cinema" in Post-colonial Malaysia: The Films of U-Wei Bin Hajisaari as Counter-Narrations of National Identity'. *Inter-Asia Cultural Studies* 4, no. 1: 145–54.

Chapter 7

NOSTALGIA AND MEMORY: REMEMBERING THE MALAYAN COMMUNIST REVOLUTION IN THE ONLINE AGE

Jason Sze Chieh Ng

The term *communism* invokes a multitude of reactions in Malaysia today, ranging from open hostility to guarded curiosity, depending on with whom one speaks. The dearth of readily available information on this somewhat taboo subject has contributed to these divergent views, which at times are delineated along ethnic lines. However, with the proliferation of affordable Internet access and somewhat more liberal attitudes towards online content by the Malaysian Communications and Multimedia Commission (MCMC), information on communism has become unrestricted and accessible to the public. As a result, the history of Malaysia's relationship with communism as remembered by the Malayan communists is now available online, and they reveal a version of history that does not necessarily align with the contemporary Malaysian national narrative. Social networking sites such as Facebook and Twitter have also allowed for the dissemination of communist history and knowledge much more swiftly and freely than traditional communication methods. The Internet has become the new stage for retired Malayan communists to present their side of history. For the purpose of this chapter's discussion, Malaya refers to the pre-1963 territories of the Malay Peninsula; the Malayan Communist party (MCP) technically does not recognize the Federation of Malaysia, as it excludes Singapore but includes the Borneo states of Sabah and Sarawak. The latter two states are historically not part of the former colonial holdings of British Malaya.

With the rising importance of social media in the public sphere, many Party retirees see this as the perfect time to re-engage with a new generation of Malaysian youth who have grown up untainted by the fears and prejudices of the Cold War. The retirees hope that those who will inherit the nation one day might understand their reasons for advocating communism for Malaya. To that end, the MCP's fraternal organization, the 21st Century Old Friends Association (21世纪老友联谊会; 21OF), opened a public website (www.of21.com) aimed at educating the Malaysian public about their past.[1] Unfortunately, this effort is hamstrung by its purely Mandarin language content, limiting its effectiveness to the ethnic Chinese community only. The website is managed by a retired party member living in Kuala Lumpur with writing contributions from fellow retirees, many of whom were former members of the Malayan Peoples' Army (the military arm of the MCP). Moreover, the website provides downloads of rare and original materials that have never been available to the public, with some material not found within government archives in London, Singapore or Kuala Lumpur. This has allowed party retirees to continue to project their presence into the post-insurgency era without fear, and to propound their views to contemporary society. The 21OF website, like many other online portals of social groups, also invites the public to participate in commemorating the MCP's past, ensuring the memories are preserved into the future through hearing, reading and viewing their artefacts online (Roth 2011, 61).

On viewing the 21OF website, operated by and dedicated to the MCP and its ideals, initially it appears as if the 'defeated' communists are clinging on to the last vestiges of an outdated ideology by projecting their propaganda online. However, the website also functions as a multipurpose social platform that connects and informs its members. In addition, the site acts as an open digital depository for declassified Party documents. Several retirees even took the opportunity to chronicle memories of their struggle, which then became articles shared on the website. These collected life stories that not only are from the collective history of the MCP, but which constitutes the retirees' best opportunity to pass on their legacy to the next generation so that their sacrifices and their beliefs will be remembered (Egerton 1994, 4).

This chapter proposes that the establishment of the 21OF website is an attempt by MCP retirees to identify with the current generation of Malaysians in the hope of establishing an empathic link with them. It is the retirees' hope that their experiences and convictions, triumphs and losses, are adequately transmitted into the future, and that their identity – the voice of a vanishing minority – might be preserved long after they have passed away. Most importantly, the website seeks to reaffirm the MCP's nationalistic creed through

---

1 All translations of the website and subsequent Mandarin language materials are done by me.

the many articles and blog posts that criticize the latest political crises gripping Malaysia. Even so, the Mandarin-only content on the website severely restricts its impact, limiting its access to the Chinese community. Comments and statements from my interviews with the 21OF webmaster and several Party retirees are included to establish the rationale and objectives of the website and its cultural importance. These are then juxtaposed with discussions on online memory and commemoration, but within the context of the history of Malayan communism.

The Malayan Communist Party

According to the current Malaysian secondary school history curriculum, Malaya (the general name for the Malay Peninsula and Singapore Island before their independence in 1957 and 1965 respectively) was once a British colony. Under colonial rule the British exploited the Malayan hinterland, which was rich in tin and later would become a major site of the empire's rubber industry. Needing cheap labour, the British imported workers from China and India to mine the tin and work on the plantations. With independence achieved, the ethnic Malays, claiming indigenous (Bumiputera; sons of the soil) status, had their special privileges enshrined in the constitution, while the ethnic Chinese and Indians were 'graciously' given citizenship despite their *pendatang* (immigrant) roots. This, according to the history books, resulted in a multicultural Malaysia based upon harmonious compromise and tolerance (Cheah 2003; Shuib 2009).

In reality, an unofficial ethnic stratification was put into practice that saw Malays dominating public service, security and politics, while the Chinese focused primarily on economic pursuits with the Indians relegated to blue-collar labour (Noel 1968, 157). Moreover, non-Malay citizens are constantly reminded that Malaysia is *Tanah Melayu* (Malay Land) and that their citizenship is a privilege – not a right. Non-Malays are also told that they should be grateful to their Malay 'benefactors' through loyalty to the Sultans and to never question the ethnic status quo. This ethnic stratification is a legacy of British 'divide and rule' policy, which eventually led to over-emphasis on Malay primacy during the lead-up to independence. The contentious issue of anti-colonial resistance is also something that the history books have failed to adequately address.

Historically there have been several attempts by ethnic Malays at colonial resistance based around distinctive political ideologies or religious dogma. Some of the earliest anti-British activities can be traced back to 1874 with the signing of the Pangkor Treaty that saw aggressive expansion of British influence in Malaya and the beginning of an active Malay resistance (Nonini 1992,

62). These acts of colonial confrontation through passive non-cooperation lasted well into the twentieth century and greatly frustrated the British colonizers. Meanwhile, Chinese and Indian labourers were brought in to work the mines and plantations, and they too suffered under the exploitative colonial system. To seek redress, the migrant labourers turned to labour agitation and were often influenced by the rising communist ideology of the early twentieth century. Communism was brought to Malaya in the 1920s via Chinese Communist Party (CCP) members who founded the Nanyang Communist Party (NCP) to act as a branch of the CCP (Yong 1997). In 1930 the NCP was directed by the Communist International (Comintern) to be dissolved and replaced with the Malayan Communist Party (MCP) in order to prevent the CCP from extending its influence into Southeast Asia. The new Party's goals were anti-colonialism and independence through socialism and, unlike the NCP, it had Malay and Indian members. But the MCP was unable to operate fully due to effective British suppression. Most of its early members (all ethnic Chinese) were arrested, executed or deported to China. Despite this, the Party rose to prominence during the Japanese invasion of Malaya when they were trained and equipped by the Allies to fight the invaders. After World War II, the party was rewarded with semi-legal status by the returning British, which they fully exploited by instigating trade union strikes and work stoppages in the hope of forcing London to grant independence. The labour and economic unrest continued until the outbreak of the Malayan Emergency in 1948.

After three European estate managers were murdered allegedly by MCP agents, the colonial government declared a state of Emergency on 16 June 1948 and immediately outlawed the MCP. Its members were forced to escape to the jungles and began what the Party calls the 'anti-British war'. The British colonial government quickly racialized the Emergency, blaming the Chinese community for supporting communism and, by extension the CCP, who were at the time winning the Chinese Civil War in China (Hanrahan 1971, 30). After Malaya became independent in 1957, the nascent Federation of Malaya government inherited the anti-communist stance of their former colonial masters and viewed the Chinese community with suspicion, convinced that the insurgency was an ethnic-Chinese rebellion with foreign support. Although the war concluded in 1989 with the signing of the tripartite Haadyai Peace Agreement between the governments of Malaysia and Thailand with the MCP, fears of a resurgent communist movement in Malaysia lingers as demonstrated by government responses to the recent mass movements by non-governmental organizations (NGOs) in Malaysia calling for political reforms (Dol 2011). Despite revelations that significant numbers of leftist Malays had joined the party and formed an all-Malay guerrilla regiment, and that the current MCP chairman, Abdullah Che Dat, is also ethnic Malay, these facts still failed to deter popular apprehensions about the party's alleged anti-Malay agenda (Wong 2005).

With the Haadyai Peace Agreement, the long war between the MCP and the Malaysian government came to an end. As part of the agreement, the government of Thailand granted land near the Malaysia–Thai border to Party members, and these settlements are known today as the 'Peace Villages'. However, the Party retirees, mostly ethnic Chinese, still view themselves as undefeated simply because they never surrendered. While the Malaysian government was relieved to finally close a long and bloody chapter of the nation's history, the MCP has neither forgotten the past nor does it intend to stay silent about its own history and struggle. In the 25 years since the peace agreement, the Party has turned its focus to the welfare and well-being of its members by providing legal assistance for those who wish to return to Malaysia or by supporting those who wish to remain in the Peace Villages. The official support mechanism for the members is the 21OF, established by fellow retirees in 2001.

Social Memory, Collective Memory and Social Organizations

Roxana Waterson and Kwok Kian-Won (2012, 17) argue that memory is intrinsic to the construction of collective identities, just as memory is integral to the individual's sense of self. This is because memory is integrative as it links the past, the present and the future. It allows social groups to identify, frame and reconstruct their identities within related contexts and associations in an attempt to assert historical credibility. Additionally, 'social memory' functions within the collective consciousness, although one significant danger is that the accuracy and truth of events can become complicated over time. Social elements such as race, class and gender directly influence how individuals remember particular historical events and, consequently, memories are influenced by the groups they belong to (Olick 1999, 340). Therefore, memory distortions, omissions and fabrications are sometimes unavoidable; however, it is the need to preserve and transmit memory into the future that drives the commemorative efforts of social organizations today. Social organizations are a group of social positions connected by social relations and perform a social role. Within the context of veteran social organizations, it becomes critical to understand that the social memories brought forth by 21OF members are the only tangible links that connect the individual and the group, while at same time connecting the group to the broader society. Exploring these social groups and their internal and external links can potentially explain the importance of these groups to themselves, as well as their significance to the preservation of shared social memories within a society (i.e., Malaysia) and within an ideology (i.e., communism).

Although memories are constantly evolving phenomena, expressed differently in different times, in different locations and for different purposes, nonetheless they are also a unifying experience, tying and linking individuals into a group with a shared collective memory. This assertion is in agreement with Robert Bevan's theory of collective memory as a bundle of individual memories that coalesce by means of exchanges between people – exchanges that then develop into a communal narrative (Bevan, cited in Roth 2011, 58). Indeed, social organizations facilitate this exchange by providing a physical or virtual platform that enables social groups to select and organize representations of the past. Structured formally, social organizations preserve the collective memory by encouraging member participation in remembrance and commemoration activities designed to relive shared experiences. This also means that these social exchanges validate the memories carried by members and fleshes them out for internal and public consumption. This does not represent a purely performative memory at work, but rather is a consequence of exposing memory to the public, evoking emotive responses.

At the same time, Marianne Hirsch and Leo Spitzer (2010, xix) argue that the histories and narratives collected allow us to reflect on how memory and transmission work, to both reveal and conceal certain traumatic episodes, and on how incomplete the past can be. Social organizations are also sites of collective memory veneration and what Tessa Morris-Suzuki (2005, 22) calls an attempt 'to re-establish a personal connection with a vanishing heritage'. Pierre Nora (1996, 626) has traced the evolution of memories of the past in which he notices the current trend of commemoration that has replaced base historical interest. This is because subsequent generations are often driven by non-altruistic motivations that rely on speculative identification and understanding of memory. Maurice Halbwachs would argue that the main social categories that generate collective memory are religious community, social class and family (cited in Roth 2011, 60). It is into the social class that the 21OF falls, as it is a grouping of individuals whose shared experiences are what define them as a separate but unique collective.

The 21st Century Old Friends Association

Although the technically defunct MCP remains an outlawed political entity, it maintains a close network of support groups across Malaysia through the 21OF. Today, these associations service the scattered Party retirees in each state, but they were initially independent of each other although they maintained close contact for special events or joint celebrations. According to the

21OF webmaster, during the annual Family Day gathering in 2000 held in the state of Pulau Pinang, the idea to link these scattered groups with their old comrades in the Peace Villages under an umbrella organization was hatched by the retirees themselves.[2] This is because over the years since the peace agreement, many of their former comrades had lived all over Malaysia and some even settled abroad, making the task of keeping contact quite daunting. As a result, the 21OF was founded on New Year's Day 2001, designated a social organization. Its purpose, however, is to maintain fraternal links between members and to commemorate the Party's past struggles. The official website was launched in August 2006, giving the association an online presence.

Unlike contemporary anti-government and radical groups who employ social media to facilitate online resistance and the airing of political views, 21OF members mostly use social media to voice their views on the latest international crises while drawing attention to pressing domestic issues, such as commentaries on the Malaysian Education Blueprint (21OF 2013a) and the 21OF's support for moderation in Malaysia (21OF 2015). Due to national Internet laws that are unable to impact on the content of websites without infringing upon issues of net neutrality and freedom of information, the website exists in a legal grey area. This is because despite the Malaysian government's explicit anti-communist stance (even after the signing of the Peace Agreement), enforcement of said policies seems to not have extended to the Internet. At the same time, the website sidesteps controversy by avoiding communist symbolism and imagery in its presentations and, instead projects, itself as a special-interest group. This may have provided the association and its website some measure of immunity from persecution. According to eight retired party members I interviewed, the 21OF is the central fraternity for MCP retirees, and the website is merely meant to present their side of history. So far, the 21OF website has not attracted the Malaysian government's attention, and there have been no attempts to censor or block access to it.

According to the 21OF webmaster, the reason that the website is in Mandarin only is because this has been the main language used in the Party, despite the broader Malaysian Chinese community speaking a wide variety of dialects. Although the Party maintained it has consistently promoted ethnic equality, it is an interesting anachronism to have an exclusively Mandarin-language website in Malay-dominated Malaysia. Interviews with the 21OF members have indicated that language is of secondary concern even to their Malay comrades because ideology is the unifying element of the Party. They

---

2   The webmaster is one of the hundreds of Party retirees allowed to return to Malaysia. He mostly manages the online component of the 21OF.

further claim that cultural or religious differences are no barriers to unity and harmony within the Party. Furthermore, since all Marxist education materials were imported from China, it is more pragmatic to employ Mandarin as the Party's language. It should be noted, however, that Malay-language translations are provided where possible.

The 21OF Website and Its Objectives

The website's self-described purpose is dual: to inform and to educate the (mainly Malaysian) public. The website claims that one of its key purposes is to rectify the history of Malaysia and Singapore, which had long been twisted by British colonialists (21OF 2014a). The other core objective of the website is to share collected historical materials with the public and to welcome history aficionados and researchers to objectively study the struggles of those who they believe fought for the nation's independence and the people's democracy. Curiously, the website also claims that they are unaffiliated with any political parties or community organizations. Upon my query, the webmaster simply reiterates this disclaimer without further elaboration. This seems disingenuous because, firstly, this is an official website for Party retirees to keep abreast of latest developments affecting them and fellow comrades; and, secondly, it is the 'go-to place' for official MCP information in the form of uploaded documents, essays, articles, sound recordings and video clips.

The website consists of three sections: the blog (部落格), the monument (纪念碑) and the wiki section (维基资料库). The blog contains news article links and opinion pieces written by contributors who are also Party retirees and have returned to Malaysia as civilians. The monument section lists the names of 'martyrs' (烈士) and is organized into the four major periods of the party: pre-World War II (1930–1940), the Anti-Japanese War (1941–1945), the Anti-British War (1948–1957), and Post-Independence (1958 onwards). The bulk of the website is the wiki section. This section was built using the Wikipedia template and contains the most extensive information on the Party to date. The data available there is currently the only MCP counter-narrative to the official government narrative of the counter-insurgency war in Malaya/Malaysia, and its value to researchers is self-evident despite being laced with hagiographic elements. This is a meticulously updated section with the latest 21OF news announcements, such as upcoming book releases, obituaries and links to articles related to the party and to Malaysian politics in general.

Under the Perspective (视角) sub-section, Party retirees post opinion pieces on domestic and global issues, including criticisms the West (namely the United States and its allies), under artistically inspired and often whimsical pseudonyms such as Ocean (海), Mountain (方山) and River (川) while peppering their statements with praise and admiration for the Party's years of struggle and the Party leadership, especially Chin Peng, the late MCP secretary general. The 13 October 2013 article commemorating the late Party leader's passing is entitled, 'Asleep in the Glorious Memory of the Masses–Condolences From Afar', and illustrates the website's hagiographic slant (21OF 2013b). Blog contributors such as 'Mountain' and 'Ocean' adopt rhetoric typical of many hard-line leftist Chinese journals in which criticisms of Western capitalism, free enterprise, democracy, gender issues and labour rights of the world appear daily, and in substantial form. However, Malaysian issues form the bulk of the writings with opinion pieces discussing headline news events, such as the controversy surrounding the 2013 Malaysian General Election or the Malaysian Ministry of Education's controversial Education Blueprint 2015–2025, which allegedly will erode vernacular education in all national schools. Otherwise, the articles can be read as a socialist opinion editorial column coloured with extensive anti-Western views.

One of the most valuable and distinctive sections of the website is the 'Historical Data Downloads' (21OF 2014b) section. Here, selected rare and out-of-print books discussing the anti-Japanese and anti-British wars have been scanned and posted online. This section also contains a plethora of primary sources such as collected internal Party files never before translated or captured by government forces. For example, minutes of a meeting from before the outbreak of the Malayan Emergency can be found here, thus allowing the public to glean the Party's motives prior to the armed struggle. Essays, short stories and other works of literature by the more learned members of the Party have been uploaded here as well. According to the webmaster and other interviewees, the availability of these documents reasserts the Party's policy of openness following the end of the struggle. In fact, they claim that the MCP no longer wishes to hide from the world because to do so is counter-productive to their goal of claiming their rightful place in Malaysian history.

As political outsiders, the MCP retirees as 21OF members are now better able to participate in the national debate on contemporary issues through the online publication of their writings. This is fascinating considering the Party's strict secrecy since the outbreak of the insurgency in 1948. Hardly any writing by Party members surfaced until recently, with the surprise revelation that the late MCP secretary general, Chin Peng, had not only released a memoir but had actually spoken to scholars in Australia about his exploits and the Party. This was the beginning of a renewed interest in the Malayan Communists. As such, the 21OF website is simply the next logical step in ensuring their voice is heard online by the public. This time, however, they could do so without fear of censorship and persecution. Social media and the digital century has become the new battleground for the MCP retirees to draw attention to their past struggles.

Relevance of the 21OF

It is no secret that the 21st Century Old Friends Association seeks to justify the sacrifices of the Malayan Communist Party by portraying it as a nationalist and anti-colonial organization. This is achieved through effective projection of their purpose as a bridge or platform that enables historical connectivity between the old comrades and the general public, while at the same time acts as a source of knowledge for visitors to gain some 'historical sense-generation'. Rusen (2012, 45) defines historical sense-generation as the mental procedure in which the past is interpreted to make sense of the present and to anticipate the future. In essence, rather than attempting to convince or persuade visitors of the righteousness of the party, the 21OF website posits questions that get visitors to consider the Party's connection with Malaysian history and historicity. In other words, the website hopes to provoke critical evaluation of historical events that still reverberate today, such as the controversial issue surrounding Chin Peng's death. Malay right-wing groups and certain circles within the Malaysian government still vehemently oppose allowing his ashes to be brought back to Malaysia on the grounds that to do so would lead to the 'terrorist' leader's martyrdom (Chik 2013). Value judgments notwithstanding, one of the core functions of the website is to connect visitors to history whether or not they are consciously aware of it. No doubt, history is fundamental to the ways individuals think about themselves; through the website, the 21OF strives to enable public understanding of how they view themselves and the world. Looking at Malaysian history through the lens of the 21OF, one may be surprised to discover they are not as moribund as previously thought by scholars and the Malaysian public. Examples of their vibrancy can be seen at the annual gatherings and activities organized by the 21OF in the Peace Villages and in Kuala Lumpur, which are advertised on the website.

Within the context of the communist armed struggle, the contest between historical consciousness and formal history has created a divergence in the Malaysian historical tapestry. This in turn has resulted in the story of Malaysia's official history becoming exclusive and skewed, principally a tool to support the current rulers (Hunter 2013). The 21OF sought to address this captive national narrative by presenting themselves as the keepers of lost Malayan history – keepers who 'won' the armed struggle by refusing to fade into obscurity. Secondly, the association's website takes advantage of the current surge of interest in the Party by the Malaysian public by offering their interpretation of the events that led to the country's independence.

Danger of Challenging the Malaysian National Narrative

The official story of Malaysia's founding is predicated on unity, compromise and tolerance between the Malays, the ethnic Chinese and the Indians during the drafting of the Federation Constitution. In reality, non-Malays were seen and continue to be seen, as unwelcomed immigrants. The inclusion of ethnic Chinese and Indians in the constitution and the granting of their citizenship were done reluctantly in the interest of gaining independence as soon as possible. As a result, the deconstruction of Malaysia's founding 'myth' has been a focus of the 21OF website.

At the same time, academics and military veterans from Malaysia and Great Britain continue to endorse this 'myth' and defend it as a model for developing the concept of 'unity among diversity' (Shuib 2009, 91, 98). The persisting narrative states that ethnic compromise, or social contract (for lack of a better term), was instrumental in paving the way to nation building. Advocates of 'the roads not taken' (referring to the alternative constitutional proposal by the left-leaning AMCJA–PUTERA coalition), such as disgruntled members of the public and political activists are attempting to draw some political advantage out of this 'lost' history to further their own cause. Historian John Tosh (2008, 6) cautions against the convergence of popular history and official 'History' in that there is a difference between thinking about history and being immersed in and influenced by the past. In this context, Malaysian political opposition groups are courting disaster whenever they invoke the communist past to garner support for their agenda. This is because in the past the Malaysian government has abundantly demonstrated its willingness to exercise wide-ranging powers to silence any presumed challenges to its legitimacy, and does so always in the name of 'peace and stability'.

Online Communism in the Age of Social Media

On the surface, it seems that the MCP retirees are stubbornly holding on to the last vestiges of their struggle, and that the 21OF website is an attempt to ride contemporary cultural and social trends. I believe, however, that this is not the case. Rather, the website seems to be a virtual extension of the association's platform for collective remembrance. The articles and blog posts reflect a subdued, conciliatory tone – a dramatic transformation from the angry revolutionary rhetoric of the pre-1989 MCP. While the site has many criticisms of the government, none of the writings exhort rebellion or promote violent uprisings against the Government of Malaysia. The site does not present any overt or covert subversive messages, but rather a frustration and displeasure at the current political situation, abundantly expressed within the Chinese cultural context of 'speaking out against injustice' (打抱不平) for the people. The non-confrontational attitude of the 21OF website can be explained as a form of collective self-renewal, which Dennis Jaffe (1985, 103) defines as a response to the traumatic experiences of war. Regardless, the association and website are often referenced by individual Mandarin-language Facebook users and social groups, such as the Malaysian Chinese Forum (Malaysia 2014) and independent online discussion groups such as Malaysia Chinese Net (Malaysia 2005). To date, there has been no other website with more authority and with a more comprehensive database on the MCP than the 21OF website. This has meant it has become a major resource contributing to the discourse on Malayan Communism and its history.

It is the MCP's aim to convey the truth as they remember it, while surreptitiously avoiding addressing any atrocities committed during the armed struggle. The main political and social themes that emerge in political discourse around the website are related to timing, social capital and a new beginning. Enough time had passed since the end of hostilities that the retired and elderly Malayan communists felt they could rejoin mainstream society in the form of a veteran association dedicated to peace in Malaysia rather than as resurgent malcontents.

Nonetheless, the 21OF's attempts to cast itself – and by extension the MCP – as ardent nationalists and not hardcore Maoist rebels (doing so by means of projecting a counter-narrative through its website) are no longer mere historical curiosities limited to academia and special-interest groups. With increasing political activism among contemporary Malaysians since the retirement of former Prime Minister Mahathir Mohamad in 2003, there has been a growing interest in the history of the old Malayan left. Of particular interest to the activists is the 1946–1948 interregnum when the MCP attempted to influence Malaya's future via constitutional means by infiltrating the left-leaning All-Malaya Council of Joint Action–Pusat Tenaga Rakyat (AMCJA–PUTERA) alliance.

In 1946, AMCJA–PUTERA authored the People's Constitutional Proposal as an alternative to the British-supported Constitutional Proposals for Malaya (Yeoh 1973, 320). The British saw the leftist alliance as mere facades for the MCP and summarily ignored their proposal. However, with the Emergency regulations in effect following the outbreak of the armed struggle, communists, leftists and their sympathizers were arrested en masse, and the alliance was dissolved. Nonetheless, disappointment at the continuing political reign of the ruling National Front (also known as BN or *Barisan Nasional*) alliance, coupled with greater political awakening among the new generation of Malaysians, led to a desire for an 'alternative' political ideology to replace it (Noor 2012). Additionally, the 2013 general elections saw a surge of interest in leftist ideology, and this was also evident in excited online discussions on the 'rediscovered' People's Constitutional Proposal of 1946. But there has been no overt declaration for communism among Malaysians, as elements of the old Emergency regulations are still in effect – although subtle respect for the MCP does exist among opposition political parties such as the Socialist party of Malaysia (Devaraj 2011). This has forced dialogue regarding the MCP and its legacy to be held at the national level, albeit fraught with controversies. The topic still remains a taboo in the public sphere, and when Chin Peng's death mistakenly thought to coincide with Malaysia Day (15 September 2013) it sparked further debate that drew proponents from both sides of the political spectrum to engage in a war of words via social media.

Although, strangely, the 21OF website has neither a forum nor a chat room to allow direct interaction between Party retirees and visitors, it does have an abundance of editorials, opinion pieces and other original texts. It is here that visitors are intimately confronted with the frustrations of the retirees, who see the homeland they proclaim to love suffer continuous crises due to the tumultuous state of Malaysian politics. This feeling is captured in a quote by a Peace Village retiree who told me that he hoped his comrades' writings will raise the Malaysian people's awareness of the need for political reform and progressiveness by moving away from communal-based politics:

> I hope my more learned comrades' articles could make the people support reform and support progressiveness. Ethnic politics will hurt everyone eventually. (Lao Jiang)[3]

Nevertheless, this unease and worry for the future of Malaysia is not restricted to the Malaysian Chinese community but encompasses all other ethnic communities as well. The 21OF website supports this by posting these writings on the blog with the hope of igniting further understanding from the public.

The 21OF and Malaysian Memory

In Malaysia, there is a successfully constructed unitary and coherent version of the past. In fact, an entire generation of citizens has grown up convinced the version of history being taught in schools is the only plausible version. According to James Wertsch (2002, 125), this perpetuation and promotion of

---

3   Lao Jiang (老江) is one of several retirees I interviewed in the Peace Village in Betong. Despite his advanced age, he is keenly aware of current affairs in Malaysia and Singapore and his mind is as sharp as ever.

a singular version of history is a hallmark of collective memory manipulation in which the dogmatic commitment to one – and only one – account persists. This is because the national collective memory is constructed to ignore all discrepancies and irregularities. Museums, national commemoration days and propaganda activities disguised as informal education have been used to script the Malaysian government's version of history, and with devastating effectiveness. Countries such as Japan, China and Singapore are notorious for doing the same: whitewashing any parts deemed unfavourable to the regime. This has meant that suppression of alternate experiences, perspectives and interpretations must be carried out, especially those that feature the historical actors.

Due to Malaysia's national narrative, which denies the MCP's contribution to modern Malaysia, any definitive description or assessment of communism's role in the nation is not only impossible to ascertain but also triggers knee-jerk reactions by the Malaysian government, which perceives such queries as imagined subversive threats. This is where the 21OF and its website come into play. The association's unique status as a social organization and the website as an online resource centre are helping to build an official narrative of the Party without limits imposed by government censors. More importantly, the website is projecting itself as a historical research entity that is not espousing communist ideology, making it harmless to online watchdogs. The website actually strives to 'set the record straight' on behalf of the MCP once and for all, doing justice to both surviving and deceased Party members as well as to Malaysian historiography. Therefore, the knowledge presented by the website is valuable to scholars and to the public because the social memory of communism is still being preserved, a memory that allows objective interpretations of its ideology to be reached.

Issues with the National Narrative

When analysing the archived MCP documents from the 21OF website, it became apparent that the national narrative is incomplete and deeply flawed. Although the moralizing tone and 'factual' descriptions of the MCP documents may not guarantee its public acceptance, it needs to undergo what Keith Jenkins (1991, 33) calls 'interpretative understanding' before it can be meaningful. For example, among the numerous documents, common themes such as full national independence and breaking away from foreign influences into Malaya's economy and sovereignty are ubiquitous. Yet, these MCP objectives must be understood within the temporal context when they were created. During the period of undefined national identity following the end of World War II, Malaya was slowly edging towards nationhood, yet it was unclear what form the new nation should take. The MCP provided their solution, believing that it was the best recourse given the economic, societal and political turmoil of the time. It was rejected by the British in favour of a pro-British communal alliance led by the conservative Malay political party UMNO (United Malays National Organization). In essence, it is insufficient to simply label communism as 'evil', 'illegitimate', or 'traitorous' just because its message clashes with the Malaysian master narrative. The conservative attitude of the Malaysian government, a vestige inherited from British colonialism, discourages active discourse on communism save to propagate the same anti-communist rhetoric that has served the regime well over the last five decades.

However, it must be noted that official national narratives are insulated from the challenges of contradictions, paradoxes and other alternative interpretations of the past due to its privileged status as the 'master' narrative. Hannah Arendt (2006, 241) agrees with this when she said: '[T]he modes of thought and communication that deal with truth are necessarily domineering; they don't take into account other people's opinions'. Admitting the contradictions in the national narrative, no matter how trivial, has dire consequences for the ruling elite. Hence, their version must be stubbornly defended, no matter how erroneous it may be. Therefore, using public notions of morality and rational discourse in constructing the national narrative is insufficient to reconstruct the entire history. It is understood that the process of creating official national narratives is grounded on political processes that support the national identity. Nonetheless, this process unfairly denies alternative social meanings and ways of constructing visions of the past. Although the Malaysian Ministry of Education's official version of history offers one of many excellent insights into Malaya/Malaysia's past, it fails to take fully into account that creating and maintaining narratives of social memory is essentially an incomplete and lifelong work-in-progress.

Demonizing Communism in Malaya/Malaysia

Attaching a value quantifier to communism is problematic, as it signifies an acknowledgement of the MCP's moral position as 'glorious victims' now that the war had ended. This is because the Malaysian government argues that communism was an alien ideological order that is inherently incompatible with the peaceful nature of Malaysians (Khoo 2010, 261). The 21OF website instead argues that communism enjoyed wide support before the Emergency or was, at the least, not outright rejected by the Malayan people (He 2014).

Scholars have described the Party as a social and historical menace that threatens the multi-ethnic 'harmony' of Malaysian society (Cheah 2002; Noor 2002; Amoroso 2003). Their arguments are predicated on the MCP as a foreign (read Chinese) subversive force that threatens the peace and 'ethnic harmony' of the nation. As a result, we are presented with a version of history that is equally heavy-handed in its judgment and in its analysis of Malaya/Malaysia's relationship with communism. To address this imbalanced historiography, the bulk of knowledge available from the website could be used to reconstruct representations of Malayan communist history. especially since it contains a mixture of experiences and insights that originate from the immediate participants. Previously established narratives from the victorious side of the war could then be co-opted to become the mirror narrative that both augments and enhances the new history of the communists and communism in Malaya/Malaysia by offering diametrically opposite perspectives. The modality proposed here is therefore based on accepting the Party retirees' lived experiences and narratives as genuine and that its inclusion into mainstream historical tapestry must be done via reconciliation.

Sharing Communist Life Stories Online

It can be argued that the lived experience constituting the narratives that make up a life story calls into question issues of morality, justice, and so forth. The core issue is not how the life story was remembered and chronicled, but rather the subject matter that is being questioned. It should not be surprising that moral and political tensions were triggered when the public first learned of the association's existence. Furthermore, the life stories of Party retirees being shared on the website leads to two dilemmas: How do the narratives reconcile with what is being disseminated by the government's propaganda machine? And how can the history of a notorious period be accepted without inviting political repercussions? These questions naturally lead to contention on the impact of communism on Malaya/Malaysia. Unfortunately, such open discourse is controversial, to say the least. But on the other hand, it is safe to say that the communist 'threat' can only be experienced as a lived experience formed by various forms of witnessing, testimonies and other public sources of memory (Santasombat 1998, 67). Whether any tangible threat exists is up to the individual to decide. Coming to terms with this controversial past can only come from both sides of the conflict. The 21OF website, therefore, is ideal for facilitating the sharing of collective memory that may eventually lead to long-term understanding through offering evidence of different versions of events.

Public Reactions to the MCP

Public opinions sampled from online news portals reflect the divisive attitude in Malaysia over the MCP's legacy. One contributor to *The Malaysian Insider* wrote shortly after Chin Peng's passing that despite struggling to liberate the nation from colonialism, the Malayan communist insurgency 'was unable to integrate itself with the value of nationalism', while noting that communists in China and Vietnam were treated much differently (Khoo 2013). On *New Straits Times Online*, a commentator called the MCP 'a group of traitors', and Chin Peng was their leader who died a traitor's death (Sabri 2013). The disparity in viewpoints is neither inherent nor spontaneous, but merely reflections from the entrenched conservatism of segments of the Malaysian public versus the emerging counter-culture of political opposition groups embracing anti-BN political attitudes. To confound matters, these contributors are ethnic Chinese and Malay, respectively.

There is also a striking and intriguing phenomenon at work in which BN opponents seem to hold a 'nostalgic' view of the MCP. In fact, PSM Central Committee Member, Jeyakumar Devaraj (2011), stated in a blog post on the PSM website that he sees the MCP leaders as freedom fighters, and that they were committed to an independent Malaysia. The 21OF made no mention of this on their news or blog sections, however. On the other hand, genuine respect for the Party's vision for a different Malaya/Malaysia should not be confused with uninformed worship of communist ideology. Whereas official Malaysian expectation is based around a shared moral national valuation of the social memory of communism, the highly contested nature of memory must also be taken into account. This can be seen from the intense debates raging within the public sphere in regard to addressing the communist past. In the context of the 21OF website, the vitriolic statements attacking the MCP are bereft of educated reasoning which, as a result, conjures the image of a divided public sphere dominated by irrational fear of communist dominance.

Perils of Remembering Malayan Communism

For researchers, there is no 'nostalgia' for communism aside from the fascination of uncovering long-hidden or lost memories of the period. In fact, the dominant narrative that coloured and guided Malaysian social consciousness does not tolerate dissent or criticism. With the existence of the 21OF and, more importantly, its website, uncomfortable questions began to emerge that both the British and Malaysian government are reluctant to face. Nostalgia for the communist past is currently being abused by Malaysian leftists and oppositional groups in an attempt to (erroneously) invoke days when political freedoms were not curtailed as strongly. But as David Lowenthal (1989, 21) argued, nostalgia is both a 'generic' explanatory category and a description of a temporal orientation, a veiled desire to search for a 'simple and stable past as a refuge from the turbulent and chaotic present'. This is dangerous because it is predicated on an assumed or constructed idealism that never existed. At the same time, nostalgia risks falsifying the past and threatens the present. Nonetheless, the 21OF and its website is not dedicated to cultivating celebratory nostalgic feelings that may run counter to those who embrace the communist past as a form of regressive utopian stance, longing for an idealized past (Pickering and Keightley 2006, 919). This 'passive escapism' of nostalgia for communism cannot address the general discontentment of the Malaysian public. The 21OF and its website do not carry nor reflect an affirmative solution for current ills of Malaysian society. The most they could provide is a prayer and hope for a better future, although they may still criticize and accuse.

At the same time, the 21OF website came into existence because there was a need to make the aging retirees' presence known to the world as well as to act as a digital depository to safeguard their writings. The website's function is to preserve the collective memory of the MCP and to direct its members toward obtaining, maintaining or changing their own social status or the status of the group. In other words, the members themselves are representations of the past. The collective memory contained in digital form on the 21OF website is a knowledge base assembled from social actors who intentionally and strategically produced 'documents of memory' in relation to their past, their current identity and their political legitimacy. The online availability of the digitized materials encourages debate and facilitates greater public participation in the discussion. The new trend of social media will then deconstruct the standard historical medium of history books into fragmented pieces consisting of party documents, statements, testimonials, memoirs, biographies and so forth. These memories are linked under the shared experiences of the old comrades, experiences that are also the collective memories of the Party.

Reconstructing the Silenced Memory

The production of memory in the form of documents and recordings construes only half of the greater field of collective memory. The mere act of accessing these memories means members of the public are interacting with the producers of memory, which in turn contributes to the shared representation of the past. If these memories are accepted, then this makes the producers members of that particular community of memory (Arthur 2008, 7). No doubt the MCP memories will evoke feelings of unease, confusion or hostility from the public and especially from the government. As the Malaysian people mature politically, there will be a growing need to revisit the nation's past and come to terms with its contentiousness. Unfortunately, this exercise is rejected as revisionism by the BN regime, and the mere act of questioning the past concatenates on issues of the Malays' special privileges, which in turn is tantamount to sedition. In reality, the rejection is an attempt to demarcate and define the communists as the alien 'other' that has no place in the national narrative. But this has inadvertently created a spectacle of manipulating the national narrative, creating what Michel Foucault (1977, 161) calls 'a concerted carnival' of history.

Unfortunately, the line between history and memory is a fuzzy one, and for the history of Malaysia it is much more pertinent. E. J. Hobsbawm (1987, 3) defined this fuzzy line as a twilight zone in which 'the past as a generalized record which is open to relatively dispassionate inspection and the past as a remembered part of, or background to, one's own life'. Malaysian history books today depict the past as a world of moral clarity, with the independence struggle, especially, described as a self-evident alignment with the democratic West and away from tyrannical communist (read Chinese) domination. But from the historical narratives uploaded to the 21OF website, two things emerge: the moral currency of the British for fighting the guerrillas is suspect, and the MCP may not have been as hardcore as previously thought. The Malayan communist narratives claim that the British were harsh in their treatment of the Malayan people during the war, often committing atrocities such as murder, rape and robbery under the guise of crushing the MCP and their sympathizers. The narratives also reveal the strong anti-colonial and pro-independence stance of the MCP which, despite its name, was more focused on national liberation than on communist revolution. The Batang Kali incident, for example, in which 24 innocent villagers were gunned down in cold blood by a platoon of the Scots Guards under the pretext of being MCP sympathizers, is decried by the website as a war crime (21OF 2008). Yet the soldiers never faced court martial, and all British government inquiries quietly ceased, despite the perpetrators having publicly admitted their involvement. In Malaysian history books, the Batang Kali massacre is unsurprisingly not mentioned. Hence, within a unique event, the contrary roles of hero and criminal are inextricably entwined, intersecting within Hobsbawm's twilight zone of memory and history.

In retrospect, the MCP armed struggle seems to have been the latest in a series of anti-colonial uprisings since the arrival of the Portuguese in 1511, except for its distinctive objectives and ideology. Yet, the communists are reviled much more because they clashed with the national narrative, challenged the ethnically driven *social contract* and were predominantly ethnic Chinese. Nonetheless, it was not the fear of communism that forced the conservative Malays to reject the MCP; rather it was the fear of cultural contamination and domination by the immigrant Chinese that drove the Malays to support British plans for Malaya's independence.

Lingering Communist Threats to the Social Contract

As mentioned previously, enshrining Malay primacy (*Ketuanan Melayu*) is paramount in Malaysia, but it is done at the expense of other ethnic communities. The quid pro quo social contract 'stipulates' Malay entitlement in political and administrative authority to be unchallenged in return for Chinese dominance of the economy. Since the MCP is against such a non-egalitarian agreement, the communists were naturally seen by Malay conservatives as traitors. Moreover, when taking into account Chin Peng's ethnicity and images of *ethnic Chinese* guerrillas in uniforms and wielding firearms, the link between communism and ethnicity can be conveniently forged to devastating effect. At the same time, the British '*Tuan*' (Malay for master or lord) who, before the insurgency, was the hated foreign interloper, suddenly became the venerated benefactor and protector, heroically defending the Malays and their land from the marauding Chinese communist 'terrorists'. This stemmed from British policy of recognizing the Malays as the sole inheritors of the land (**B**umiputera) and viewing the other ethnic communities as transient. Although the policy was technically defunct with the Federation of Malaya Constitutional Proposal of 1957, the inclusion of provisions guaranteeing the special position of the Malays effectively maintained the racialized status quo and divided the nation through reverse affirmative action.

Thus, the political elites and conservatives of Malaysia's maintenance of the perennial provisions do not provide an avenue for reconciliation but, instead, divide the nation ethnically and stunt social development. At the same time, there is a resurgence of interest in communism; it has been triggered by the passing of Chin Peng. This led the Malaysian government to quickly suppress materials deemed 'sensitive' or 'seditious' (Shankar and Woon 2013). But as more writings and party documents surface through the 21OF website, that troubled past will not diminish, but has been strengthened as a result. As long as the memory remains, there will always be a need to address it, or history will remain fractured and incomplete.

Mechanisms and Controversies of Social Media Control in Malaysia

Until the death of former MCP secretary general Chin Peng on 16 September 2013, terms associated with the Party and communism were never buzzwords within the social networks. But once news broke of Malaysian Public Enemy No.1's demise, all manners of discussions related to the elderly revolutionary mushroomed overnight through social media. Facebook and Twitter were abuzz with emerging details of the circumstances surrounding his death, while various instant messaging applications disseminated the news to those unaware of it. In a matter of days, topics related to communism were excitedly discussed, debated and dissected by netizens in Malaysia and the world. Noticeably, following the furore over this arguably historic affair, the Malaysian government did not attempt to ban or censor online discussions of the Party and its late leader. They did make it clear, though, that Chin Peng is still not forgiven, nor is communist ideology welcomed in Malaysia (Kaur 2013; Brown 2016). The rapidity with which the news circulates speaks volumes about the reach and impact of social media in Malaysia and, coupled with the lack of active governmental restrictions, this new medium has become the latest digital congregation of minds. Moreover, the rate at which the topic of the day dominates the virtual sphere essentially discloses the potency of social media as well as its addictiveness to Malaysian netizens, whose number and mastery over the medium will only advance over time.

One of the most direct effects of the continuous penetration of Internet accessibility in Malaysia is the rapidly growing number of social media users. This evolving trend is no doubt supported by the affordability of smartphones and tablet computers on top of 'traditional' forms of Internet access – namely desktop and laptop computers – which offers an incredible level of user-friendliness and portability. Moreover, social media applications (apps) with their simplified interface and forgiving controls make online interactions convenient, effortless. This in turn allows anyone from pre-teens to senior citizens to connect and share their thoughts with the world in an intimate level unseen in the previous century. Naturally, opposition politicians, critics, and activists find this situation ideal for their purposes as nothing is able to reach the public so widely and immediately as the ubiquitous social media. Consequently, the Malaysian government have every reason to be wary of this new media, for it is unable to fully control distribution or completely police the people's free exchange of ideas. Both netizens and the government are keenly aware of the unrestricted freedom social media provides. Dissenters and political opposition thrive online, as it is utilized as an alternative medium of expression, free of government oversight and manipulation (Liu 2014, 45).

One prime example of social media's potency in Malaysia can be seen during the lead-up to the 2013 Malaysian General Election and the various *Bersih* ('clean', in Malay, which here refers to the rallies of the non-governmental organization known as the Coalition for Free and Fair Elections) rallies. It was through apps such as Whatsapp, LINE, WeChat, Instagram and popular social networking websites such as Facebook and Twitter that the organizers were able to rally supporters quickly, while at the same time instantly publicizing the event worldwide. The result was a massive turnout in support of electoral change in Malaysia (Roughneen 2011; *Malay Mail* Online,

2015). But social media is a double-edged sword, as pro-government supporters utilized the same method in organizing counter-protests, albeit with some degree of success. The *Himpunan Rakyat Bersatu* (Assembly of the United People), commonly known as the 'Red Shirt' rally after the organizer's choice of red clothing to contrast *Bersih* supporters' yellow T-shirts, was launched on 16 September 2015. The rally was chiefly led and organized by extreme right elements within the ruling UMNO party, who reached out to supporters via similar methods, exhorting Malays to participate in the name of 'defending *hak Melayu* (Malay Rights)'. Interestingly, following warnings from the government, the websites and posts inciting Malays to turn out in droves in a 'show of force' seemingly disappeared (Bernama 2015). These rallies were powered by the extreme convenience and relatively little-to-no cost to utilize the apps. This fact has made social media a part of daily existence for many Malaysians, and as long as these conditions remain true, social media users will be able to connect with one another online, sharing and spreading ideas and views freely and without fear.

The Malaysian Communications and Multimedia Commission (MCMC) is the government agency tasked with policing Internet usage in Malaysia, and its mandate has been to curb fear-mongering and the spread of hate and disharmony by irresponsible individuals or groups. Often, these 'disrupting' elements of society are critical of the government, which leads to online censorship or legal action being taken against them. Yet, the Malaysian government has had experience in battling its critics in the online battlefield. Dubbed 'cyber troopers', pro-government social media groups such as the 1Malaysia Social Media Volunteers (myVO1CE) or the Sensible and Ethical Malaysians United Troopers (Semut) are used to 'trawl' (to use the fishery term) the Internet for comments considered to be seditious to the powers in Putrajaya (Case 2015, 12). The modus operandi of the 'troopers' would be to highlight the 'offenders' and file lawsuits in the name of defending the good names of Malaysia and its government. These 'social media troopers' are essentially thinly veiled government apparatuses operating under the guise of vigilantism and in the name of 'patriotism'.

But the Malaysian government has taken direct action against websites that purportedly cast the nation and its leaders in negative light, and this trend seems to be on the rise since 2015. Following an article that alleged Prime Minister Najib Tun Razak's administration was corrupt and guilty of embezzlement of the nation's sovereign fund, the *Asia Sentinel* news website was blocked to users from Malaysia. This came after the banning of investigative news website, the *Sarawak Report*, which has been carrying out an exposé of the alleged widespread financial scandal involving the prime minister and his cronies (Malaysiakini 2016). *The Malaysian Insider*

(TMI), another popular Malaysian online news website, was banned by the MCMC on 25 February 2016 for 'national security' reasons (*The Malaysian Insider* 2016a). This has led to intense speculation online that the critical investigative approach by *The Malaysian Insider* journalists had triggered the ban. TMI has vowed to continue to report the truth, regardless of the ban. In contrast to its liberal attitude towards social media, local online news outlets seem to be the target of tightening suppression, with the London-based *Sarawak Report* being the only foreign news website banned. On the other hand, the US-based *Wall Street Journal* has published a number of critical pieces on Prime Minister Najib and the ongoing 1MDB sovereign fund scandal since 2015 but has yet to suffer repercussions aside from the prime minister threatening to sue the news company for 'criminal defamation' (*The Star* Online 2015).

The government's egregious attempts to silence critics have been met with equally aggressive resistance, leading to a stalemate that at times is lively and restive. Denial-of-service attacks and defamation suits by the government became frequent at the cost of international condemnation of curtailing civil liberties and free speech (Gray 2013). This condemnation has not deterred the government, which sees 'keyboard warriors' (moniker for online activists) as serving selfish interests when posting their 'lies' online with the intention to incite (*The Malaysian Insider* 2016b). The political opposition responded by continuing its criticisms and challenging the legality of government suppression by mobilizing its own 'cyber troopers' to voice its dissent (Shukry 2013). Former Malaysian prime minister, Mahathir Mohamad, can be considered another social media 'trooper' whose criticism of the government has captured the Malaysian people's imagination. In the last several years, Mahathir's blog has been a platform of grievances and disapproval that focuses on scandals and crises that plague current Prime Minister Najib Tun Razak's administration. Mahathir's comments have garnered so much public attention that the government has made subtle threats to investigate him or censor his blog. To the former statesman's supporters, who flocked to his 'banner' to support his condemnation of the current government's faults and failures, any attempts to arrest or legally harass him will signal the severe erosion of his prestige and political clout which, in turn, signifies the end of free speech for social media users. Despite the situation, the former prime minister has vowed to continue to speak out, claiming it his constitutional right to do so. Ironically, Mahathir disapproved of criticism during his own premiership, as seen when he ordered the shutdown of several newspapers for a year following the publication of pro-opposition articles in the 1980s.

At the moment, Malaysian social media and its users are at the mercy of the government. But until more draconian measures are fully implemented, online civil liberties still prevail to a certain degree, and Malaysian netizens will continue to exercise their rights to dissent and to criticize until such time as they are muzzled by the censors. Although the MCMC has announced it will not restrict social media access, there are plans to take sterner actions against social media 'abusers' along with wider, but not clearly defined, 'specific powers' being granted to authorities to block websites (*The Malaysian Insider* 2015; Naidu 2016). It remains to be seen how far the Malaysian government will tolerate dissent and criticism. But time is running out, and so far only website bans upon requests from law enforcement agencies have been carried out by the MCMC. Time will tell if Malayan Emergency-era restrictions on free speech will return once more to silence those deemed 'enemies of the state' – just as the Malayan communists were once the target.

Conclusion

Despite having endured hardship, first as rag-tag guerrillas and later as social outcasts living in the Thai–Malaysia borderlands, the retired Malayan Communist Party members have over the last 25 years successfully carved out a place for themselves in the new millennium thanks to the advent of social media. Although deemed irrelevant since 1989, the Party's resurgence as a popular topic among netizens is an example of cunning adaptation into current social trends. By staking an online presence, the Party, through the 21OF and its website, successfully prevented obscurity and instead has ensured its longevity in the public conscience. On the other hand, the 21OF website is also a tool to project the retirees' devotion to Malaya/Malaysia by sharing their thoughts through their writings. Most importantly, it is a site of remembrance and commemoration for and by both the living and the departed. Nonetheless, their status as political minorities often intertwines with their ethnicity (the majority of Party members are ethnic Chinese), despite their objective to be a true multi-ethnic movement. As one Party retiree told me, it was happenstance that the Chinese community was the most eager to support anti-colonial efforts because they suffered the most under British rule.

As Dennis Walder (2009, 938) argued, it is not enough to simply remember the past and turn it into a personal narrative. Too many nations and cultures had advocated certain events that they claim to define themselves as distinct from others. Projecting an impeccable image via a 'glorious' past only serves to arouse suspicions of one's true history. It is also very important to be ethical when interrogating the memories, or one may risk falling into narcissistic nostalgia and neglecting other equally significant memories. Therefore, remembering entails some responsibility from the producer, as memory can also be shared among its proponents – such as in the MCP's case the shared legacy of an armed struggle for independence. The nostalgia contained and promoted by the 21OF website could then be understood as more than only a justification for their ideology or a vindication for giving up the armed struggle; it is a form of agency projection and preservation of their silenced narratives. The MCP may be a diminished entity today, but it still managed to cling on to public consciousness through effective use of the Internet and, in the end, let their voices be heard.

References

Amoroso, Donna J. 2003. 'Making Sense of Malaysia'. *Kyoto Review of Southeast Asia*. Online: http://kyotoreview.org/issue-3-nations-and-stories/making-sense-of-malaysia/ (accessed 2 December 2014).

Arendt, Hannah. 2006. *Between Past and Future: Eight Exercises in Political Thought*. New York: Penguin Books.

Arthur, Paul. 2008. 'Pixelated Memory: Online Commemoration of Trauma and Crisis'. *National Academy of Screen and Sound* 4: 1–19. Online: *Interactive Media: E-Journal of the National Academy of Screen and Sound*. http://imjournal.murdoch.edu.au/?media_dl=413 (accessed 17 March 2015).

Bernama. 2015. 'MCMC to Act against Those Inciting People to Join Red Shirt Rally – Salleh'. Bernama, 10 September. Online: http://www.bernama.com/bernama/v8/newsindex.php?id=1169921 (accessed 10 February 2016).

Brown, Victoria. 2016. 'IGP: No to Marxism course'. *The Star* Online, 28 February. Online: http://www.thestar.com.my/news/nation/2016/02/28/igp-no-to-psm-marxism-course/ (accessed 28 February 2016).

Case, William. 2015. *Routledge Handbook of Southeast Asian Democratization*. New York: Routledge.

Cheah, Boon Kheng. 1979. *The Masked Comrades: A Study of the Communist United Front in Malaya*. Singapore: Times Books International.

———. 2002. *Malaysia: The Making of a Nation*. Singapore: ISEAS.

———. 2003. 'Ethnicity, Politics, and History Textbook Controversies in Malaysia.' *American Asian Review* 21, no. 4: 229–52.

———. 2012. *Red Star Over Malaya: Resistance and Social Conflict During and After the Japanese Occupation of Malaya, 1941–46*. Singapore: NUS Press.

Chik, Hasbullah Awang. 2013. 'Don't Upset Malays with Chin Peng Issue, Perkasa Warns MCA'. *The Malaysian Insider*, 20 September. Online: http://www.themalaysianinsider.com/malaysia/article/dont-upset-malays-with-chin-peng-issue-perkasa-warns-mca (accessed 7 January 2014).

Devaraj, Jeyakumar. 2011. 'T-shirts Found on the PSM Bus?' *Socialist Party of Malaysia*, 31 August. Online: http://partisosialis.org/en/node/2046 (accessed 12 November 2014).

Dol, Haris. 2011. 'Resurgence of Communism: Bersih Supporters Going Overboard.' *Malaysian Digest*, 28 June. Online: http://www.malaysiandigest.com/archived/index.php/25-features/commentary/29561-resurgence-of-communism-bersih-supporters-going-overboard.html (accessed 15 November 2013).

Egerton, George. *Political Memoir: Essays on the Politics of Memory*. London: Frank Cass.

Foucault, Michel. 1977. *Language, Counter-Memory, Practice: Selected Essays and Interviews*, edited by Donald F. Bouchard. Oxford: Blackwell.

Gray, Rosie. 2013. 'Malaysian Government Critic Faces DDoS Attack.' BuzzFeedNews, 12 April. Online: http://www.buzzfeed.com/rosiegray/malaysian-government-critic-faces-ddos-attack#.egGZM2PpN (accessed 11 February 2016).

Hack, Karl and C. C. Chin. 2004. *Dialogues with Chin Peng.* Singapore: Singapore University Press.

Hanrahan, Gene Z. 1971. *The Communist Struggle in Malaya.* Kuala Lumpur: University of Malaya Press.

Hirsch, Marianne and Leo Spitzer. 2010. *Ghosts of Home: The Afterlife of Czernowitz in Jewish Memory.* Berkeley: University of California Press.

Hobsbawm, E. J. 1987. *The Age of Empire: 1875–1914.* London: Weidenfeld and Nicolson.

Hunter, Murray. 'Malaysia: Desperately Needing a New National Narrative'. Dissident Voice, 30 August. Online: http://dissidentvoice.org/2013/08/malaysia-desperately-needing-a-new-national-narrative (accessed 15 September 2014).

Jaffe, Dennis. 1985. 'Self-Renewal: Personal Transformation Following Extreme Trauma'. *Journal of Humanistic Psychology* 25, no. 4: 99–124.

Jenkins, Keith. 1991. *Re-thinking History.* New York: Routledge.

Kaur, Jeswan. 2013. 'Umno in no mood to forgive Chin Peng'. Free Malaysia Today, 19 September. Online: http://www.freemalaysiatoday.com/category/opinion/2013/09/19/umno-in-no-mood-to-forgive-chin-peng/ (accessed 20 February 2016).

Khoo, Gaik Cheng. 2010. 'Filling in the Gaps of History: Independent Documentaries Re-present the Malayan Left.' In *Cultures at War: The Cold War and Cultural Expression in Southeast Asia,* edited by Tony Day et al.: 247–64. Ithaca, NY: Cornell Southeast Asia Program Publications.

Khoo, Ying Hooi. 2013. 'Was Communism all that Bad, Really?'. *The Malaysian Insider,* 23 September. Online: http://www.themalaysianinsider.com/opinion/khoo-ying-hooi/article/was-communism-all-that-bad-really (accessed 27 March 2014).

Liu, Yangyue. 2014. *Competitive Political Regime and Internet Control: Case Studies of Malaysia, Thailand, and Indonesia.* Newcastle-upon-Tyne: Cambridge Scholars Publishing.

Lowenthal, David. 1989. 'Nostalgia Tells It Like It Wasn't'. In *The Imagined Past: History and Nostalgia, edited* by Christopher Shaw et al.: 18–32. Manchester: Manchester University Press.

MalayMail Online. 2015. 'Politweet: Social Media Chatter on Bersih 4 Trumps Past Rallies, But No Guarantee of Attendance.' *Malay Mail* Online, 28 August. Online: http://www.themalaymailonline.com/malaysia/article/politweet-social-media-chatter-on-bersih-4-trumps-past-rallies-but-no-guara (accessed 6 February 2016).

Malaysiakini. 2016. 'Putrajaya Blocks Another News Site Critical of Najib'. Malaysiakini, 21 January. Online: https://www.malaysiakini.com/news/327657 (accessed 9 February 2016).

Morris-Suzuki, Tessa. 2005. *The Past Within Us: Media, Memory, History.* New York: Verso.

Naidu, Sumisha. 2016. 'Malaysia to Take "Stern Action" against Social Media Abuse'. Channel NewsAsia, 20 January. Online: http://www.channelnewsasia.com/news/asiapacific/malaysia-to-take-stern/2441588.html (accessed 22 February 2016).

Noel, Donald. 1968. 'A Theory of the Origin of Ethnic Stratification.' *Social Problems* 16, no. 2: 157–72.

Nonini, Donald M. 1992. *British Colonial Rule and the Resistance of the Malay Peasantry, 1900–1957.* New Haven: Yale University Southeast Asia Studies.

Noor, Farish. 2002. *The Other Malaysia: Writings on Malaysia's Subaltern History.* Kuala Lumpur: Silverfishbooks.

———. 2012. 'Political Change in Malaysia and Uncertainty in the Future: Sobering Lessons from Indonesia.' New Mandala, 9 August. Online: http://asiapacific.anu.edu.au/newmandala/2012/08/09/political-change-in-malaysia-and-uncertainty-in-the-future-sobering-lessons-from-indonesia/ (accessed 23 August 2014).
Nora, Pierre. 1996. *Realms of Memory: Rethinking the French Past*, vol. 3. New York: Columbia University Press.
Olick, Jeffrey K. 1999. 'Collective Memory: The Two Cultures.' *Sociological Theory* 17, no. 3: 333–48.
Peng, Chin. 2003. *My Side of History*. Singapore: Media Masters.
Pickering, Michael and Emily Keightley. 2006. 'The Modalities of Nostalgia'. *Current Sociology* 54, no. 6: 919–41.
Roth, Marty. 2011. *The Cultures of Memory: Memory Culture, Memory Crisis and the Age of Amnesia*. Palo Alto: Academica.
Roughneen, Simon. 2011. 'Social Media Plays Major Role in Motivating Malaysian Protesters.' MediaShift, 18 July. Online: http://mediashift.org/2011/07/social-media-plays-major-role-in-motivating-malaysian-protesters199/ (accessed 6 February 2016).
Rusen, Jorn. 2012. 'Tradition: A Principle of Historical Sense-Generation and its Logic and Effect in Historical Culture'. *History and Theory* 51, no. 4 (December): 45–59.
Sabri, Sugiman. 2013. 'DEATH OF EX-MCP CHIEF: Chin Peng Fled as a Traitor'. *New Straits Times* Online, 19 September. Online: http://www2.nst.com.my/latest/death-of-ex-mcp-chief-chin-peng-fled-as-a-traitor-1.358753 (accessed 27 March 2014).
Santasombat, Yos. 1998. 'Oral History and Self-Portraits: Interviewing the Thai Elites'. In *Oral History in Southeast Asia: Theory and Method*, edited by P. Lim Pui Huen et al.: 66–85. Singapore: ISEAS.
Shankar, Athi and Leven Woon. 2013. 'Police Nab Duo with Chin Peng Items'. Free Malaysia Today, 25 September. Online: http://www.freemalaysiatoday.com/category/nation/2013/09/25/police-nab-duo-with-chin-peng-items (accessed 16 October 2013).
Shuib, Md. Shukri, Mohamad Faisol Keling and Mohd Na'eim Ajis. 2009. 'The Implications of Cold War on Malaysia State Building Process'. In *Asian Culture and History* vol.1, no. 2: 89–98.
Shukry, Anisah. 2013. 'We Don't Know Who the Red Bean Army Is'. Free Malaysia Today, 4 July. Online: http://www.freemalaysiatoday.com/category/nation/2013/07/04/we-don%E2%80%99t-know-who-the-red-bean-army-is%E2%80%99/ (accessed 20 February 2016).
The Malaysian Insider. 2015. 'Putrajaya Has No Plans to Block Social Media'. *The Malaysian Insider*, 19 November. Online: http://www.themalaysianinsider.com/malaysia/article/putrajaya-no-plans-to-block-social-media (accessed 7 February 2016).
The Malaysian Insider. 2016a. 'TMI Banned on Grounds of National Security'. *The Malaysian Insider*, 25 February. Online: http://www.themalaysianinsider.com/malaysia/article/tmi-turns-8-cut-off-from-selected-net-providers (accessed 26 February 2016).
The Malaysian Insider. 2016b. 'News Portals Serve Their Own Agendas, Says Najib'. *The Malaysian Insider*, 26 February. Online: http://www.themalaysianoutsider.com/malaysia/article/news-portals-serve-their-own-agendas-says-najib (accessed 26 February 2016).
The Star Online. 2015. 'Najib Expected to File Suit against WSJ'. *The Star* Online, 5 July. Online: http://www.thestar.com.my/news/nation/2015/07/05/najib-to-sue-wsj/ (accessed 20 February 2016).
Tosh, John. 2008. *Why History Matters*. New York: Palgrave Macmillan.

Walder, David. 2009. 'Writing, Representation and Postcolonial Nostalgia'. *Textual Practice* vol. 23, Issue 6: 935–46.

Waterson, Roxana and Kwok Kian-Won. 2012 'The Work of Memory and the Unfinished Past: Deepening and Widening the Study of Memory in Southeast Asia'. In *Contestations of Memory in Southeast Asia*, edited by Roxana Waterson et al.: 17–50. Singapore: NUS Press.

Wertsch, James. 2002. *Voices of Collective Remembering*. New York: Cambridge University Press.

Wong, James Wing On. 2005. *From Pacific War to Merdeka: Reminiscences of Abdullah CD, Rashid Maidin, Suriani Abdullah, and Abu Samah*. Petaling Jaya, Malaysia: SIRD.

Yeoh, Kim Wah. 1973. *Political Development of Singapore, 1945–1955*. Singapore: Singapore University Press.

Yong, C. F. 1997. *The Origins of Malayan Communism*. Singapore: South Seas Society.

Persatuan Kawan Karib Johor. 2011. 'Mǎláixīyà 21 shìjì liányì huì jiǎnjiè' 马来西亚21世纪联谊会简介 (21st Century Old Friends Association Brief Introduction), *Róufú zhōu lǎo yǒu liányì huì* 柔佛州老友联谊会, 20 November. Online: http://laoyou.org.my/index.php?option=com_content&view=article&id=75%3A21&catid=26%3A21&Itemid=22 (accessed 20 November 2014).

21OF. 2008. 'Yīng jūn túshā bā dōng jiālǐ píngmín, zuìzé nàn táo!' 英军屠杀巴东加里平民, 罪责难逃! ('The British Army cannot escape their crime of the Batang Kali civilian massacre!'), *21Lǎo yǒu bùluò gé* 21老友部落格, 17 September. Online: http://blog.of21.com/?p=29880 (accessed 11 December 2013).

21OF. 2013a. 'Quánlì zhīchí dǒng zǒng hàozhào de fǎnduì 《jiàoyù dà lántú》 qiānmíng yùndòng' 全力支持董总号召的反对《教育大蓝图》签名运动 ('Fully Supporting Dong Zhong's signature campaign to protest against the "Education Blueprint"'), *21Lǎo yǒu bùluò gé* 21老友部落格, 6 September. Online: http://blog.of21.com/?p=28380 (accessed 15 July 2014).

21OF. 2013b. 'Ānmián zài dàzhòng guāngróng de huíyì zhōng–jì zì yuǎnfāng de dàoniàn'. 安眠在大众光荣的回忆中–寄自远方的悼念 ('Asleep in the Glorious Memory of the Masses–Condolences'), *21Lǎo yǒu bùluò gé* 21老友部落格, 13 October. Online: http://blog.of21.com/?p=28444 (accessed 15 July 2014).

21OF. 2015. 'Dú bào suíbǐ: Kàngjí jíduān zhǔyì lì tǐng zhōngyōng yùndòng'. 读报随笔：抗击极端主义 力挺中庸运动 ('Newspaper Essay: Fight extremism, support the moderation movement'), *21Lǎo yǒu bùluò gé* 21老友部落格, 8 January. Online: http://blog.of21.com/?p=28380 (accessed 18 February 2015).

21OF. 2014a. 'Wǎngzhàn shēnmíng'. 网站申明 ('Website Disclaimer'), *21Lǎo yǒu* 21老友, 11 December. Online: http://www.of21.com/doku.php?id=申明 (accessed 12 December 2014).

21OF. 2014b. 'Lìshǐ zīliào xiàzài'. 历史资料下载 ('Historical Material Download'), *21Lǎo yǒu* 21老友, 11 December. Online: http://www.of21.com/doku.php?id=申明 (accessed 12 December 2014).

He, Qicai 何启才. 2014. 'Zhàn qián mǎ lái yà zuǒyì yùndòng shǐ' 战前马来亚左翼运动史 ('History of left-wing movements in pre-war Malaya'), *21Lǎo yǒu* 21老友, 22 May. Online: http://www.of21.com/doku.php?id=magong_lishi:zhan_qian_shiqi:zhan_qian_malaiya_zuoyi_yundong_shi (accessed 29 May 2014).

Malaysia Chinese Forum. 2014. Dà mǎ huárén lùntán. 大马华人论坛. Online: https://www.facebook.com/page/大马华人论坛/144721845542332 (accessed 11 September 2014).

Malaysia Chinese Net. 2005. Dà mǎhuá大马华. Online: http://www.malaysia-chinese.net/ (accessed 22 December 2014).

Chapter 8

NEW AND TRADITIONAL MEDIA IN MALAYSIA: CONFLICTING CHOICES FOR SEEKING USEFUL AND TRUSTED INFORMATION IN EVERYDAY LIFE

Sandra Hanchard

Traffic jams are the bane of existence in Kuala Lumpur. As people commute to and from work each day in unpredictable conditions (flash floods are common), sitting in traffic is part of everyday life. At least one has access to the radio. BFM Malaysia, an independent business radio station, cycles out acronyms of its name to keep listeners amused: 'Building First-World Mindsets', 'Bribe-Free Malaysia', 'Balming Frustrated Minds', and so forth. Talkback radio attracts all sorts to debate the national concerns of the day. Alternatively, drivers in a traffic jam can use their smart phones to voice their opinions. Complaining about traffic on social media instils feelings of camaraderie; solidarity through suffering. Why not use news feeds to see if your friends are similarly afflicted and get updates on congested areas before the mainstream media scrambles to cover the event? Or perhaps just use the time to catch up on personal news. Malaysian media celebrity Niki Cheong recounts, 'When a car doesn't move at traffic lights, mum used to say the driver must be on phone. Now, she says, must be "playing" Twitter'.[1] Each day, Malaysians are exposed to different information sources and have choices as to which media they use to take action (perhaps choose a different traffic route based on feedback from other drivers). Information media is pervasive in everyday life, even in traffic jams.

This chapter situates social media information in the wider Malaysian media ecology by surveying traditional and new media choices that users have in their search for everyday information. The rise of global media

---

1   https://twitter.com/nikicheong/ (posted 11 March 2014)

platforms and local regulatory frameworks are both factors that influence how Malaysians consume different types of media. I argue that Malaysian users prefer different forms of media for trusted or useful information-seeking in everyday life, reflecting a complex and sometimes confusing media environment. Information-seeking in everyday life refers to day-to-day information practices that serve purposeful outcomes, helping users to maintain order in their lives (Savolainen 1995). Everyday information in the media has value when the user regards it as useful or trustworthy. Useful information has relevancy to users in their objectives for meeting everyday outcomes. Trusted information is generally provided by a source that is regarded as credible or knowledgeable on a certain subject. This chapter asks: What is the value of social media in the wider Malaysian media environment for affording useful and trusted information? Social media has distinct properties from other information and communication channels such as television, newspapers, radio and also other forms of online media. Users, for example, have the ability on social media, unlike other media, to curate their news feed based on relevant social networks. The Malaysian Communications and Multimedia Commission (MCMC 2011) estimates upwards of 80 per cent of Malaysian Internet users are active on social media. Malaysians spend at least one-third of their time on social networking websites (comScore 2011). With the mainstream adoption of social media in Malaysia and high engagement levels, there is a need to understand everyday practices on platforms in more detail.

More widely, new media has offered the possibility for Malaysians to gain information and news that has not been filtered by authorities. However, an emerging constraint on open information sharing through social media by Malaysians is the fear of being seen as seditious. Credibility and censorship of information influence how and why Malaysians access different types of media. Existing media scholarship in Malaysia emphasizes the relevance of traditional media. Salman et al. (2011) assert that Malaysians still prefer to get their news through print newspapers, radio and television. Based on an online questionnaire of 400 Malaysian users, I provide data that supports the argument that social media is an important alternative information source for Malaysians. My findings show that social media platforms are a valued option for Malaysians to seek and share useful, and to some degree trusted, information in everyday life. Secondly, I demonstrate that there are socioeconomic divides in user preferences for traditional and new media types, where rural users and users of lower educational and income levels demonstrate a preference for traditional media. This divide has significant implications for democratic participation in Malaysian society. This chapter begins by outlining political, socio-economic and cultural factors shaping the Malaysian media landscape. I then adopt a networked media framework to illustrate the differences between traditional and new media. Social media is discussed in terms of how platforms and architectures afford everyday information-seeking and sharing. Given a rapidly changing global media environment, the preferences for new and traditional media by Malaysians need to be re-examined.

Political, Socio-economic and Cultural Factors Shaping Malaysian Media

Traditional media in Malaysia is tightly controlled by the government, despite the appearance of a liberal media environment. In his Vision 2020 policy, former prime minister, Mahathir Mohamad, advocated the democratic use of media and information technology towards ensuring prosperity for all Malaysians.[2] However, these initiatives did not necessarily mean a more open and transparent Malaysia. The ensuing rapid economic growth of this period and the expansion of the middle classes were in parallel with state moves towards authoritarianism (Loo 2008). Media analyst Zaharom Nain (1994) points out that despite the proliferation of new press titles in the 1990s, there was in fact a concentration of ownership at the time between two local media publications, the *New Strait Times Press* (*NSTP*) and *Utusan Melayu*. This concentration of media ownership, at least for the traditional press, continues today. The Printing Presses and Publications Act (1984) for the press, and the Communications and Multimedia Act (1998) for the broadcasting industry and the Internet, directly empower ministers to determine who can own and operate mainstream and broadcasting outlets (Salman et al. 2011). In the television industry, for example, the major media conglomerate Media Prima owns all major private stations – they are also linked to the major Malay political group, United Malays National Organisation (UMNO). Traditional media plays a powerful role in propagating ideology in Malaysia (Ahmad et al. 2012). For example, the government-owned news agency Bernama was used as an outlet for government propaganda during the last general election in 2013 (Houghton 2013). Many Malaysians assume that the traditional media is a mouthpiece for the government.

Malaysian online media outlets have emerged and flourished in recent years as an alternative to traditional media. For example, news websites Malaysiakini and Free Malaysia Today purport to be free from partisan ownership constraints and to offer independent, critical analysis of the government. Ahmad et al. (2012) argue that social media in particular affords a space

---

2 The Vision 2020 policy can be found on the official website of Prime Minister's Office of Malaysia: http://www.pmo.gov.my/.

for Malaysians to critically engage in national topics of debate and to spread information widely at a local level. Social media potentially alters the relationship between the nation and 'the people' by providing new spaces for discourse and information-sharing. In the 1990s Mahathir promised, through the Bill of Guarantees, that the Internet would be free from government controls and censorship (Salman and Hasim 2011, 3). Journalism academic Cherian George (2005) cautioned, however, that Internet users were still not guaranteed immunity from security laws covering seditious or libellous content. Further, there was no certainty over how long the government would honour the no-censorship guarantee. While social media has allowed Malaysians to express their views with more freedom, justified concerns remain regarding government monitoring and censorship. According to the Centre of Independent Journalism (2012), amendments to the Evidence Act – which holds intermediaries liable for seditious content – are part of efforts to 'tame the Internet', which allows critical views of the government to circulate widely.

Of further concern are socio-economic divides between Malaysian users who can tap into global networked resources for information and media consumption. The Malaysian government has attempted to close technology and socio-economic gaps by ensuring accessibility to the Internet. This includes a campaign of 'one house/one computer', tax reductions for computers, providing affordable wireless connectivity to both urban and rural areas, and free laptops to those who are not able to afford them (Rahim et al. 2011, 9). Malaysian scholars have recognized, however, that gaps are based not only on access, but on the quality of participation on new media (Rahim et al. 2011; Salman and Rahim 2012). For example, the effectiveness of Internet adoption by users is influenced by factors such as the formal education of users (Hargittai and Hinnant 2008). Differences in access to information and communication technologies between rural and urban users in Malaysia have political consequences. For example, the fact that rural voters supported the ruling *Barisan Nasional* (National Front) coalition during the 2013 general election was attributed to rural users' lack of access to online newspapers that were critical of the government (Malott 2013). After the election, other commentators questioned whether it might have instead been the impact of ethnic Malay (rather than rural) voters supporting the government, given that smaller rural seats with lower population density tend to have more Malay voters (Ong 2014). A study by Ng et al. (2015) found, however, that both urbanization and ethnicity are effects in Malaysian voting preferences.

Not only is traditional media in Malaysia tightly controlled by the government, it is siloed along racial lines, with each group having identifiable news media preferences across newspapers, television channels and radio stations (Firdaus 2006). For example, the newspaper *Utusan Malaysia* is popular with

Malays, *Sinchew Daily* with the Chinese and *Vanakkam Malaysia* with Tamil Indians. These preferences are likely to be influenced by language and cultural choices. Government policies have been introduced to address socio-economic and ethnic divides across spheres in everyday life. The New Economic Policy (NEP) was introduced to support an emerging Malay middle-class and to facilitate the redistribution of wealth in the context of the perceived political and economic status of the Chinese (Jomo 2004). 1Malaysia, a key policy of Prime Minister Najib's administration, calls for a united multicultural *rakyat* (ordinary people). The rationale behind 1Malaysia is that economic progress depends on ethnic unification. I examine whether there are socio-economic, residential and cultural digital divides of traditional and new media use.

Distinguishing New from Traditional Media

What makes new media different from traditional media when seeking everyday information? Terms such as 'interactivity' and 'connectivity' characterize new media (Cubitt 2013). Interactivity refers to the ability of users to interact with content producers, for example – readers can reciprocate sharing information with the original author or publisher. Connectivity refers to the ability of users to interact with other users: for example, members of a forum can share informational tips with each other. Networked environments that enable multiple interactions are a critical component of digital media, where information flows in multiple directions, unlike traditional broadcast media. This changes the relationship between publisher and reader; however, some of the differences between new and traditional media are blurring. Van Dijck and Poell (2013 11) argue that social media is not a niche, specialized media; it has broad appeal and influence in everyday life. In particular, they write that 'mass media and social platforms can hardly be seen as separate forces when it comes to controlling information and communication processes'. Affordances for social interaction further distinguish social media from other types of media. Lüders (2008, 685) contends that personal media is distinguishable from mass media because of social rather than technical, features. Mass media no longer has the monopoly on providing general information. Users access information through personal networks, where 'meaning' is derived from the social functions of use; however, information choices made by users are mediated in social media environments by technical features.

Social media platforms are sociotechnical environments for user interactivity and connectivity. New media scholar Tarleton Gillespie (2010) argues platforms should be understood in similar terms to traditional media. He writes that the term 'platform' has been loosened from its original computational etymologies to now reference new media forms, such as user-generated content.

The 'architectures' of platforms refer to the design features that shape user behaviours, such as 'like' buttons (users acknowledge a post) in social media, user lists for curating content (only news 'feeds' from certain social networks are consumed), and privacy options (news feeds are shared with certain social networks). Socio-technical elements are designed by platform owners who have their own commercial imperatives, but users make their own choices as to how they interact within these architectures. The term 'networked publics' refers to discourse in public environments between connected individuals and is often political in content. danah boyd (2011, 41) argues that networked publics reorganize the interaction between users; that is, architecture and design mediates information-flow on social media. Papacharissi (2011) uses the metaphor of a 'networked self' to contextualize online individual activity in social groups. My approach differs from a 'networked self' and 'networked publics' perspective by focusing on information practices in everyday contexts on social media, beyond motives of sociality and self-presentation. I emphasize that everyday information-seeking on social media can serve outcomes in everyday life; information is not purely exchanged for the sake of socialization. Further, it should be observed that the concept of a 'networked self' is highly individualistic. How self-presentation on social media translates to a collectivist Southeast Asian context deserves examination in future studies (see related work by Postill, 2008, who critiques networked individualism and its overemphasis on egocentric networks.).

Affordances are the mechanisms through which new media can influence everyday life (Hogan 2009). danah boyd (2011, 46) provides a breakdown of the affordances that networked technologies introduce: these are persistence (archiving of content), replicability (content can be duplicated), scalability (visibility of content) and searchability (content can be indexed). Papacharissi and Gibson (2011) suggest a fifth structural affordance, shareability, where networked technologies encourage sharing rather than withholding of information. The design features of social media platforms prompts users to rethink what everyday information they choose to share across their social networks; that is, their audience. Marwick and boyd (2011) identify the need to reconceptualize audiences on new media, in particular the phenomenon of 'context collapse' on micro-blogging websites. The authors describe how social media platforms collapse multiple audiences into single contexts, giving users new challenges in managing their social worlds. New problems in relevancy have been created as users juggle the balance between 'public' and 'private' content; in particular, how much of their private lives they should be exposing to public audiences through their sharing practices. Information-seeking for useful and trusted information on social media is constrained by the mediation of social relationships through platform architectures.

Measuring Usefulness and Trust

This chapter examines the value of everyday information-seeking and sharing in traditional and new media that is based on relevancy criteria determined by users; I will focus on 'usefulness' and 'trust'. I suggest that the usefulness of information is amplified when the source is regarded as trustworthy; conversely, information that is not trusted is rendered less useful to the user. I examine whether different sources are perceived as more likely to distribute information that is reliable, accurate and credible. I suggest that trust is a rarer commodity than usefulness. Earning trust involves fact-checking, editing, peer validation and more. Both usefulness and trust of information are dependent on the relevance of the source to the situation at hand. There is a substantial body of information-assessment research on Internet use, particularly in terms of credibility (Flanagin and Metzger 2007; Hargittai et al. 2010; Goldspink 2010; Menchen-Trevino and Hargittai 2011; Niederer and van Dijck 2010). The attribute of 'trust' is an important component of credibility-assessment research (Blanchard et al. 2011). Trust has been linked to expertise, social status and relevancy (Stewart 2011). Walther et al. (2011, 23) argue that the perceived expertise and trustworthiness of a source, rather than the channel or media, is the most important factor for why users accept information. A study on credibility and micro-blogging by Schmierbach and Oeldorf-Hirsch (2010) found that content related to current events posted on Twitter is considered less trustworthy than content posted on news websites. The topic of information quality on social media is substantial and deserving of ongoing study, given the evolving nature of platforms.

I chose to implement an online questionnaire to determine perceptions of usefulness and trust towards media, drawing on a rich body of Internet and everyday life studies (Anderson and Tracey 2008; Ewing and Thomas 2010; Howard et al. 2002; Quan-Hasse et al. 2002; Wellman and Haythornthwaite 2002). My questionnaire was distributed through Effective Measure, a commercial Internet measurement firm operating in Malaysia for census-level online behavioural data.[3] During March 2012, Effective Measure had more than 200 websites 'tagged' with their software in Malaysia, with demographic profiles on more than 85,000 users. Their data are extrapolated to represent the total Internet population in Malaysia, using government census data to ensure that it is weighted accurately. The demographics I asked to be provided included; gender, age, residence, education, monthly household income and occupation.[4] I collected answers from 400 respondents, divided evenly between

---

3   http://www.effectivemeasure.com
4   Income brackets were provided from Effective Measure in USD. I performed a rough conversion to Malaysian Ringgit (MYR) using an online currency converter.

Bahasa Malay, Chinese, Indian and English speakers (primary language spoken at home), across a wide cross-section of demographic profiles.[5] Overall, the sample of social media users I collected suggests a group of users that have advantages in terms of income, education and occupation, when compared to the general population that accesses the Internet. Middle-class Malaysians were well-represented in my sample. The sample was also younger and more likely to be urban. The income, education and urban differences of this group suggest digital divides in users who participate in social media. The Malaysian Communications and Multimedia Commission (MCMC 2012) data report similar trends in important categories such as age, education and income. I also asked respondents two multiple-choice questions about which media sources they could get useful information from for their everyday life; and which media sources they generally trusted.

In my analysis, I have categorized social media, search engines, online news websites and blogs as 'new' media; and television, radio and newspapers (print) as 'traditional' media. I identified 'new media' using Cubitt's (2013) definition, which encompasses networked technologies. Given that the Internet has enjoyed mainstream use for more than a decade, it is debatable as to whether online media forms should be termed, *new*. However, in the context of Malaysian scholarship (Salman et al. 2011) the Internet and online media are still regarded as new. The categories of media types that I provided to respondents were not exhaustive (respondents could select 'Other'). I do not discuss important media forms such as advertising, filmmaking, music, festivals and so on; other scholars in Malaysia have covered the cultural and national importance of these types of media (Hopkins and Lee 2012; Yeoh 2010). Rather, I focus on contextualizing social media as a type of information media that influences how users take action in their everyday lives. The approach I take establishes a measure of 'value' of social media information compared to other media, although there are certainly other valid criteria. I offer a contribution to understanding the changing information and media environment in Malaysia, particularly evolving attitudes towards new media.

I then based 'Low', 'Middle' and 'High' groupings based on Economic Planning Unit 2012 data on Mean Monthly Gross Household Income of Top 20%, Middle 40% and Bottom 40% of Households by Ethnicity and Strata, Malaysia, 1970–2012. A category, 'Very high' was created for mean household income per month above approximately 15,000 MYR. See: http://www.epu.gov.my/documents/10124/37cd593e-916c-4938-865f-d727201cbd05

5   My original questionnaire consisted of 21 questions that were used for my doctoral thesis – soon to published as 'Social media information and everyday life in Malaysia'. Only two of these questions were used for this chapter.

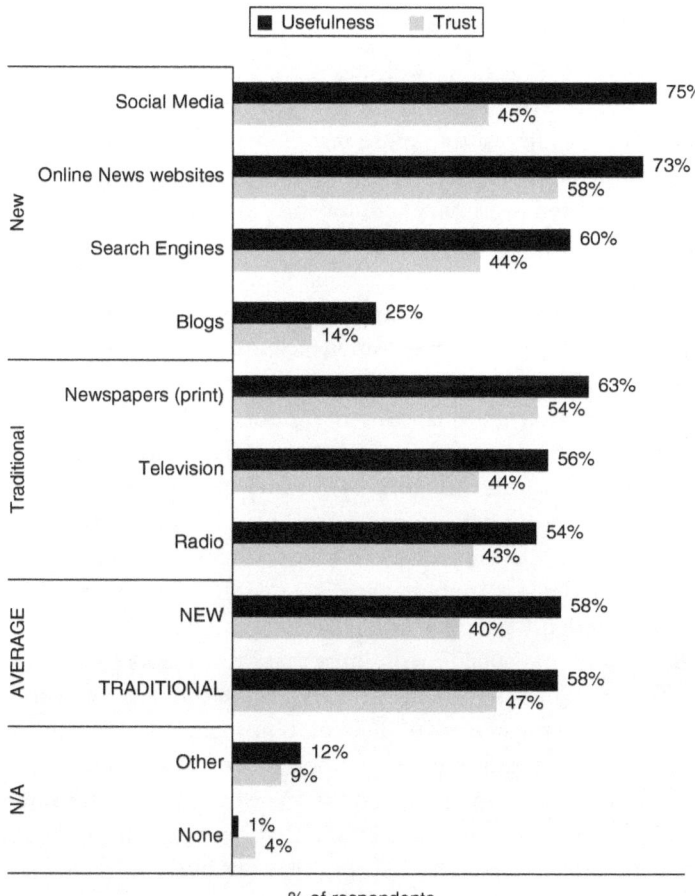

Figure 8.1 Comparison between usefulness and trustworthiness of media sources. *Source*: Hanchard, October 2012, n = 400.

Findings

Figure 8.1 shows that, overall, both traditional and new media are regarded as a source of useful everyday information by an equal proportion of Malaysian users (58%). However, more Malaysian users in this study trust traditional media over new media (47% and 40%, respectively). This could be because users value editorial processes provided by traditional publishers that may be lacking in new media. Overall, Malaysian users were more likely to value both media sources for useful, rather than trusted, everyday information. Notably, the biggest differences between usefulness and trust could be seen in the users' perception of new media: social media (30% difference) search engines (16%) and online news websites (15%).

The most useful types of media

Social media and online news websites were regarded by Malaysian users as the most 'useful' type of media for everyday information (75% and 73% respectively). It is of interest that more respondents selected social media over search engines (60%) as a source of useful information, particularly as search engines are considered a primary tool for information-seeking. This could be because information is being 'pushed' to users from personal sources through the architectures of social media platforms. More respondents selected online news websites (73%) versus print newspapers (63%) for useful information, suggesting that online content has somewhat more relevance to respondents' everyday lives. This could also reflect different editorial priorities of online news producers versus traditional content producers. Further, users have more opportunities to control the information they can curate for their everyday needs on the Internet (refer to work by Sunstein, 2007, on polarization). In traditional media, respondents were more likely to select print newspapers over television and radio for useful everyday information. This list of media provided to respondents was not exhaustive, demonstrated by the fact that 12 per cent of respondents selected 'Other'.

Table 8.1 shows that social media information was more likely to be considered useful among young Malaysian users, while online news websites were more likely to be useful sources of information for users over the age of 45. While the reasons for this difference are unclear, we can speculate that younger users are more likely to value information received from social sources, while older users prefer information from sources that have been accredited through formal editorial processes. Urban users were more likely to value online news websites, while rural users favoured traditional media forms for useful information (print newspapers, television and radio). Television was more likely to be valued by Bahasa speakers as a source of useful information when compared to the average of all respondents; this possibly reflects that the national networks tailor much of their content to Bahasa speakers. My data also point to socio-economic divides in terms of preferences for traditional and new media. For example, tertiary-educated users were more likely to value search engines and online news websites as sources of useful information. Low-income users were the most likely value traditional media forms. High-skill white-collar users were more likely to find search engines useful, compared to low-skill white-collar users, who were more likely to find television and print newspaper sources useful.[6]

6   I describe 'high-skill white-collar' roles as being typically office-based, requiring a high level of education, and usually attracting a higher income. 'Low-skill white-collar' roles are similarly office-based, requiring lower levels of education, and usually attracting

Table 8.1 Percentage of users who identified media types as 'useful' sources of information; shown are the major differences (5% or greater) between demographic groups or between a demographic group and the average of all respondents.

Demographic	Media	Category (high)	%	n	Category (low)	%	n
Age	Social media	15–24 years	86	86	45–54 years	62	32
	Online news websites	45–54 years	87	45	15–24 years	61	61
		55+ years	93	14	–		
Residence	Online news websites	Urban	74	247	Rural	63	43
	Newspapers – print	Rural	71	48	Urban	61	204
	Television	Rural	72	49	Urban	52	174
	Radio	Rural	66	45	Urban	51	170
Language	Television	Bahasa Malay	67	67	Average of total	56	400
Education	Search engines	Tertiary	62	210	Non-tertiary	47	29
	Online news websites	Tertiary	75	255	Non-tertiary	56	35
Income	Newspapers – print	Low-income	75	56	Average of total	61	341*
	Television	Low-income	72	54	Average of total	53	341*
	Radio	Low-income	69	52	Average of total	53	341*
Occupation	Search engines	High-skill white-collar	66	135	Low-skill white-collar	52	35
	Newspapers – print	Low-skill white-collar	75	50	High-skill white-collar	59	122
	Television	Low-skill white-collar	63	42	High-skill white-collar	51	104

Source: Hanchard; October 2012; n= 400

*Dependents were not included in the income analysis.

Trusted media types

Looking at Figure 8.1 we can see that, overall, online news websites were the most trusted media source (58% of all respondents). In contrast to my findings on 'useful information', social media was not the most trusted media source of everyday information – only 45 per cent of respondents trusted social media sources. Furthermore, blogs were the least likely media source to be trusted for everyday information (14%). This is likely due to the lack of editorial review procedures on blogs. While formal verification processes are generally also absent from social media content, users know on what level they have established a level of intimacy with the connection providing information, so they can possibly make better-informed value judgements. It is notable that, overall, respondents were only slightly more likely to trust online news websites (58%) over print newspapers (54%). This slight difference could be attributed to the perceived editorial independence of online media outlets in Malaysia. It should be noted that some newspapers have both online and print versions, such as *The Star*, which enjoys a national daily readership. There are other major news outlets that only exist online, such as Malaysiakini. The general preference for online versus print newspapers may also be influenced by factors of accessibility, affordability and users' content preferences.

Online news websites were more likely to be considered sources of trusted information by tertiary-educated and urban users, as well as by English and Chinese speakers (see Table 8.2). For content and language diversity, online media might better suit minority groups. In the context of debates around media programming in the national language and cultural identity in Malaysia, Rahim (2010) has argued for greater language diversity – the Internet may be able to support such goals given the relative affordability of creating online content. The difference between urban and rural users in terms of their trust of new media sources provides further evidence of a digital divide. Low-income users were more likely than high-income users to trust traditional media overall. Similar trends were found across occupational classifications. For example, low-skill white-collar users were more likely to trust information from all forms of traditional media.

lower income levels. High-skill white-collar roles include: associate professional and technical roles, director, CEO, COO, CFO, large company owner and senior and middle management. Low-skill white-collar roles include: administrative and secretarial, sales and customer service roles. There were not enough respondents in my sample in the 'blue-collar' category for indicative data.

Discussion

Social media is an important part of the Malaysian media ecology for users seeking useful everyday information. The architectures of platforms afford information-seeking and sharing within and between social networks that have relevance to users' everyday lives. However, social media lacks the verification processes of traditional media. Consequently, information on social media is less likely to be trusted compared to other types of media, despite government interference and issues of independence with traditional media. Indeed, Malaysian scholars expect that traditional and new media will continue to coexist (Salman et al. 2011). There are clear differences between groups of socio-economic advantage and disadvantage in their respective preferences towards new and traditional media in Malaysia. I have shown that traditional media is regarded as more useful and trusted by users of lower educational and occupational attainment. Further, rural users were also more likely to value traditional media forms for useful information. A lack of political participation online may compound the economic disadvantages of rural Malaysians (Gibbons and Kasim 1990).

Social media information is curated by and for the user, who is the locus of interaction on each platform (Papacharissi 2011, 306). The architecture of platforms predict what information the individual will find relevant to their social networks. New dynamics of usefulness and trust emerge on social media because there is a remixing of information flow between producers and consumers of information. On traditional media, the lack of networking affordances means that readers have to exert greater effort to interact with publishers. Social media allows information-seeking behaviours for Malaysian users in ways that are limited, or not possible, via traditional media in Malaysia. The reshaping of social worlds through affordances of social media potentially has outcomes that benefit Malaysian society. For example, the opportunity to share everyday information between social networks affords awareness of other cultural traditions. Malaysian users may be more likely to be exposed to the religious and cultural festivities of other ethnic groups through photos and traditional greetings that are shared on social media. Malaysians will express goodwill in the traditional terms of 'other' cultures at appropriate times in the year on social media. Examples of cultural and religious expressions that can be seen include 'Gong Xi Fa Cai' to say Happy Chinese New Year; 'Selamat Hari Raya', signifying a day of celebration at the end of Ramadan, the Islamic month of fasting; 'Happy Deepavali' during the Hindu Festival of Lights; and 'Merry Christmas'. Further, new media in Malaysia allow minority groups to express themselves and receive news relevant to their specific communities; whereas traditional media may be dominated by the cultural values of the

Table 8.2 Percentage of users who identified media types as 'trusted' sources of information; shown are the major differences (5% or greater) between demographic groups or between a demographic group and the average of all respondents.

Demographic	Media	Category (high)	%	n	Category (low)	%	N
Residence	Online news websites	Urban	60	198	Rural	47	32
Language	Online news websites	English	72	72	Indian	48	48
		Chinese	59	59	Bahasa	51	51
Education	Online news websites	Tertiary	60	202	Non-tertiary	45	28
Income	Newspapers – print	Low-income	64	48	Average of total	52	341*
	Television	Low-income	57	43	Average of total	41	341*
	Radio	Low-income	52	39	Average of total	42	341*
Occupation	Newspapers – print	Low-skill white-collar	67	45	High-skill white-collar	49	100
	Television	Low-skill white-collar	55	37	High-skill white-collar	38	78
	Radio	Low-skill white-collar	46	31	High-skill white-collar	39	80

Source: Hanchard; October 2012; n = 400

*Dependents were not included in the income analysis.

majority ethnic group. The architecture of social media platforms allows users to reduce social distances by exchanging information with different social networks, even those with whom they have weaker ties (Granovetter 1973).

It should not be assumed that all affordances of social media have social benefit. For example, affordances for amplifying, recording and spreading information (boyd 2011) can mean that harmful ideas, including hate speech, spread more quickly. Racial polarization on media can escalate during times of political upheaval, facilitated by the viral qualities of social media. Racism on social media was at a fervent high during the Malaysian 2013 general election. There were incidences of citizens, mobilized on social media to monitor fraudulent activity at polling booths, harassing legitimate voters who did not 'look Malaysian' (Malaysiakini 2013), while Bangladeshi foreign workers were accused of voting illegally in the service of the ruling coalition (Zahiid 2013). An environment of online persecution and fear followed the election. The MCMC targeted individuals on social media who were protesting the election result by accusing them of inciting racial hatred (The Edge 2013).

The net benefit of protecting cultural diversity in allowing Malaysians to share and seek information freely on social media should be valued, and not curtailed by heavy-handed control of information that we know already hampers traditional media. New media is compelling because it offers a space for users to share their experiences of events that constitute the social imaginary, or public culture, of the nation (Leong 2014). Periods of crisis and events of historical significance can be intensely experienced on social media. During the events of the missing Malaysia Airlines flight MH370 in March 2014 and the downed flight MH17 in July 2014, global outpourings of grief and anger contributed to a volatile information environment in which unverified information spread rapidly on social media. This was despite efforts by authorities as they scrambled to provide official versions of events. Online information distribution around these events served to illustrate that Malaysians do indeed live in a global media environment, with access to reporting from new media sources, independent of local authorities. My study also raises implications as to whether global technologies such as social media promote dominant Western values to the detriment of cultural diversity. It prompts questions about the cultural neutrality of platforms in allowing users of different language and values to share information in ways that are appropriate to them. Many of the major social media platforms that are used in Malaysia originate from the United States, such as Facebook and Twitter. However, social media platforms are transformed by use; shared content and social meaning is supplied by users who bring their own local values (Postill 2011).

Information-seeking and sharing on new media allows users to participate in the political life of a country. Media freedom is a pressing development issue in Malaysia. Sani (2005, 345) explains that the tight governmental control over the media in Malaysia is rationalized by the nation's development agenda. The Malaysian Social Science Association (2014) asserts that academic freedoms, under threat by the application of the Sedition Act, are required for a 'mature democratic society'. Of concern is the particularly zealous application of the Sedition Act of 1948, a legacy from the British colonial era, punishing individuals for expressing criticism of government figures on social media (Lim 2014). The April 2015 passing of the Prevention of Terrorism Bill (POTA) and amendments to the Sedition Act, allowing mass surveillance, effectively established strong censorship of the Internet (Asohan 2015). As Cherian George (2005) feared, this does not bode well for Internet freedoms and civil society in Malaysia. The Malaysian government recognizes the Internet as a mainstream media outlet and therefore seeks to monitor and manage public communication through it, especially criticism of officials; a difficult task given that many of the popular social media platforms are owned in the United States, and the sheer volume of user content generated on a daily basis. There have been worrying arrests in 2015 of high-profile targets for their commentary on social media, including media figures – notably the cartoonist, Zunar, charged with sedition for his criticism of the ruling coalition posted on Twitter in February 2015. The desire to control new media sits in tension with techno-utopian aspirations in Malaysia and parallel notions of democracy and freedom of speech.

Malaysian users have more reasons to be cautious about what they say online amongst their social networks; given the affordances of shareability on social media, users can never be too sure how far their content is distributed, and whether their communications may be watched by authorities (Hanchard 2016). Online research is needed documenting to what degree Malaysian users have toned down any open criticism of the government on social media. In response to increased online monitoring by authorities, civil rights groups, notably Sinar Project, have proactively organized digital and security workshops for the public. Their inaugural workshop in August 2015 was predominantly attended by journalists who were given technical steps for online identity protection, such as the use of Virtual Private Networks (VPNs). These security practices are increasingly relevant to a politically mobilized middle-class amid widespread dissatisfaction with the Malaysian government over allegations of corruption, especially the 1Malaysia Development Berhad (1MDB) scandal involving suspected misappropriation of state funds to the personal account of Prime Minister Najib Razak. Over the Merdeka national holiday weekend in August 2015, protestors in the *Bersih* 4 movement calling for a clean and transparent government were savvy in their use of 'underground' apps, such as Firechat and Prime by Malaysiakini, to avoid fears of communication-blocking by authorities.

Affordances of seeking and sharing information across social networks on social media have implications for grassroots cultural movements. Social media opens up possibilities for new forms of activism. Kavanaugh et al. (2005, 120) argue that users are more likely to act on information shared by their personal connections rather than through mass media. Furthermore, users may be influenced to take part in political activities by their peers on social media. In *Spreadable Media*, Jenkins et al. describe these structural affordances in wider cultural terms. They highlight the participatory nature of contemporary media and the implications on business, politics and everyday life. The propensity to share is a cultural consequence of new media use. Global values are transmitted to diverse local contexts through participation on social media, Malaysia notwithstanding. Ahmad et al. (2012) discuss the propagation of information on social media and changing public values in Malaysia. They write in reference to the Arab Spring and democratic movements in the Middle East, as reflected by activism on social media. In Malaysia, they highlight shifting cultural values that by global use are influenced towards democratization and also towards greater accountability from the Malaysian government. Social media does not cause social change, but it can enable it to occur more quickly and widely. This is especially pertinent where traditional media in Malaysia is limited in its ability to instigate change because of government controls and censorship constraints.

Limitations and Future Work

This chapter has offered a preliminary comparison between traditional and new media in Malaysia. In particular, this research prompts further investigation into measures of quality information-seeking and sharing on social media. Trust is particularly an important area for future research in social media information environments. It is of high interest whether platforms evolve to include more features for authentication, possibly leading to greater trust in information shared by connections. There have been recent attempts to standardize use by platform owners: for example, Twitter showcasing stories and potential 'uses' for newly initiated members, and Facebook providing editorial guides, such as highlighting satirical content (Machkovech 2014). Some of the motivation to shape social media use is monetization, but it is also to make Twitter more accessible to a wider group of the population, beyond a technical audience (Puschmann and Burgess 2013, have written on the political economy of Twitter). In this study I have compared social media participation across demographic categories; the known limitation was a deep qualitative analysis of the personal motivations and circumstances that determine whether information on social media is used successfully to meet everyday needs for each user. Further, the questionnaire measured respondents' evaluations of social media generally, rather than specific platforms. A comparison of social media users against non-users or ex-users would be of benefit in examining digital divide issues in more detail (see Blank and Dutton 2013, on ex-users of the Internet).

Conclusion

Malaysians choose media for useful and trusted information in everyday life by weighing up the relevance and credibility of information from both traditional and new media sources. We can speculate that users trade off factors of trust and usefulness in choosing between traditional media sources, which have editorial processes, versus new media that gives users greater choice in the content they can customize to suit their everyday needs. Social media is often global platforms, but the uses and information practices that occur on those platforms are often localized to the societal contexts of users. While it offers multilayered social, communication and information functionality, social media is significant because it plays a central role in how users meet purposeful needs in their everyday lives. Information that is shared on social media can be chaotic, reflecting complexity in everyday life. Users need to determine how to make increasing volumes of user-generated data relevant to them; they can do this by filtering for useful and trusted information. Social media is unique from other types of information channels in that users have access to a range of human sources and curators that they know on various levels of intimacy. Friends and family (collectivist social structures) through to acquaintances and strangers (individualist social structures) may offer information that can benefit the user in a range of tasks. An increasingly restricted regulatory environment for online activity in Malaysia may prompt Malaysians to be more careful in the information they choose to seek (and especially share) with their connections on social media. Social media has appeal as a democratic space for discourse and information, but presently is at risk of falling under the same censorship restrictions that govern traditional media in Malaysia.

References

Ahmad, Fauziah, C. P. Kee, Normah Mustaffa, Faridah Ibrahim, Wan Amizah Wan Mahmud and D. Dafrizal. 2012. 'Information Propagation and the Forces of Social Media in Malaysia'. *Asian Social Sciences* 8, no. 5: 71–76.

Anderson, Ben, and Karina Tracey. 2008. 'Digital Living: The Impact (or Otherwise) of the Internet on Everyday British Life'. In *The Internet in Everyday Life*, edited by

Barry Wellman and Caroline Haythornthwaite, 139–63. Malden, MA: Blackwell Publishers Ltd.
Asohan, A. 2015. 'Malaysia: The Velvet Glove Comes off the Iron Fist'. *Digital News Asia*, 13 April. Online: http://www.digitalnewsasia.com/insights/malaysia-the-velvet-glove-comes-off-the-iron-fist (accessed 14 April 2015).
Blanchard, Anita, Jennifer Welbourne, and Marla Boughton. 2011. 'A Model of Online Trust: The Mediating Role of Norms and Sense of Virtual Community'. *Information, Communication & Society* 14, no. 1: 76–106.
Blank, Grant, and William H. Dutton. 2013. "The Emergence of Next Generation Internet Users." In *A Companion to New Media Dynamics*, edited by John Hartley, Jean Burgess and Axel Bruns, 122–41. Hoboken, NJ: Wiley.
boyd, danah. 2011. 'Social Network Sites as Networked Publics: Affordances, Dynamics, and Implications'. In *A Networked Self: Identity, Community, and Culture on Social Network Sites*, edited by Zizi Papacharissi, 39–58. New York: Routledge.
Centre for Independent Journalism, Malaysia. 2012. *Malaysia Slips in Global Rankings of Internet Freedom*. Kuala Lumpur: Centre for Independent Journalism, Malaysia. Online: http://cijmalaysia.org/2012/10/02/malaysia-slips-in-global-rankings-of-internet-freedom/ (accessed 18 March 2013).
comScore. 2011. 'Social Networking Accounts for One Third of All Time Spent Online in Malaysia'. comScore, 17 October. Online: http://www.comscore.com/Press_Events/ Press_Releases/2011/10/Social_Networking_Accounts_for_One_Third_of_All_ Time_Spent_Online_in_Malaysia (accessed 20 October 2011).
Cubitt, Sean. 2013. 'Media Studies and New Media Studies.' In *A Companion to New Media Dynamics*, edited by John Hartley, Jean Burgess, and Axel Bruns, 439–49. Hoboken, NJ: Wiley.
The Edge. 2013. 'Police Warn against Inciting Racial Hatred through Social Sites, SMS'. Yahoo News Malaysia, 8 May. Online: http://my.news.yahoo.com/police-warn-against-inciting-racial-hatred-social-sites-084007000.html (accessed 13 December 2013).
Ewing, Scott, and Julian Thomas. 2010. *CCI Digital Futures 2010: The Internet in Australia*. Melbourne: ARC Centre of Excellence for Creative Industries and Innovation, Swinburne University of Technology.
Firdaus, Amira. 2006. 'Ethnic Identity and News Media Preferences in Malaysia'. In *ARC APFRN Signature Event. Media: Policies, Cultures and Futures in the Asia Pacific Region Conference*, 27–29 November, Perth.
Flanagin, Andrew, and Miriam Metzger. 2007. 'The Role of Site Features, User Attributes, and Information Verification Behaviors on the Perceived Credibility of Web-Based Information'. *New Media & Society* 9, no. 2: 319–42.
George, Cherian. 2005. 'The Internet's Political Impact and the Penetration/participation Paradox in Malaysia and Singapore'. *Media, Culture & Society* 27, no. 6: 903–20. doi:10.1177/0163443705057678.
Gibbons, David, and Shukor Kasim. 1990. *Banking on the Rural Poor in Peninsular Malaysia*. George Town: Center for Policy Research, Universiti Sains Malaysia.
Gillespie, Tarleton. 2010. 'The Politics of "Platforms"'. *New Media & Society* 12, no. 3: 347–64. doi:10.1177/1461444809342738.
Goldspink, Christopher. 2010. 'Normative Behaviour in Wikipedia'. *Information, Communication & Society* 13, no. 5: 652–73.

Granovetter, Mark. 1973. 'The Strength of Weak Ties'. *Journal of American Sociology* 78 no. 6: 1360–80.

Hanchard, Sandra. 2016. 'Malaysia: Global Binge-Viewing in a Restrictive State'. In *Geoblocking and Global Video Culture*, edited by Ramon Lobato and James Meese, 150–56. Amsterdam: Institute of Network Cultures.

Hargittai, Eszter, and Amanda Hinnant. 2008. 'Digital Inequality Differences in Young Adults' Use of the Internet'. *Communication Research* 35 no. 5: 602–21.

Hargittai, Ezster, L. Fullerton, E. Menchen-Trevino, and K. Thomas. 2010. 'Trust Online: Young Adults Evaluation of Web Content.' *International Journal of Communication*, no. 4: 468–94.

Hogan, Bernie. 2009. '*Networking in Everyday Life*'. PhD thesis, University of Toronto. Online: http://individual.utoronto.ca/berniehogan/Hogan_NIEL_10-29-2008_FINAL.pdf (accessed 10 January 2013).

Hopkins, Julian, and Julian Lee. 2012. *Thinking through Malaysia: Culture and Identity in the 21st Century*. Petaling Jaya: Strategic Information and Research Development Centre.

Houghton, Tessa. 2013. 'Malaysian Media – Watchdog or Running Dog?' New Mandala, 17 November. Online: http://asiapacific.anu.edu.au/newmandala/2013/11/17/malaysian-media-watchdog-or-running-dog/ (accessed 13 December 2013).

Howard, Philip E. N., Lee Rainie and Steve Jones. 2002. 'Days and Nights on the Internet.' In *The Internet in Everyday Life*, edited by Barry Wellman and Caroline Haythornthwaite, 45–73. Malden, MA: Blackwell.

Jenkins, Henry, Sam Ford and Joshua Green. 2012. *Spreadable Media: Creating Value and Meaning in a Networked Culture*. New York: New York University Press.

Jomo, Kwame Sundaram. 2004. *The New Economic Policy and Interethnic Relations in Malaysia*. Identities, Conflict and Cohesion Programme Paper Number 7. United Nations Research Institute for Social Development. Online: http://www.unrisd.org/80256B3C005BCCF9/search/A20E9AD6E5BA919780256B6D0057896B?OpenDocument (accessed 7 February 2012).

Kavanaugh, Andrea, Debbie Reese, John Carroll and Mary Rosson. 2005. 'Weak Ties in Networked Communities.' *The Information Society* 21: 119–31.

Leong, Susan. 2014. *New Media and the Nation in Malaysia: Malaysianet*. Routledge Contemporary Southeast Asia Series. Oxon: Taylor and Francis.

Lim, Ida. 2014. 'Midnight Arrest of Facebook User over "Monkey" Jibe Was Overkill, Lawyers Say'. *The Malay Mail* Online, 28 September. Online: http://m.themalaymailonline.com/malaysia/article/midnight-arrest-of-facebook-user-over-monkey-jibe-was-overkill-lawyers-say (accessed 30 September 2014).

Loo, Hong Chuang. 2008. *Contested Media Narratives: Negotiating Nationalism and Ethnicity in Malaysia*. Melbourne: University of Melbourne.

Lüders, Marika. 2008. 'Conceptualizing Personal Media'. *New Media & Society* 10, no. 5: 683–702.

Machkovech, Sam. 2014. 'Does Facebook Think Users Are Dumb? 'Satire' Tag Added to Onion Articles'. Ars Technica, 16 August. Online: http://arstechnica.com/business/2014/08/does-facebook-think-users-are-dumb-satire-tag-added-to-onion-articles/ (accessed 26 February 2015).

Malaysiakini. 2013. 'Cop's Husband, Seen as a Foreign Voter, Is Assaulted'. Malaysiakini, 5 May. Online: http://www.malaysiakini.com/news/229213 (accessed 5 May 2013).

Malaysian Social Science Association. 2014. 'Academic Freedom and the Sedition Act'. Malaysiakini, 9 September. Online: http://m.malaysiakini.com/letters/274135.html (accessed 30 September 2014).

Malott, John. 2013. 'Malaysia Elections: What Happened and What It Means'. *The Islamic Monthly* Online, 7 May. Online: http://www.theislamicmonthly.com/malaysia-elections-what-happened-and-what-it-means/ (accessed 11 July 2013).

Marwick, Alice, and danah boyd. 2011. 'I Tweet Honestly, I Tweet Passionately: Twitter Users, Context Collapse, and the Imagined Audience'. *New Media & Society* 13, no. 1: 114–33.

Malaysian Communications and Multimedia Commission. 2011. 'Household Use of the Internet Survey'. MCMC. Online: http://www.skmm.gov.my/Resources/Statistics/Household-Internet-Usage-Survey/Household-Use-of-the-Internet-Survey-2011.aspx (accessed 4 December 2012).

———. 2012. 'Internet Users Survey'. MCMC. Online: http://www.skmm.gov.my/Resources/Statistics/Internet-users-survey.aspx (accessed 28 March 2014).

Menchen-Trevino, Ericka, and Eszter Hargittai. 2011. 'Young Adults' Credibility Assessment of Wikipedia'. *Information, Communication & Society* 14, no. 1: 24–51.

Ng, Jason, Gary Rangel, Santha Vaithilingam, and Subramaniam Pillay. 2015. '2013 Malaysian Elections: Ethnic Politics or Urban Wave?' *Journal of East Asian Studies* 15, no. 2: 167–98. Online: http://papers.ssrn.com/sol3/papers.cfm?abstract_id=2395091 (accessed 6 May 2015).

Niederer, Sabine, and José van Dijck. 2010. 'Wisdom of the Crowd or Technicity of Content? Wikipedia as a Sociotechnical System'. *New Media & Society* 12, no. 8: 1368–87.

Ong, Lynette. 2014. 'Malaysia – the Best Predictors of Electoral Outcomes'. New Mandala, 13 July. http://asiapacific.anu.edu.au/newmandala/2014/07/13/malaysia-the-best-predictors-of-electoral-outcomes/ (accessed 14 July 2015).

Papacharissi, Zizi. 2011. 'Conclusion: A Networked Self'. In *A Networked Self: Identity, Community, and Culture on Social Network Sites*, edited by Zizi Papacharissi, 304–18. New York: Routledge.

Papacharissi, Zizi, and Paige Gibson. 2011. 'Fifteen Minutes of Privacy: Privacy, Sociality, and Publicity on Social Network Sites'. In *Privacy Online*, edited by S. Trepte and L. Reinecke, 75–89. Heidelberg: Springer.

Postill, John. 2008. 'The Limits of Networked Individualism'. *Media/anthropology* (blog), 5 November. Online: http://johnpostill.com/2008/11/05/the-limits-of-networked-individualism/ (accessed 25 September 2014).

———. 2011. *Localizing the Internet*. New York: Berghahn Books.

Puschmann, Cornelius, and Jean Burgess. 2013. 'The Politics of Twitter Data.' In HIIG Discussion Paper Series no. 2013-01. Online: http://ssrn.com/abstract=2206225 or http://dx.doi.org/10.2139/ssrn.2206225 (accessed 25 February 2014).

Quan-Hasse, A., Barry Wellman, J. Witte, and J. Hampton. 2002. 'Capitalizing on the Net: Social Contact, Civic Engagement, and Sense of Community.' In *The Internet in Everyday Life*, edited by Barry Wellman and Caroline Haythornthwaite, 325–58. Malden, MA: Blackwell.

Rahim, Samsudin. 2010. 'The Local Content Industry and Cultural Identity in Malaysia'. *Journal of Media and Communication Studies* 2, no. 10: 215–20.

Rahim, Samsudin, Latiffah Pawanteh and Ali Salman. 2011. 'Digital Inclusion: The Way Forward for Equality in a Multiethnic Society.' *The Innovation Journal: The Public Sector Innovation* 16, no. 3.

Salman, Ali, and Mohd Safar Hasim. 2011. 'Internet Usage in a Malaysian Sub-Urban Community: A Study of Diffusion of ICT Innovation'. *The Innovation Journal: The Public Sector Innovation* 16, no. 2.

Salman, Ali, Faridah Ibrahim, Mohd Yusof Hj Abdullah, Normah Mustaffa, and Maizatul Haizan Mahbob. 2011. 'The Impact of New Media on Traditional Mainstream Mass Media'. *The Innovation Journal: The Public Sector Innovation Journal* 16, no. 3: 1–11.

Salman, Ali, and Samsudin Rahim. 2012. 'From Access to Gratification: Towards an Inclusive Digital Society'. *Asian Social Science* 8, no. 5: 5–15.

Sani, Mohd Azizuddin Mohd 2005. 'Media Freedom in Malaysia'. *Journal of Contemporary Asia* 35, no. 3: 341–67.

Savolainen, Reijo. 1995. 'Everyday Life Information Seeking: Approaching Information Seeking in the Context of "Way of Life"'. *Library & Information Science Research* 17, no. 3: 259–94.

Schmierbach, M., and A. Oeldorf-Hirsch. 2010. '*A Little Bird Told Me, So I Didn't Believe It: Twitter, Credibility, and Issue Perceptions*'. In Annual Conference of the Association for Education in Journalism & Mass Communication (AEJMC). Denver, CO.

Stewart, James. 2011. 'Local Experts in the Domestication of Information and Communication Technologies'. *Information, Communication & Society* 10, no. 4: 547–69.

Sunstein, Cass. 2007. *Republic 2.0*. Princeton: Princeton University Press.

Van Dijck, José, and Thomas Poell. 2013. 'Understanding Social Media Logic'. *Media and Communication* 1, no. 1: 2–14.

Walther, Joseph, Caleb Carr, Scott Choi, David DeAndrea, Jinsuk Kim, Stephanie Tong and Brandon Van Der Heide. 2011. 'Interaction of Interpersonal, Peer, and Media Influence Sources Online'. In *A Networked Self: Identity, Community, and Culture on Social Network Sites*, edited by Zizi Papacharissi, 17–37. New York: Routledge.

Wellman, Barry, and Caroline Haythornthwaite, (eds). 2002. *The Internet in Everyday Life*. Malden, MA: Blackwell Publishers Ltd.

Yeoh, Seng Guan. 2010. *Media, Culture and Society in Malaysia*. Hoboken, NJ: Taylor & Francis.

Zaharom, Nain. 1994. 'Commercialization and Control in a "Caring Society": Malaysian Media "Towards 2020"'. *SOJOURN: Journal of Social Issues in Southeast Asia* 9, no. 2: 178–99.

Zahiid, Syed Jaymal. 2013. 'Bangladesh Denies Claims Its Workers Were Phantom Voters.' *The Malaysian Insider*, 3 June. Online: http://www.themalaysianinsider.com/malaysia/article/bangladesh-denies-claims-its-workers-were-phantom-voters (accessed 5 October 2014).

NOTES ON CONTRIBUTORS

Panizza Allmark is the associate dean of arts and humanities at Edith Cowan University. She is an associate professor in media and cultural studies. Panizza is also the chief editor of *Continuum: Journal of Media & Cultural Studies* and has published in the field of visual culture, photography, gender, transnationalism and urban space.

Catherine Gomes is a senior lecturer at the Royal Melbourne Institute of Technology (RMIT University) and in 2016 completed an Australian Research Council DECRA (Discovery Early Career Research Award) fellowship. Her work covers migration, transnationalism and diasporas, particularly transient migration in Australia and Singapore with special interests in international students, their well-being, their social networks and their media and communication use. In addition, Catherine has written on identity, gender, ethnicity and race in Chinese cinema. Catherine is founding editor of *Transitions: Journal of Transient Migration* and leader of the Migration and Digital Media Research Lab in the Digital Ethnography Research Centre (DERC) at RMIT. Her book, *Multiculturalism through the Lens: A Guide to Ethnic and Migrant Anxieties in Singapore*, was published in 2015. Catherine also teaches Asian Studies and Communication Studies.

Cate Gribble is an internationally recognized expert on international higher education. Cate's current research focuses on international student mobility, migration and employability. In 2015 Cate was awarded the inaugural World Association for Cooperative Education (WACE) research award to investigate international students' experiences of work-integrated learning (WIL) in Australia and Canada. Other current projects include an investigation of employability in different cultural contexts (funded by the UK Society for Research in Higher Education) and the 'New Colombo Plan: Australians as international students in Asia' with colleagues from Deakin University and the University of Adelaide. Cate is the author of *Enhancing the Employability of International Graduates: A Guide for Australian Education Providers* (Sponsored by the Victorian Government Department of Economic Development, Jobs, Transport and Resources and the Australian Government Department of Education and Training).

Sandra Hanchard completed her PhD at the Swinburne Institute for Social Research, Swinburne University in Melbourne. She is a senior visiting lecturer for the master of communication program at Taylor's University, in Kuala Lumpur, Malaysia. Her research interests include new media and technologies in everyday life, racial polarization and hate speech online, and digital methods. Residing in Malaysia for the past six years, Sandra is actively involved with industry and community groups related to big-data analytics and data visualization. She has infographics and a case study on Malaysia featured in the book, *Geoblocking and Global Video Culture*, published in 2016. She is also the director of DataViz My, which facilitates the Data Science Primer Course for the Malaysian Global Innovation and Creativity Centre (MaGIC), a government agency dedicated to fostering the start-up ecosystem.

Larissa Hjorth is an artist and digital ethnographer in the School of Media and Communication, RMIT University. Hjorth's books include *Mobile Media in the Asia-Pacific* (2009), *Games and Gaming* (2010), *Online@AsiaPacific* (2013), *Understanding Social Media* (2013), *Gaming in Social, Locative and Mobile Media* (2014), *Digital Ethnography* (2016) and *Screen Ecologies: Art, Media, and the Environment in the Asia-Pacific Region*. Research projects include: *Locating the Mobile*: http://locatingthemobile.net/ and *Games of Being Mobile*: http://gamesofbeingmobile.com/.

Susan Leong is research fellow with Curtin University in Western Australia, and author of *New Media and the Nation in Malaysia: Malaysianet* (2014). Current research projects focus on business migration from China into Australia, Asian new media including Chinese social media, ethno-religious minorities and coexistence in Malaysia and Singapore. Susan has published in *Critical Asian Studies*, *New Media & Society* and *Crossings* as well as in *Continuum* on the notion of Internet time, the theoretical frameworks of social imaginaries and franchise nation, Malaysia's Multimedia Super Corridor (MSC) mega project and the Australian–Chinese diaspora. Susan is associate editor of *Transitions: Journal of Transient Migration*, co-editor of the book series: Media, Culture and Communication in Asia-Pacific Societies and part of the Management Board of the Australia–Asia-Pacific Institute at Curtin.

Loo Hong Chuang is currently an assistant professor at University Tunku Abdul Rahman, Malaysia, and teaches broadcasting, communication theory, journalism and film studies. His research focus is on the role various media play in transforming and maintaining the intertwining relationships, as well as tensions, between ethnicity and nationalism in multi-ethnic Malaysia. His latest academic and film projects explore the influences of tourism on ethnic minorities in world, as well as national, heritage sites in Malaysia.

Floris Müller is a media scholar and psychologist, working as a freelance researcher and therapist in Amsterdam. His recent research projects focus on anti-racism in the media, production processes of documentary film and the representation of minorities in news and entertainment.

Jason Sze Chieh Ng is a PhD candidate at the University of Melbourne's School of Historical and Philosophical Studies. His current research is on memory and historical representation within the life stories of the retired members of the Malayan Communist Party.

Ly Thi Tran is a senior lecturer in the School of Education, Deakin University, and an Australian Research Council DECRA fellow. Ly's research and publications focus on international students, pedagogy and curriculum in international education and Vietnamese higher education. She has been awarded three grants on international student mobility and staff professional development in international education by the Australian Research Council. She is a lead investigator of the 'New Colombo Plan' with Cate Gribble and Glen Stafford. Her book, *Teaching International Students in Vocational Education: New Pedagogical Approaches*, won the 2014 International Education Association of Australia Excellence Award for Best Practice/Innovation in International Education.

Irfan Wahyudi received his PhD from Edith Cowan University's School of Arts and Humanities and is also a lecturer in media studies on the faculty of social and political sciences, Universitas Airlangga. His research interests including community and media engagement, media activism and migrant-worker movements.

Joshua Wong is a PhD candidate at RMIT University's School of Media and Communication, as well as a member of the Young and Well Cooperative Research Centre. His research lies at the intersection of well-being, mobility and the usage of media technologies in the everyday lives of international students.

INDEX

Abbott, Jason 10
ABC News (Australia) 32
Abdullah C. D. 172–73
Adriana, Anis 35
Ahmad, Fauziah 199–200, 213
Al Jazeera, 32, 133
'Allah,' use of in Malaysia
   'Bible incident,' 119, 124, 128
   etymology of 119–20
   historical background 122–26
   overview 12, 119–22, 134–36
   social media and 126–34
Allmark, Panizza 11
Amnesty International 30, 34
Anderson, Benedict 43, 106
Arab Spring 213
Arendt, Hannah 183
Arnold, Michael 21, 28, 51, 96
Arrighi, Giovanni 43
Article 19 (NGO) 133
Asian Migrant Centre (NGO) 19, 23–24, 27–28
Asian Migrant's Coordinating Body (Hong Kong activist group) 28, 31
Asia Pacific Mission for Migrants (NGO) 35
Asia Sentinel (Malaysian online news portal) 190
Association of Chitty Melaka (Singapore) 148, 149
Association of Indonesian Migrant Workers in Hong Kong 25
Association of Southeast Asian Nations (ASEAN), temporary migrant workers from Vietnam in 70–71
Australia
   Cronulla Riots 7
   international students in, social media and transnational mobility
      case studies 47–48
      home connections, maintaining 48–50
      'inauthentic' connections 52–55
      increased cultural exposure of 42–43
      life narratives, sharing 50–52
      online communities of diaspora 55–59
      overview 5, 11, 42–44, 59–60
      Singapore compared 101
      vicarious hanging out 50–52
      well-being of 43–46
   multicultures in 7
   National Strategy on International Education in Australia 91n4
   skilled workers in 5–6
   Vietnam, migrants from
      generally 64–65
      students 68
Australian Research Council 97n10

Badawi, Abdullah Ahmad 125
Bangladesh, foreign domestic workers from 4–5
Barr, M. D. 125
Batang Kali Massacre 187
Baym, N. 54–55
Bernama (Malaysian news agency) 199
Bevan, Robert 174
BFM Malaysia (radio station) 133, 197
Blackburn, Susan 23
Blogspot 9
Bok, David 148, 148n10
boyd, danah 202
Brubaker, Rogers 21

Brunei
  Hudud law in 131
  as part of Malaysia 145n3
Buddhism in Malaysia 123
Burma
  foreign domestic workers from 4–5
  students from 5

Cambodia, temporary migrant workers from Vietnam in 70
Canada
  students in 5
  Vietnam, migrants from 64–65
capability approach to well-being 45
Casey, Anton 103
Castoriadis, C. 121
Centre of Independent Journalism 200
Ceradoy, Aaron 35
Chan, Carol 21, 23, 30
Chen, K. H. 43
Cheong, Niki 197
Chia, Philip 158
China
  Chinese Students and Scholars Association 78
  Communist Party (CCP) 77–78, 172–73
  Cultural Revolution 105
  disenfranchised persons, social media and 46–47
  foreign domestic workers from 4–5
  Haiyang Shiyou 981 oil rig 79–80
  Hong Kong. *See* Hong Kong
  social media in 9, 41, 77–78
  students from 5
  temporary migrant workers, social media and 46
  transnational mobility in 4
  Vietnam, students from 68, 80–81
  whitewashing of memory in 182
Christianity in Malaysia 123
CNN 32
Coalition of Indonesian Migrant Workers' Organisations 27, 28
Collective memory 174
Collins, Francis Leo 88–89
Colombo Plan 5
Communism in Malaysia
  demonizing of 183–84
  lingering threats from 188
  perils of remembering 185–86
  public reactions to 184–85
  reconstructing memory 186–87
Community and Everyday Life (Day) 1–2
Constable, Nicole 25, 27, 28, 32
Cubitt, Sean 204
Cui, Litang 9

The Daily Mail, 32
Day, Graham 1–2
Devaraj, Jeyakumar 185
DeWind, J. 107–8
De Witt, Dennis 146, 162
Disenfranchised persons, social media and 46–47
Domestic workers. *See* Foreign domestic workers
Dongpo News (Korean online news portal) 76

Effective Measure (Internet research firm) 203, 203n4
The Effing Show (Malaysian social media program) 135
The Emergence of Modern Southeast Asia (Owen) 3–4
Eriksen, Thomas H. 159–60
eudaimonic approach to well-being 44

Facebook
  Australia, transnational students in using 52, 53–54, 55, 59
  in China 9
  Erwiana Sulistyaningsih and 30–33
  generally 10
  in India 41, 78
  Indonesian female domestic workers
    in Hong Kong using 11, 20–21, 26–27, 28–30
  in Malaysia
    'Allah,' use of and 121–22, 128–30, 131–32, 133
    Melaka City and 144, 155–56, 158–59, 160–64
  traditional media versus 211, 213
  21st Century Old Friends Association and 180, 188–92

in Singapore 77, 99–101, 100t4.2
in Vietnam 76, 79–81
Vietnamese community and 80
Fake Malaysia News (Malaysian online news portal) 130
Federalism in Malaysia 123
Findlay, A. M. 47
Flickr
  in India 78
  in Singapore 77
Fong, Vanessa L. 88–89
Ford Foundation 80
Foreign domestic workers
  generally 4–5
  Filipina domestic workers in Hong Kong 24, 25, 27
  Indonesian female domestic workers in Hong Kong. *See* Hong Kong
Foucault, Michel 187
France, migrants from Vietnam in 64–65
Fraser, Nancy 21
Free Malaysia Today (Malaysian online news portal) 199

George, Cherian 200, 212
Gibson, Paige 202
Gillespie, Tarleton 201
Global Social Media Impact Study 101
Gomes, Catherine 11–12
Google + in Malaysia 128–29
Govindasamy, A. R. 125
Gribble, Cate 6, 11
The Guardian, 32

Haadyai Peace Agreement (1989) 172–73
Halbwachs, Maurice 174
Hall, J. A. 54–55
Hall, Stuart 135
Hanafi school of Islam 122–23
Hanbali school of Islam 122–23, 130–31
Harchard, Sandra 13
Hedonic approach to well-being 44
Hendrickson, B. 108
Hidayah, Anis 29
Hinduism in Malaysia 123
Hirsch, Marianne 174
Hitchcock, Michael 154

Hjorth, Larissa 11, 21, 28, 51, 96
Ho, Nga Thi Thuy 75
Hobsbawn, E. J. 187
Hong, Lysa 105–6
Hong Kong
  Filipina domestic workers in 24, 25, 27
  generally 2–3
  Indonesian female domestic workers in
    activism by 26–27
    Erwiana Sulistyaningsih. *See* Sulistyaningsih, Erwiana
    human rights abuses 20–21
    issues encountered by 21–23
    overview 11, 19–21, 36
    social media, use of 11, 20–21, 26–27, 28–30
    stereotypes of 23–25
  labour organizations in 27–28
  transnational mobility in 4
  Umbrella Revolution 19
Hong Kong Confederation of Trade Unions 32, 34
Houben, V. J. H. 122
Hsia, Hsiao-Chuan 24–25
Hua, Hsieh Bao 22
Huang Jianli 105–6
Huat, Chua Beng 43
Human Rights Watch 22, 26–27

Ice Bucket Challenge 8–9
IMA-Europe (NGO) 33
India
  disenfranchised persons, social media and 46–47
  foreign domestic workers from 4–5
  Ministry of Overseas Indian Affairs 78
  Public Diplomacy Division 78
  social media in 41, 78–79
  students from 5
  transnational mobility in 4
Indonesia
  foreign domestic workers from
    female domestic workers in Hong Kong. *See* Hong Kong
    generally 4–5
  New Order Regime 105
  skilled workers from 5–6
  social media in 41

Indonesian Migrant Workers Union
    26, 27, 31
Instagram
    generally 9
    in Malaysia 189–90
    in Singapore 100t4.2
InterAcademy Council 82
International Domestic Workers
    Federation 34
International students. *See* Students
Islam
    Hanafi school 122–23
    Hanbali school 122–23, 130–31
    Malaysia, use of 'Allah' in
        'Bible incident,' 119, 124, 128
        etymology of 119–20
        historical background 122–26
        overview 12, 119–22, 134–36
        social media and 126–34
    Maliki school 122–23
    Shafi'i school 122–23, 130–31
    Sunni branch 122–23
    Wahhabi branch 130–31
Islamic State in Iraq and Syria (ISIS) 8–9
Islamic State in Libya and Levant
    (ISIL) 8–9
Ismath, Khalid 130
Ito, M. 50
Iwabuchi, Koichi 43

Jaffe, Dennis 180
Japan
    Vietnam, students from 68
    whitewashing of memory in 182
Jenkins, Henry 29, 213
Jenkins, Keith 182

Kadir, Abdullah bin Abdul (Munshi
    Abdullah) 120
KakaoTalk (Korean social media)
    generally 59
    in Singapore 99, 100t4.2
Kampong Boy: Yesterday and Today (Lat) 1
The Kampong Boy (Lat) 1–2
Kansas State University 9
Kavanaugh, Andrea 213
Khalid, Mohammad Noor (Lat) 1–2
Kian-Won, Kwok 173

Kim, Youna 88–89
King, Victor T. 150–51, 152
Komito, Lee 26
Kony, Joseph 8
Korea. *See* South Korea
Korean.net (Korean social media) 76
Kulkarni, Rama 34

Lao Jiang 181n3
Laos, temporary migrant workers from
    Vietnam in 70
Lat (Mohammad Noor Khalid) 1–2
Law, Lisa 28, 31
Leong, Susan 6, 12
Lim, Merlyna 29, 32, 33, 130
LINE (Japanese social media)
    generally 59
    in Malaysia 189–90
LinkedIn in Singapore 100t4.2
Loo, Hong-Chuang 12–13
Loone, Susan 130
Lowenthal, David 185
Lüders, Marika 201

Malaysia
    'Allah,' use of in
        overview 12, 119–22, 134–36
        etymology of 119–20
        historical background 122–26
        social media and 126–34
    All-Malaya Council of Joint Action—
        Pusat Tenaga Rakyat Alliance
        179, 180
    Assembly of the United People 189–90
    Australia, transnational students in. *See*
        Australia
    Baba in 147, 147n9
    Batang Kali Massacre 187
    Bersih 4 movement 189–90, 212
    'Bible incident,' 119, 124, 128
    Bill of Guarantees 128, 200
    Buddhism in 123
    Bumiputera policy 6, 7
    Bumiputeras in 123, 144–45, 145n4
    Chinese Communist Party and 172–73
    Chinese in 147n9, 148
    Christianity in 123
    civil war in 172–73

INDEX

colonial period 3n1, 171–72
Communications and Multimedia Act (1998) 199
communism in
  demonizing of 183–84
  lingering threats from 188
  perils of remembering 185–86
  public reactions to 184–85
  reconstructing memory 186–87
Constitution
  Article 3 128
  Article 11 128
  Article 121 125
  Article 121A 125
  Article 160 123–24
Department of Islamic Development of Malaysia 125
Education Blueprint 175, 177
Emergency (1948) 172–73
ethnic groups in 123, 144–45, 145n4
Evidence Act 200
federalism in 123
Federation of Malaya Constitutional Proposal (1957) 188
generally 2–3
Georgetown as World Heritage Site 143
Haadyai Peace Agreement (1989) 172–73
Hinduism in 123
historical background 145n3, 171–73
Home Ministry 127
Internal Security Act 125–26
Islam, arrival of 122–23
Islam Hadhari (civilizational Islam) 125
Kelantan State
  Hudud law in 121, 126, 131–32
  Syariah Criminal Code II (1993) 126
Kuala Lumpur City, social media in 128–29
Malayan Communist Party (MCP) 169–73, 179–81, 182–85, 186–87, 188
Malayan People's Army 170
Malay Reservations Act (1913) 123–24
Malaysian Communications and Multimedia Commission (MCMC) 169, 190–92, 198, 204, 211
Malaysian People's Movement Party 131–32

Melaka City, multicultures in
  authenticity, engaging 156–60
  Chitty Melaka in 145, 147–49, 147n8, 155–56, 157–60, 162–64
  community, repositioning of 160–64
  Dutch Eurasians in 145–47, 146n7, 154, 155–57, 160–62
  heritage conservation 149–52
  Kampung Chitty in 149, 157–58, 159
  overview 12–13, 143–44, 143n1, 164–65
  perkanan communities 147–48
  Portuguese Eurasians in 146, 146n6, 154, 160–62
  social media and 155–56
  theme park quality of 144, 154
  tourism development 149–52
  transformation from ethnocentric to multiculturalist site 152–55
  as World Heritage Site 143–44, 151, 153, 154–55
Ministry of Culture, Arts and Heritage 153n12
Ministry of Education 183
Ministry of Tourism 153n12
multicultures in 3, 6, 7
Nanyang Communist Party (NCP) 172
National Front (*Barisan Nasional*) 125n5, 180, 200
national narrative
  dangers of challenging 179
  issues with 182–83
Negeri Sembilan State, Islam in 123
New Cultural Policy 151
New Economic Policy 124, 151–52, 201
new media versus traditional media in
  analysis of 209–13
  cultural factors shaping 199–201
  distinguishing 201–2
  future research 213–14
  limitations of study 213–14
  measuring usefulness and trust 203–4
  overview 13, 197–99, 214
  political factors shaping 199–201
  socioeconomic factors shaping 199–201
  trust, findings regarding 208–10
  usefulness, findings regarding 206–7

Malaysia (*cont.*)
  Nyonyas in 147, 147n9
  1Malaysia Development Berhad
    scandal 212
  1Malaysia policy 125–26, 201
  Orang Asli in 145n5
  Pan Malaysian Islamic Party (PAS) 124–25, 125n5, 126, 131, 132
  Peaceful Assembly Act (2011) 125–26
  People's Alliance 125n5
  People's Constitutional Proposal (1946) 180–81
  Prevention of Terrorism Act (2015) 125–26, 212
  Printing Presses and Publications Act (1984) 199
  protests in 28
  'Red Shirt' rallies 189–90
  religion in 123
  Sabah State
    Bibles in 124
    Christianity in 123
  Sarawak State
    Bibles in 124
    Christianity in 123
    social media in 128–29
  Security Offences (Special Measures) Act (2012) 125–26
  Sedition Act (1948) 129–30, 133–34, 212
  Selangor State, Islamic Affairs Department 119, 124
  Socialist Party of Malaysia 181
  social media in
    control of 188–92
    defamation and 129–30
    elections and 128, 129, 189–90, 211
    statistics 128–29
  students from 5
  syariah law in 125
  Thailand, conflict with 172–73
  Tourism Malaysia 150
  transnational mobility in 4
  21st Century Old Friends Association
    dangers of challenging national narrative 179
    issues with national narrative 182–83
    life stories, online sharing of 184

Malaysian memory and 181–82
  overview 13, 169–71, 174–76, 192–93
  perils of remembering communism 185–86
  relevance of 178
  social media and 179–81, 188–92
  as social organization 174
  website 176–78
United Malays National Organisation (UMNO) 124–25, 125n5, 126, 143, 151–52, 183, 189–90, 199
Vietnam, temporary migrant workers from 70
Vision 2020 policy 199, 199n2
Visit Malaysia campaigns 149–50, 153
Malaysiakini (Malaysian online news portal) 129, 133, 199, 208, 212
Malaysian Airlines
  MH 17 downing 211
  MH 370 disappearance 211
Malaysian Dutch Descendants Project (MDDP) 146–47, 155–57, 160–62
The Malaysian Insider (Malaysian online news portal) 184–85, 190–91
Malaysian Social Science Association 212
Maliki school of Islam 122–23
Marichal, Jose 31
Martin, Fran 42, 88–89
Marwick, Alice 202
Media Prima (Malaysian media conglomerate) 199
Melaka City. *See* Malaysia
Merdeka Center (polling firm) 131
Migrant Care (NGO) 29
Migrante Europe (NGO) 33
Migrante International (NGO) 33
Migrant Forum in Asia (NGO) 28
migrant workers
  foreign domestic workers
    Filipina domestic workers in Hong Kong 24, 25, 27
    generally 4–5
    Indonesian female domestic workers in Hong Kong. *See* Hong Kong
  skilled workers
    in Australia 5–6
    from Indonesia 5–6
    in New Zealand 5–6

from Philippines 5–6
from Vietnam 5–6, 65–67
temporary migrant workers
    social media and 46
    from Vietnam 70–71
migration
    social media and 46–47
    from Vietnam. *See* Vietnam
Miller, Daniel 51, 101
Mission for Migrant Workers
    (NGO) 35–36
mobility. *See* transnational mobility
Modi, Narendra 79
Mohamad, Mahathir 7, 125, 128, 134, 191, 199, 200
Montgomery, D. W. 45
Morley, David 55
Morosov, E. 31
Morris-Suzuki, Tessa 174
Müller, Floris 12–13
multicultures
    in Australia 7
    in Melaka City. *See* Malaysia
    overview 6–8
    in Singapore 3, 6–7, 93–96
    social media and 10
Munshi Abdullah (Abdullah bin Abdul Kadir) 120
Muslims. *See* Islam
Myanmar
    foreign domestic workers from 4–5
    students from 5
myVO1CE (Malaysian social media group) 189–90

Nadarajah, Y. 127
Nain, Zaharom 199
Nair, Sheila 151
New Media and the Nation in Malaysia (Leong) 121
News.com, 32
NewsForAfrica, 32
New Straits Times Online (Malaysian online news portal) 185
New Straits Times Press (Malaysian newspaper) 199
The New York Times, 32
New Zealand, skilled workers in 5–6

Ng, Jason Sze-Chieh 13, 200
Nguyen, Chi Hong 70
Nora, Pierre 174
Nurchayati, N. 23

Obama, Barack 8
objective well-being 44–45
Oeldorf-Hirsch, A. 203
One Billion Rising for Justice (NGO) 34
One Vietnam (Vietnamese social media) 75, 80–81
Ong, Aihwa 22, 32
Organisation of Economic Co-operation and Development (OECD) on Vietnam 74
Overseas Korean Times (Korean online news portal) 76
Owen, Norman G. 3–4

Pangkor Treaty (1874) 171–72
Papacharissi, Zizi 202
Parnwell, Michael 152
Paul, A. M. 25
Paulsen, Eric 130
Peng, Chin 176–77, 178, 181, 184–85, 188–89
PewDiePie (video game commentator) 8–9
Pham, Thu 73–74
Phan, Alan 80
Philippines
    foreign domestic workers from 4–5, 24, 25, 27
    skilled workers from 5–6
    temporary migrant workers, social media and 46
Piper, Nicole 21
Poell, Thomas 201
Portes, A. 107–8
Projek Dialog (Malaysian social media advocacy group) 133
Prosser, Michael 9
Pue, Giok Hun 147

QQ (Chinese social media)
    generally 9, 41
    in Singapore 99, 100t4.2

Rahim, Samsudin 208
Rahman, Tunku Abdul 135, 145n3
Ramli, Rafizi 130
Ravichandran, Moorthy 147, 147n8, 148
Razak, Najib Tun 124, 125–26, 129, 130, 190, 191, 201, 212
Reza, Fahmi 130
Rizvi, Fazal 88–89
RMIT University 9, 97n10
Rusen, Jorn 178

Sani, Mohd Azizuddin Mohd 212
Sarawak Report (Malaysian online news portal) 190, 191
Saudi Arabia, *Hudud* law in 131
Sawir, E. 108
Schlesinger, Philip 160
Schmierbach, M. 203
Semut (Malaysian social media group) 189–90
Sen, Amartya 45–46
Setyo, Anik 26
Shafi'i school of Islam 122–23, 130–31
Shamsul, A. B. 147
Sharom, Azmi 130
Sheller, M. 43
Sinanan, Jolynna 51
Sinar Project (Malaysian civil rights group) 212
Sinchew Daily (Malaysian newspaper) 200–201
Singapore
  ASEAN Foundation Scholarships in Development, Environment, and IT 90
  Australia, transnational students in. *See* Australia
  Chinese in 93
  CMIO racial categorization 93, 112
  Employment Pass (E-Pass) 92n7
  foreign domestic workers in 4–5, 4n2
  generally 2
  Global Schoolhouse Initiative 89–90
  Immigration and Checkpoints Authority 102
  Indians in 93
  industry in 91n5
  international students in, social media and transnational mobility
    attitudes of 106–9
    attractiveness as destination 91–93
    Australia compared 101
    Chinese cultural bias 103–6
    empirical study of 96–97
    identity connections with nationality and home 109–11
    overview 11–12, 87–89, 111–13
    social media use 97–103
  Inter-Racial and Religious Confidence Circle 94
  languages in 104n12
  Malay in 93
  Media Development Authority 102
  Ministry of Education 90
  Ministry of Manpower 91–92, 92n7
  multicultures in 3, 6–7, 93–96
  Overseas Singaporean Unit 77
  as part of Malaysia 145n3
  Penal Code 94, 102
  People's Action Party 6–7, 94–96, 96n9, 103, 105
  Population White Paper: A Sustainable Population for a Dynamic Singapore, 94–96
  Prophet Muhammad Birthday Riots (1964) 93
  protests in 28
  Singapore Education Brand 89–90
  Singapore Government Scholarships 90
  'Singapore Story,' 105–6
  Singapore 21 project 77
  Skilled Pass (S-Pass) 92n7
  social media in 76–77, 101n11
  Speak Mandarin Campaign 105
  Student Pass 102–3
  students from 5
  transnational mobility in 4
  universities in 89–91
  Vietnam, students from 68, 80–81
  whitewashing of memory in 182
  xenophobia in 94–96, 94n8, 102–3
skilled workers
  in Australia 5–6
  from Indonesia 5–6
  in New Zealand 5–6

INDEX 231

from Philippines 5–6
from Vietnam 5–6, 65–67
Skype
   Australia, transnational students in using 48–51, 52
   generally 9–10
slacktivism 31
Snapchat in Singapore 100t4.2
social media. *See also* specific app or network
   Australia, international students in and. *See* Australia
   in China 9, 41, 77–78
   disenfranchised persons and 46–47
   as ethnographic tool of inquiry 8–9
   in India 41, 78–79
   in Indonesia 41
   in Malaysia
      control of 188–92
      defamation and 129–30
      elections and 128, 129, 189–90
      statistics 128–29
   migration and 46–47
   multicultures and 10
   Singapore, international students in and. *See* Singapore
   in Singapore 76–77, 101n11
   in South Korea 76
   temporary migrant workers and 46
   in Thailand 41
   transnational mobility and 9–10, 46–47
   in Vietnam 41, 79–81
social memory 173–74
social organizations, memory and 174
South China Morning Post, 32
South Korea
   disenfranchised persons, social media and 46–47
   Overseas Korean Foundation 76
   social media in 76
   students from 5
   Vietnam, migrants from
      students 68
      temporary migrant workers 70
Spitzer, Leo 174
Spreadable Media (Jenkins) 213
Squires, Catherine 36

Sri Lanka, foreign domestic workers from 4–5
The Star (Malaysian newspaper) 208
Startup Vietnam project 74
Stockton University 9
students
   Australia, international students in. *See* Australia
   from Burma 5
   in Canada 5
   from China 5
   from India 5
   from Malaysia 5
   Singapore, international students in. *See* Singapore
   from Singapore 5
   from South Korea 5
   from Thailand 5
   transnational mobility and 5
   in United Kingdom 5
   in United States 5
   from Vietnam 5, 65, 67–70
subaltern counterpublic 21
subjective well-being 44–45
Sukarno 105
Sulistyaningsih, Erwiana
   generally 11, 21
   human rights abuses 20–21
   international support for 33–36
   overview 30, 36
   social media and 30–33
Sunni branch of Islam 122–23
Sun Yat-sen 105
Sze, Yuni 31

Taiwan
   protests in 28
   Vietnam, temporary migrant workers from 70
Tan, Tony 96n9
Tapsell, Ross 59
temporary migrant workers
   social media and 46
   from Vietnam 70–71
Thailand
   foreign domestic workers from 4–5, 24
   Malaysia, conflict with 172–73
   social media in 41

students from 5
transnational mobility in 4
Thanapal, Sangeetha 7
Thomas, K. J. 119–20
Thuy, Bui Thu 79
Time 32
Ting, Helen 151–52
Tong, Goh Chok 77
Tosh, John 179
Town Boy (Lat) 1
Tran, Ly Thi 6, 11, 69, 71
Transnational mobility
  Australia, international students in and.
    See Australia
  in China 4
  foreign domestic workers 4–5
  in Hong Kong 4
  in India 4
  in Malaysia 4
  overview 4–6
  Singapore, international students in and.
    See Singapore
  social media and 9–10, 46–47
  students and 5
  in Thailand 4
Tuan, Nguyen Van 80
Turkle, Sherry 46
Turner, Bryan 43
21st Century Old Friends Association. *See*
  Malaysia
Twitter
  Australia, transnational students in
    using 55
  generally 9
  in India 78, 79
  in Indonesia 41
  in Malaysia
    'Allah,' use of and 121–22,
      128–29, 133
    traditional media versus 197, 203,
      211, 212, 213
    21st Century Old Friends Association
      and 188–89
  in Singapore 77, 100t4.2
  Vietnamese community and 80

Ulhaque, Zulfikar Anwar (Zunar) 130, 212
Ultraman (comic character) 127

United Kingdom
  students in 5
  Vietnam, students from 68, 80–81
United Nations Department of Economic
    and Social Affairs (UNESCO)
  generally 4
  Melaka as World Heritage Site 143–44,
    151, 153, 154–55
  on Vietnamese students 65
United States
  students in 5
  Vietnam, migrants from
    generally 64–65
    students 68, 80–81
University College London 9
University of Hawai'i 108
Urry, J. 43
Utusan Melayu (Malaysian newspaper)
  199, 200–201
Uychiat, Rowena 35

Vanakkam Malaysia (Malaysian
  newspaper) 200–201
Van Dijck, José 201
Varia, Nisha 22
Verma, Vidhu 151
VietAbroader (Vietnamese social media)
  73–74, 75, 80–81
Vietnam
  Department of Overseas Labour 70
  Đổi Mới reforms 65–66, 67, 68, 70
  Ease of Doing Business Report on 72
  Foreign Investment law (1988) 66
  generally 2
  Haiyang Shiyou 981 oil rig 79–80
  Ministry for Education and Training 68
  Ministry of Foreign Affairs 67
  Ministry of Labour, Invalids and Social
    Affairs 71
  OECD on 74
  overseas migration from
    attractive conditions for returnees,
      providing 73–75
    blogs 80
    boat people *(thuyền nhân)* 65
    corruption, eradicating 72
    foreign domestic workers 4–5
    harnessing diaspora 71–72

overview 11, 63–64, 81–82
phases of 64–65
potential contributions of, tapping 73
skilled workers 5–6, 65–67
social media and 75–76
students 5, 65, 67–70
temporary migrant workers 70–71
transparency, improving 72
war-related migrants (*Việt kiều*) 65–67
resolution 36, 66–67
social media in 41, 79–81
Strategy for Education Development 68
Vietnam Silicon Valley 74
Vimeo 9
virtual private networks (VPNs) 212

Wahhabi branch of Islam 130–31
Wahyudi, Irfan 11, 20, 26
Walder, Dennis 192
Walk Free (NGO) 34
Wall Street Journal, 191
Walther, Joseph 203
Waterson, Roxana 173
Webcam (Miller & Sinanan) 51
WeChat (Chinese social media)
  Australia, international students in using 59
  generally 9, 41
  in Malaysia 189–90
  in Singapore 99, 100t4.2
Weibo (Chinese social media)
  Australia, international students in using 59

generally 9, 41, 78
in Singapore 99, 100t4.2
Weiss, M. L. 128
well-being
  alternative approaches 45
  Australia, transnational students in 43–46
  capability approach 45
  defining 45
  eudaimonic approach 44
  hedonic approach 44
  media and 45–46
  objective well-being 44–45
  subjective well-being 44–45
Wertsch, James 181–82
WhatsApp
  generally 26
  in Malaysia 121–22, 133, 189–90
Wong, Joshua 11, 42
Worden, Nigel 152

Yamanaka, Keiko 21
Yew, Lee Kuan 105, 145n3
Young and Well CRC 42
YouTube
  generally 9
  in India 78
  in Malaysia 121–22, 128, 133
  in Singapore 77, 100t4.2

Zawawi, Ibrahim 151
Zunar (Zulfikar Anwar Ulhaque) 130, 212